The CENTRALITY of CHRIST

IN CONTEMPORARY MISSIONS

OTHER TITLES IN THE EMS SERIES:

No. 1 *Scripture and Strategy: The Use of the Bible in Postmodern Church and Mission*
David J. Hesselgrave

No. 2 *Christianity and the Religions: A Biblical Theology of World Religions*
Edward Rommen and Harold A. Netland, eds.

No. 3 *Spiritual Power and Missions: Raising the Issues*
Edward Rommen, ed. (out of print)

No. 4 *Missiology and the Social Sciences: Contributions, Cautions, and the Conclusions*
Edward Rommen and Gary Corwin, eds.

No. 5 *The Holy Spirit and Mission Dynamics*
C. Douglas McConnell, ed.

No. 6 *Reaching the Resistant: Barriers and Bridges for Mission*
J. Dudley Woodberry, ed.

No. 7 *Teaching Them Obedience in All Things: Equipping for the Twenty-first Century*
Edward J. Elliston, ed.

No. 8 *Working Together with God to Shape the New Millennium: Opportunities and Limitations*
Kenneth B. Mulholland and Gary Corwin, eds.

No. 9 *Caring for the Harvest Force in the New Millennium*
Tom A. Steffen and F. Douglas Pennoyer, eds.

No. 10 *Between Past and Future: Evangelical Mission Entering the Twenty-first Century*
Jonathan J. Bonk, ed.

No. 11 *Christian Witness in Pluralistic Contexts in the Twenty-First Century*
Enoch Wan, ed.

The CENTRALITY *of* CHRIST

IN CONTEMPORARY MISSIONS

Edited by
Mike Barnett and Michael Pocock

Evangelical Missiological Society Series
Number 12

visit us at missionbooks.org

The Centrality of Christ in Contemporary Missions

Copyright 2005 by Evangelical Missiological Society
All Rights Reserved

No part of this book may be reproduced, stored in a retrieval system, or transmitted in any form or by any means—electronic, mechanical, photocopy, recording, or otherwise—without prior written permission from the publisher, except brief quotations used in connection with reviews in magazines or newspapers. For permission, email permissions@wclbooks.com. For corrections, email editor@wclbooks.com.

Scripture taken from the HOLY BIBLE, NEW INTERNATIONAL VERSION®. Copyright © 1973, 1978, 1984 International Bible Society. Used by permission of Zondervan. All rights reserved.

Scripture taken from the NEW AMERICAN STANDARD BIBLE®, Copyright© 1960, 1962, 1963, 1968, 1971, 1972, 1973, 1975, 1977, 1995 by The Lockman Foundation. Used by permission.

Published by William Carey Publishing (formerly William Carey Library)
10 W. Dry Creek Cir
Littleton, CO 80120 | www.missionbooks.org

William Carey Publishing is a ministry of Frontier Ventures
Pasadena, CA | www.frontierventures.org

Cover design: Mike Riester

ISBN: 978-1-64508-525-6 (paperback)

Printed Worldwide
27 26 25 24 23   2 3 4 5 6   IN

Library of Congress Cataloging-in-Publication Data on file with the publisher

To the One whom God has highly exalted,

whose name is above all names,

the Lord Jesus Christ

Philippians 2:9, 11

Contents

Author Profiles   9

Foreword   Michael Pocock   13

Introduction   Mike Barnett   15

I. THE CENTRALITY OF CHRIST

1. *Is Jesus Christ Really the Only Way?*
   George Murray   19

2. *The Uniqueness of Christ and Missions*
   Patrick Cate   37

3. *Christ Centered Epistemology: An Alternative to Modern and Postmodern Epistemologies*
   Michael Pocock   69

4. *The Relevance of Jesus as the Source of Salvation and Mission for the Twenty-First Century Global Context*
   William J. Larkin   101

II. CHRIST IN CONTEMPORARY MISSIONS

5. *Mission and Jesus in a Globalizing World: Globalization and the Pluralistic Jesus*
   Harold Netland … 121

6. *Mission and Jesus in a Globalizing World: Mission as Retrieval*
   Harold Netland … 145

7. *Jesus and the Pagan West: Missiological Reflections on Evangelism in Re-enchanted Europe*
   Michael T. Cooper … 165

8. *WDJS—What Does Jesus Say . . . About Receptivity?*
   Cecil Stalnaker … 195

III. MISSIOLOGICAL INSIGHTS

9. *A Christocentric Understanding of Linguistic Diversity: Implications for Missions in a Pluralistic Era*
   Samuel Larsen … 233

10. *Leadership and Teams in Missions—Jesus Style*
    Mike Barnett … 247

11. *The Inescapable Christ: The Significance of E. Stanley Jones' Christology for Twenty-first-Century Missiology*
    John Moldovan … 271

12. *How Do They Think? Understanding and Teaching Religious Belief Systems for Twenty-first-Century Missions*
    Norman Allison … 293

Author Profiles

Norman Allison served as a missionary with the Christian and Missionary Alliance in the Arab Middle East prior to teaching Anthropology in the School of World Missions at Toccoa Falls College, which he directed from 1976-2003. He studied at the American University of Beirut, and received the Ph.D. in Anthropology from the University of Georgia where he concentrated in Religious Belief Systems. He served as president of the EMS from 2001-2004.

Mike Barnett and his wife, Cindy, served twelve years with the IMB. He was a church planter in North America, has a business background and continues to work in international business development. He currently serves as the Elmer V. Thompson Professor of Missionary Church Planting at Columbia Biblical Seminary and School of Missions. Mike earned a Ph.D. in Church History from Southwestern Seminary in Fort Worth, Texas. He has published on leadership and teams and creative access platforms in missions and is currently vice president for the Southeast Region of EMS.

Patrick Cate and his wife, Mary Ann, served in Iran from 1974 to 1979 and Egypt from 1984 to 1989. Pat served as the new personnel director from 1980 to 1984 and later assumed the presidency of Christar in September of 1989. Pat has a Ph.D. in Islamics from Hartford Seminary

Michael T. Cooper served for thirteen years as a missionary in Central and Eastern Europe, and currently researches the revival of pre-Christian European religions in Western Europe and North America. He is assistant Professor of Biblical Studies and Christian Ministries at Trinity International University. He is published in *Mission Studies, Christian Education Journal, Global Missiology* and *Common Ground Journal* and has presented papers on Paganism at various academic venues.

William J. Larkin is Professor of New Testament and Greek at Columbia Biblical Seminary and School of Missions. He received his Ph.D. in 1975 from University of Durham, England. He wrote *Culture and Biblical Hermeneutics: Interpreting and Applying the Authoritative Word in a Relativistic Age* (1988) and *Acts* for the IVP New Testament Commentary Series (1995). He co-edited *Mission in the New Testament: An Evangelical Approach* (1998). He has published numerous articles or essays on biblical-theological subjects related to missions. He is an ordained minister in the Presbyterian Church in America and has taught in Zimbabwe, Portugal, Korea, and Germany.

Samuel Larsen is Academic Dean and Samuel Patterson Professor of Missions and Evangelism at Reformed Theological Seminary (RTS) in Jackson, Mississippi, where he has taught since 1998, after receiving his Ph.D. in Intercultural Studies from Trinity International University. Sam is also Vice President for International Doctoral Programs at RTS. His areas of special interest include globalization and intercultural education. He is a retired Navy Chaplain and also has a decade of service in Kenya and Australia, first under World Presbyterian Missions and later under Mission to the World. Sam and his wife, Louise, have three grown children and nine grandchildren.

Author Profiles 11

John Moldovan is Assistant Dean for Evangelism and Missions at Southwestern Baptist Theological Seminary. He also teaches from the George W. Bottoms Chair of Missions and directs the MA Missiology. He served as Associate Professor of Missions and Evangelism at the Criswell College in Dallas, Texas from 1989 to 2003. John endured harsh persecution in Romania and was forced into exile for his ministry by the Romanian dictator Nicolae Ceausescu. His understanding of suffering offers a unique perspective on missions.

George W. Murray has been President of Columbia International University since January 2000. Previous to this he was the Executive Director of The Evangelical Alliance Mission (TEAM). He and his wife, Annette, also served as missionary church planters in Italy for thirteen years. He received his D.Miss from Trinity International University.

Harold Netland is Professor of Philosophy of Religion and Intercultural Studies at Trinity Evangelical Divinity School. He has lived much of his life in Japan, teaching at Tokyo Christian University. Previous publications include *Dissonant Voices: Religious Pluralism and the Question of Truth* (Eerdmans,1991) and *Encountering Religious Pluralism: The Challenge to Christian Faith and Mission* (InterVarsity, 2001).

Michael Pocock is Senior Professor of Missions and Chairman of the Department of World Missions and Intercultural Studies at Dallas Theological Seminary. He served for sixteen years with The Evangelical Alliance Mission (TEAM), beginning in Venezuela and continuing in mobilization for the organization. He has served as President of EMS and is currently vice president for the South Central Region of EMS. Books include: *Cultural Change and Your Church* (Baker, 2002) and *The Changing Face of World Missions* (Baker, 2005).

Cecil Stalnaker serves with Greater Europe Mission and as Associate Professor of Missions and Evangelism at Tyndale Theological Seminary, located near Amsterdam, The Netherlands. Additionally, he is a visiting professor at the Theological Biblical Academy in Krapina, Croatia. He received his doctoral education from the Evangelische Theologische Faculteit in Heverlee/Leuven, Belgium. Prior to teaching at Tyndale he ministered with his wife and two children in French-speaking Belgium at the Institut Biblique Belge and in church planting.

Foreword

The Centrality of Christ in Contemporary Missions: Was there really any doubt? Jesus claimed he was indispensable for salvation saying: "I am the way, and the truth and the life. No one comes to the Father except through me." (John 14:6) That same Christ sent his disciples into the world by his own authority, calling on them to teach those who followed them to do everything he had commanded them to do. (Matt. 28: 18-20).

The Apostle Paul understood his own mission centered on the proclamation of Christ as the Son of God, even though he clearly understood the Trinitarian reality that God the Father, and the Spirit of holiness and power were the basis of his ministry (Romans 1:1-7).

Jump 1700 years ahead to the fathers of the modern, Protestant, mission movement. The Moravians were Christ-centered if they were nothing else. After the Thirty Years War in Germany, they were tired of the dissentions wracking the church, and wished only to base their spiritual life and health on a relationship with Christ and personal piety rather than doctrinal formulations. They were not entirely balanced in this, but their emphasis became the "inextinguishable blaze" that ignited the modern evangelical missionary movement. Their contagious passion for Christ was passed from Zinzendorf, to Wesley and on to William Carey. It enjoyed the full appreciation of Great Awakening preachers and missionaries like Whitefield, Brainerd and Jonathan Edwards.

Fredrik Franson, who founded some fourteen mission agencies in Europe and North America in the late 19th Century, including what would become the Evangelical Alliance Mission, promoted as his life ambition: "Constant, Conscious,

Communion with Christ." This was the echo of Scandinavian pietism, and of the Moravians. It was still the heartbeat of the evangelical missionary movement.

Contemporary Evangelicals maintain that Christ is still the center of their mission and message. But will Christ be explicitly proclaimed as the indispensable Center when faced with an increasingly pluralistic world? A world where exclusive claims of any kind are unwelcome? What will be the impact of multiple world religions and new spiritualities on the evangelical heartlands? As globalization brings the majority of North American believers, and many elsewhere, into contact with those of radically different faiths, might their outspoken commitment to Christ degenerate into a more general faith in God, with few specific claims about the specific content of their faith? What would be the impact of this shift on the evangelical missionary movement?

The Evangelical Missiological Society exists to encourage reflection on the missionary task by both professional missiologists and thoughtful practitioners. The society is concerned to make the biblical gospel clear through appropriate contextualization, while avoiding the enervating effects of syncretism. That is the concern expressed in this volume. It is only as we evaluate our message and methods by the degree to which they reflect and lead to Christ that we can remain true to the One who calls and sends us.

I gratefully acknowledge the contribution of all the writers of these chapters, but am particularly indebted to Mike Barnett of Columbia International University for assuming the challenge of editing this volume. He was willing to take on what I could not do, and he was helped by the encouragement of his institution and the technical assistance of Greg Goebel and Judith Kimsey. It is appropriate that a colleague like Mike should collaborate on this particular work as part of a school whose motto is: "To know Him, and to make Him known."

Michael Pocock
Dallas Theological Seminary
June 2005

Introduction

He was a sophomore in mid-semester, spring 2001 at Baylor University in Waco, Texas. His Dad had driven down from Dallas during a rare visit to the U.S. from his base of missions service abroad. Both of them cherished these occasional visits. They offered a brief opportunity for updating and de-briefing the progress of the lives of the father, son, and family usually over a slightly rushed meal at a favorite restaurant of the student's choosing. The son was the product of a committed Christian family. He was an MK—'missionary kid'—baptized in a Baptist church at the age of nine years and raised in a community of believers. His teenage years overseas had introduced him to a bigger, more interesting if complex world. And now in the midst of undergraduate studies, he had questions.

His honest and nervous inquiries hit his father square in the gut. "How can we be sure, Dad, that we are right when we say the only way to salvation is through Jesus Christ?" "What makes us think that we have the only correct understanding of truth?" "Doesn't God love and care for a faithful Muslim or Buddhist in the same way he would a Christian?" "Why is it that we Christians often seem to live lives that are less 'Christian' than non-believers?" "Couldn't Jesus have merely been a great man, a famous prophet, a respected moral teacher?"

These are questions for today's world. The young generations of our 'post-everything' world are immersed in an atmosphere of universal, politically correct toleration and plurality. This defies a faith based on biblical absolutes and denies a Messiah, Savior, Lord and God projected as the only way to salvation, fulfillment, and eternity. These questions are totally relevant to the task of being on mission with God among all peoples through the church.

This volume of the annual EMS series offers answers to these questions and more. Is Jesus really the only way? What is unique about Christ and missions? How can a new understanding of Jesus Christ bridge the gap between modern positivism and post-modern relativism? What difference can Jesus make as the source of salvation in our twenty-first-century missions task? Where does Jesus Christ fit into this globalizing world? Can a fresh encounter with Christ transform the nominal Christian world of Europe and the West? How do people receive Jesus and what are the implications for evangelism and discipleship? Can we learn from the model of Jesus how to be more effective missions workers? The answers lie in the clear and relevant communication of the centrality of Jesus Christ.

The EMS series is truly a labor of love, a remarkable effort of volunteers from missions faculties and fields. It was a privilege to serve with co-worker, friend, and fellow editor Michael Pocock. Thank you to the society and its leadership for continuing this series. Praise God for such a talented group of contributors and authors! I want to personally thank Aaron Burt and my wife Cindy for their able proof-reading of the chapters. Thanks also to Columbia International University, especially library director JoAnn Rhodes and my dean, Junias Venugopal, for facilitating this project. Special thanks go to Judith Kimsey, my former student, a gifted writer and proof editor. And most of all to my former student and co-worker Greg Goebel who served as the assistant editor of this volume.

Our desire is that through this volume readers from around the world might learn how to better answer the heartfelt questions of their sons and daughters for the benefit of future generations and the glory of God until Jesus comes again.

Mike Barnett
Columbia Biblical Seminary and School of Missions
June 2005

I. THE CENTRALITY OF CHRIST

Chapter One

Is Jesus Christ Really the Only Way?

George W. Murray

This chapter is adapted from a chapel message delivered at Columbia International University on October 10, 2004.

Thomas asked, "How can we know the way to heaven?" Jesus answered, "I am the way and the truth and the life. No one comes to the Father except through me" (Jn 14:6 NIV). Is Jesus Christ really the only way of salvation for the whole world? And if so, isn't that rather narrow? Yes, it is. Doesn't that sound exclusive? Yes, it does.

When I was a college student I went on a summer mission trip to a place near Chicago. We rented an old Methodist tabernacle with a sawdust floor and wooden benches that seated about one thousand people. For thirty straight nights, we preached the Gospel of Jesus Christ. As a team, we rented a little cottage that was very basic. In place of a kitchen it had a hotplate and a sink in the back room. For breakfast we ate bread and jam and drank instant tea and coffee. At night we had cheese and crackers and soup. In order to have one decent meal a day, we went to a restaurant on the edge of the campground and bought a home-cooked lunch. The first day we sat at a big table, and a young lady approached us and said, "Hi, my name is Sandy, and I'm your server. Are you new here?" I said "Yes." She continued, "What are you all doing here this summer?" I replied, "We've come here to tell people about Jesus," to which she raised her eyebrows quizzically. That exchange began a very interesting series of conversations, since we ate there every day.

One day after lunch, Sandy asked, "Can I talk to you for a minute? I've been telling my friends about some of the stuff you've told me about God and Jesus, and I was wondering if we can come to your cottage one night and ask you some questions." I said, "Sure." And so twelve of them came to our little front porch and began to ask questions. I will never forget a question Sandy asked. Looking straight at me she said, "George Murray, do you believe that Jesus Christ is the only way of salvation for the *whole* world?" I said, "Yes." She replied, "Well if that is true, then what about the fact that hundreds of millions of people living right now have never once heard about Jesus Christ? What's going to happen to them when they die?"

What do you say to a question like that? Sandy did not ask me about people who don't believe in Jesus, she asked me about people who don't know there is a Jesus to believe in. What will happen to them when they die?

I said, "Sandy, what I think and what you think about that question may be right or may be wrong. But what God's Word says is always right. Based on passages like John 3:18, Romans 1-3 and other Old and New Testament passages, I believe that any man or woman, boy or girl, living anywhere in the world who is old enough to know the difference between right and wrong, and who can make a moral choice, if that person dies without putting his or her faith in Jesus Christ, that person will spend eternity in the fires of an everlasting hell." And the minute I said that, Sandy exploded. I can still hear her voice as it screamed out across the summer night, "But that's not fair!"

Many sincere Christians have come to the same conclusion as Sandy. Here is how they reason: "I agree with Sandy. As a believer in Christ I have lived next to the same neighbors for years. I've befriended them and shared my testimony with them. I've told them what Jesus means to me. I've given them literature. I've taken them to church for the Christmas program; the message was very clear. They know the way; in fact they have a Bible in their home, but they have repeatedly rejected the Gospel message. And, I believe that if my neighbors died tonight they would be separated from God forever. But, what about people who have never heard of Jesus, who have never met a Christian, who have never seen a church? What about people for whom the Bible is an unknown book, and the cross is an unknown symbol? What about people who have no Christmas and Easter on their calendars, and who, while we wait for Christ's second coming, have never heard of His first coming? Will they be separated from God when they die? That's not fair!"

So the question hangs in the air, broods in our minds, and stirs our hearts as we think of a world of over six billion people. Here is the question: "How can Jesus Christ claim to be the *only* way of salvation for the *whole* world?" The answer is two-fold: 1) because of *who* Jesus is, and 2) because of *what* Jesus did. In order to understand these two things, let's put them in the form of two questions. First question: Who *is* Jesus Christ? Second question: What did Jesus Christ *do*?

The Person of Jesus Christ

Let's look at our first question: Who *is* Jesus Christ? Answer: *Jesus Christ is God!* Not just like God, not just the way to God, not just the greatest person who ever lived. He is God Almighty himself. By asserting this, we are in no way denying or diminishing the reality or necessity of Christ's humanity. Jesus was fully human and fully divine, as clearly articulated, not only in the pages of Scripture, but in the Nicene, Calcedonian, and Athanasian creeds. As we look at Christ's astounding claim in John 14:6, we must realize that Jesus can say what he does because of who he is. Jesus is God, the second person of the trinity, co-eternal and co-equal with the Father and with the Spirit.

Some say, "I believe Jesus Christ was a good man and a worthy example, but I certainly don't believe he was God." This statement is a contradiction in terms. You cannot logically affirm it because Jesus himself openly and repeatedly claimed to be God. So, the alternatives have always been three: he is a liar, knowing that he is not God, yet claiming to be; he is crazy, thinking that he is God even though he is not; or, he is exactly who he claims to be.[1]

Listen to God's Word and let the cumulative effect of biblical evidence wash over your soul in a fresh recognition of who it is that we say we believe and follow. God's Word teaches Christ's *eternal pre-existence*. There was never a time when Jesus Christ was not. There was never a time when Jesus Christ was not God. "In the beginning was the Word, and the Word was with God, and the Word was God" (Jn 1:1). The Bible teaches Christ's *virgin birth*. "How will this be," Mary asked the angel, "since I am a virgin?" The angel answered, "The Holy Spirit will come upon you, and the power of the Most High will overshadow you. So the holy one to be born will be called the Son of God" (Lk 1:34-35). The Bible teaches his *sinless life*: Isaiah, John, Paul, Peter, all under the inspiration of the Holy Spirit, make categorical statements about the fact that Jesus Christ never sinned in thought, word, or deed (Is 53:9; Jn 7:18; 2 Co 5:21; 1 Pt 3:18). God's Word teaches Christ's *vicarious death*, meaning that he, the guiltless one, died for us, the guilty ones. God's Word teaches his *bodily resurrection*. Jesus' enemies said, "What miraculous sign can you show us to prove your authority to do all this?" Jesus answered them, "Destroy this temple, and I will raise it again in three days," and John notes that "the temple he had spoken of was his body" (Jn 2:18-20). The Bible teaches Christ's *glo-*

rious ascension. Right in the middle of his letter to Timothy, Paul bursts out in a doxology about Jesus when he exclaims, "Beyond all question, the mystery of godliness is great: He appeared in a body, was vindicated by the Spirit, was seen by angels, was preached among the nations, was believed on in the world, was taken up in glory" (1 Ti 3:16).

The record of Scripture is clear. Jesus Christ is God. Jesus healed the sick and caused the lame to walk, the deaf to hear, the dumb to speak. Jesus touched and cleansed the lepers. Jesus restored sight to the blind. The man born blind said to the Pharisees, "Nobody has ever heard of opening the eyes of a man born blind. If this man were not from God, he could do nothing" (Jn 9:32-33).

Jesus forgave sins. Four faith-filled faces on a rooftop looked down at the man that they had just lowered on a mat in front of Jesus. Jesus said to the man, "Friend, your sins are forgiven." And the cold-hearted, theologically correct Pharisees murmured among themselves, "Who is this fellow who speaks blasphemy? Who can forgive sins but God alone?" Knowing their thoughts, Jesus said, "Why are you thinking these things in your hearts? Which is easier: to say, 'Your sins are forgiven,' or to say, 'Get up and walk'? But that you may know that the Son of Man has authority on earth to forgive sins...." He said to the paralyzed man, "I tell you, get up, take your mat and go home" (Lk 5:20-25). And the man got up and went home!

Jesus Christ raised the dead. In Luke 7, the Bible presents that awful scene of a widow whose only young adult son had died. The funeral was over and the procession was making its way to the cemetery. As they came out of the city gate Jesus was coming the other way. He stopped them, scandalized the people by putting his hand on the casket of the dead person, and then spoke to the young man. Christ raised him up and gave him back to his mother, and the end of that story records these words: "And all the people said, 'God has come to his people'" (v. 16).

Jesus walked on and calmed the stormy seas. He changed water into wine. He miraculously multiplied food to feed five thousand, then another group of four thousand. He cast out demons. Those demons recognized Christ's deity. "What do you want with us, Jesus of Nazareth? Have you come to destroy us? I know who you are–the Holy One of God!" (Mk 1:24). And I am always struck by that instructive verse in Mark's Gospel where we read that Jesus "would not let the demons speak *because they knew who he was*" (Mk 1:34). (italics added)

The enemies of Jesus recognized his deity. Why did Jesus' enemies seek to put him to death, and eventually succeed in doing so? It was not because of his scathing denunciation of their hypocrisy, as withering and convicting as that was. It was not because of the miracles he performed. It was not because he cast out demons; They were doing that also. There was one reason alone that they put him to death: his claim to be God. John 10:32 records that "Jesus said to them, 'I have shown you many great miracles from the Father. For which of these do you stone me?'" Now look at their answer: "We are not stoning you for any of these," replied the Jews, "but for blasphemy, because you, a mere man, claim to be God" (10:33).

They were right. Jesus *did* claim to be God. He said, "I and my Father are one" (Jn 10:30). Jesus said, "He who has seen me, has seen the Father" (Jn 14:9). John 5:18 says that his enemies wanted to kill him because Jesus "called God his own Father, making himself equal with God." Why does this verse say his enemies wanted to kill him? It was because he called God his *own* Father. The Greek word *idion* means "unique, peculiar, in a way that nothing else is." And so, when Jesus says that God is his *idion patera*, he is identifying himself with God as no one else can. They knew exactly what he meant, and that is why they tried to kill him.

Furthermore, we read in John 8:58, "'I tell you the truth,' Jesus answered, 'Before Abraham was born, I am!'" I remember the first time I read this verse in the Roman Catholic Bible.

It reads, "Jesus answered, Amen, Amen, I say to you, before Abraham was born, I am." I wondered how the Catholic scholars decided to use the expression "Amen, Amen." It is because that is what the Greek says. "Amen" means "it is true." And Jesus uses that word here *twice*. "I tell you the truth. I tell you the truth," he says deliberately and repeatedly. In fact, Jesus is the only person in the Bible who ever used the double "amen." And Jesus always chose this double expression just before he said something that he knew his listeners would *not* believe. For example, in John 3 Jesus says: "Nicodemus, you're not going to believe this, but it's true! It's true! Amen! Amen! Except a man is born again, he cannot see the Kingdom of God!" "What?" Nicodemus said, "Can a man enter into his mother's womb and be born again?" And Jesus could have responded: "I knew you were going to say that, Nicodemus. That's why I started my declaration with the words, 'It's true! It's true!'" And again in John 13:21 Jesus says: "Gentlemen, my closest colleagues who have walked intimately with me for these last three years, you who are sitting here with me at this holy meal before I go to the cross, you're not going to believe this, but it's true! It's true! Amen! Amen! I say to you, one of you is going to betray me." And we read that his disciples looked at each other, doubting of whom he spoke.

Jesus uses this double expression again in John 8:58. In effect he says: "You're not going to believe this, but it's true! It's true! Amen, Amen. Before Abraham was born, I am!" Jesus could have said "Before Abraham was born, I *was*," and he would have been correct. Instead he says, "Before Abraham was born, I *am*." Quite apart from the fact that he is doubtless identifying himself with the Jehovah "I Am" who appeared to Moses in the burning bush, Jesus is also deliberately making a literal statement.

How can that be? It cannot be, if Jesus is not God. God is omnipotent, omniscient, and omnipresent. Speaking of his omnipresence we mean that God is everywhere at the same time. But most of the time when we talk about the Lord's omnipresence, we restrict that truth to the concept of *space*. But it is also true that God is omnipresent in *time*. And so when we talk about the Lord in terms of time, it is not only accurate to say that he *is*, that he *was*, and that he *will be*, but it is also accurate to say that he *is* is and that he *is* was and that he *is* will be! All that he was, he still is; all that he will be, he already is. Why? Because he is God! Moses affirms this in Psalm 90:2 when he says, "From everlasting to everlasting, you are God." This is also affirmed in Isaiah 57:15, where the Lord is called "the high and lofty one...who inhabits eternity." Jesus' audience in John 8 knew exactly what he was claiming, so we read in verse 59, "At this, they picked up stones to stone him."

Jesus openly received worship as God. When Cornelius tried to worship Peter, the apostle refused to let him do it since he was only a mortal man (Ac 10:25, 26). When the people of Lystra wanted to worship Paul and Barnabas, the apostles refused to let them do it, claiming they were mere men and urging the people to "turn to the living God" (Ac 14:15). When the apostle John fell down to worship at the feet of the angel through whom the amazing visions of the book of the Revelation had been given, the angel refused his worship, telling him to "worship God" (Rev 22:8).

Here is the point I am making: Peter refused the worship of people; Paul refused the worship of people; the angel in the book of the Revelation refused the worship of people. On the other hand, Jesus Christ never, ever refused the worship of people because he knew that they were recognizing him for exactly who he was. Whether it was the Samaritan man cured of leprosy, or the man born blind, or Mary of Bethany, or Thomas in the Upper Room, or the disciples on the floorboards of their boat, Jesus never said to them, "Don't do that! Get up!" Instead, he let them worship because they were recognizing him for who he is. Who is Jesus Christ? Jesus is God!

Jesus Christ and the Cross

The second question is: What did Jesus Christ *do*? Answer: *Jesus Christ died on Calvary's cross for the sins of the whole world. This* is why Jesus came. *This* is what Jesus did. *This* is why Jesus can claim to be the only way of salvation for the whole world.

So how many people in the world know about the salvation that only Christ can offer? If we study the well-documented statistics published annually in the *International Bulletin of Missionary Research*, we can conclude in broad general terms that nine out of every ten people in the world are lost, outside of personal faith in Jesus Christ; two out of every three people in the world have never heard a clear explanation of the gospel; and one out of every three people in the world are still in the "unreached" category, with no near neighbor to tell them the message of the gospel.[2]

Statistics like these make it difficult for some people to accept the fact that Jesus is the only way. These are people like the sincere woman I met in Italy, where my wife and I served as church-planting missionaries for thirteen years. One summer we decided to take a student team to one of the 31,000 cities and towns in Italy where there is still no gospel witness. We chose a city the size of Columbia, South Carolina (which has over 500 Christian churches), where there was not even one local body of believers. We did door-to-door literature distribution for ten days and covered the entire city, inviting people to a conference in a prominent downtown location. We were very excited. About 400,000 people had been contacted, but on the first night only five people came. On the second night, again, five people came. But the third night, after we had prayed together and asked the Lord to bring out the people whom we had contacted, we went out into the meeting room and there were over twenty people in attendance. We were thrilled! That night, the Italian evangelist who was working with us gave a compelling gospel message about the cross of Jesus Christ.

Afterward, a beautiful woman stood up with tears in her eyes and said, "That was one of the most beautiful and compelling descriptions of the life and death of Jesus Christ I have ever heard." The minute I heard her say that, my heart welled up, and I thought "Praise the Lord! The breakthrough has come!" But then she said, "*Ma, caro signore* (But, dear sir), I beg of you, please do *not* insist that Jesus Christ is the *only* way of salvation for the *whole* world." As we continued to talk, we discovered that she and those who came with her were adherents of the Baha'i faith – a split off of Islam that teaches that Baha'u'llah is one of a series of divine manifestations that includes Jesus, Mohammed, Zoroaster, and the Buddha. The Baha'i faith teaches that the differences in the world's religions are simply divine manifestations of one universal faith and brotherhood. For Baha'i adherents, Jesus is *one* way, but not the *only* way.

Yet, Jesus' statement in John 14:6 is clear and categorical: "I am the way and the truth and the life. No one comes to the Father except through me." When Jesus said this, it was not an expression of bigotry; it was a declaration of deity. Look at Peter's words in Acts 4:12. Peter, the man who denied the Lord, was standing before the people who had crucified Jesus and now had the power to do the same thing to him. Yet, filled with the Holy Spirit, Peter declared clearly and categorically, "Salvation is found in no one else, for there is no other name under heaven given to men by which we must be saved." These words of Peter's have been forever preserved for us in God's Holy Word. They were true then; they are true now. There is no other name. Buddha? No. Confucius? No. Mohammed? No. Baha'u'llah? No. Joseph Smith? No. Charles Taze Russell? No. Mary Baker Eddy? No. Sun Myung Moon? No. There is no other name! Look at what Jesus says about himself in John 10:7-9 "I am the gate [door] for the sheep...whoever enters through me will be saved." There is no other *way*, no other *name*, no other *door*.

Is Jesus Christ Really the Only Way?

One for All

How can Jesus Christ claim to be the only way of salvation for the whole world? It is because of *who Jesus is* and because of *what Jesus did*. I want to strongly emphasize that at this point it is important to see the indispensable connection between who Jesus *is* and what Jesus *did* and how these two things form the foundation for his exclusive claim.

Hebrews 9:26 says, "But now he has appeared once for all at the end of the ages to do away with sin by the sacrifice of himself." This verse is referring to what Jesus did through his death on the cross, and it says that that mighty act happened "at the end of the ages." The Greek expression is *sunteleia ton aionon*. In Greek literature, this expression describes the tallest peak of the tallest mountain in a range of mountains. So, when the writer to the Hebrews, under the inspiration of the Holy Spirit, chooses this Greek expression, which the New English Bible translates "the climax of history" and Barclay's translates "the consummation of history," God's Word is telling us that the sacrifice of Christ on the cross was the *highpoint* of human history. All of history past looks forward to that event. All of history future looks back to that event. That is why John Bowring wrote: "In the cross of Christ I glory/Towering o'er the wrecks of time/All the light of sacred story/Gathers round its head sublime."[3] Every time you and I take the bread and drink the cup, we are celebrating the crucifixion of Christ, the *most important fact in human history.*

John the Baptist spoke of Jesus with the sweeping statement, "Look! The Lamb of God who takes away the sin of the world!" (Jn 1:29). Centuries earlier, Isaiah prophesied, "We all like sheep have gone astray. Each of us has turned to our own way. And the Lord has laid on him the iniquity of us all" (Is 53:6). 1 John 2:2, speaking of Jesus Christ, says, "He is the atoning sacrifice for our sins, and not only for ours, but also for the sins of the whole world." This is an amazing statement regardless of your personal view of the extent of Christ's atonement!

There are two questions that every thinking Christian should ask when contemplating the cross and what Jesus did there. The first question is: How could *one* person die for *all* people?

At times I have sought to explain the biblical truth of the vicarious substitutionary atonement of Jesus Christ by reaching back into history and telling of different people who were arrested, tried and condemned to death for crimes of which they were guilty. Just before the execution took place, an innocent person would step forward and offer to die in the place of the guilty person. The innocent person's offer was accepted and the guilty person went free. There is more than one illustration of that in history, and we rightly use a story like that to explain the idea of Christ's substitutionary atonement. But, in such true life stories it is always *one* dying for *one* to be free. In the case of Jesus, it is *one* dying for *all* to be free. How can that be? It cannot be if Jesus is not God. As God, he is worth more than all human beings of all time.

Allow me to illustrate this point of Christ's infinite worth. During the Civil War, there were regular "cease fire" times, during which there would be prisoner of war exchanges. The established rules of prisoner of war exchange declared that one captain was worth sixty privates. The Bible demonstrates this "greater value" principle more than once. In 1 Chronicles 12:8-15, eleven men from the tribe of Gad defect to David in the wilderness of Ziglag. The text names them and says that they were outstanding soldiers. In fact, it says that the least of them was a match for one hundred and that the greatest of them was a match for one thousand.

An even more interesting illustration of this "greater value" principle occurs in 2 Samuel 15-19. Earlier, Absalom had rebelled against his father, King David, who is called "the captain of Israel." The battle is heating up in the forest of Ephraim, and David believes that he should lead the charge against his own son. All of his officers rise up in protest and say, "You must not go out; if we are forced to flee, they won't care about us. Even if half of us die, they won't care; but *you are worth ten thousand of us*" (18:3; italics added).

In Hebrews 2:10, Jesus is called "the captain of our salvation." One for sixty? No. One for one hundred? No. One for one thousand? No. One for ten thousand? No. One for *all*! How can that be? It cannot be if Jesus Christ is not God. But he, the one and only God, is worth more than all people of all time past, present, and future.

All Is Paid

There is a second question that every thinking Christian should ask when contemplating the cross and what Jesus did there. The question is: Did Jesus Christ pay the *full* penalty for sin? Romans 6:23 reads, "For the wages of sin is death . . ." and this awful truth is clearly taught in other Old and New Testament passages.

When the Bible speaks about death, it does so in *three* ways. The first is *physical* death. What is physical death? Physical death is separation of the spirit from the body. James 2:26 reads, "As the body without the spirit is dead, so faith without deeds is dead." James uses physical death to illustrate a spiritual truth.

Secondly, the Bible talks about *spiritual* death. What is spiritual death? Spiritual death is separation of the spirit from God. Ephesians 2:1-5 reads, "You were dead in your transgressions and sins" but God, "has made us alive with Christ." This is not talking about physical death. It is talking about spiritual death—separation of the spirit from God. Every one of us was "stillborn" spiritually speaking. Spiritual death turns to life only when we reach out by faith and receive what Jesus Christ has provided for us on the cross.

But there is a third way that the Bible talks about death, and that is *eternal* death. What is eternal death? Eternal death is eternal separation of the body and the spirit from God forever. The book of Revelation also calls it "the second death."

In Matthew 10:28, Jesus says, "Do not be afraid of those who kill the body but cannot kill the soul. Rather, be afraid of the One who can destroy both soul and body in hell."

Now we come back to the question: Did Jesus Christ pay the *full* penalty for sin? At this point we must not forget that Jesus is fully man and fully God.

Did Jesus die *physically*? Yes. In John 19 the soldiers came to break Jesus' legs to hasten the death process on the cross, but they did not have to do it because he was already dead.

Did Jesus die *spiritually*? Yes. Matthew and Mark record Jesus' words, "My God, my God, why have you forsaken me?" (Mt 27:46; Mk 15:34). Twice in the prophetic description of Christ's death on the cross, Isaiah declared that it was a *soul* sacrifice, "He shall see the suffering of his soul…and be satisfied" (53:11).

Did Jesus Christ die *eternally*? Yes. There are two answers to the question: How long did Jesus hang on the cross? Both are equally accurate. The first answer is six hours. The second answer: *eternally*! How can that be? It cannot be, if Jesus is not God. Because Jesus is God and because God is eternal, what he did in a moment of time-space history was an eternal act that paid the full penalty for sin. The cross of Christ is a fact of time and of eternity. That is why the book of Revelation reads in chapter 13, verse 8 that Jesus Christ is "the Lamb slain from before the foundation of the world." Hebrews 10:12 states, "But when this priest [Jesus] had offered for all time one sacrifice for sins, He sat down at the right hand of God." Other translations use "forever" in place of "for all time."

Even before the first of our four children was born, my wife and I determined that we would have a time of daily devotions together. Some of the most wonderful times in our family were evening devotions. During those times, our kids asked some very difficult questions. One of those questions had to do with *eternal death*. One of our children asked, "Daddy, what is hell really like?" Over the years, I have thought a lot about that question, and I have come to the conclusion that probably the greatest description of hell that you can give anyone is to point them to what happened at the cross. J. I. Packer agrees when he writes,

> Some, then, face an eternity of rejected-ness. We cannot, of course, form any adequate notion of hell and no doubt that it is good for us that this is so, but perhaps the clearest notion we can form is that derived from contemplating the cross. Look at the cross, therefore, and you will see what form God's judicial reaction to human sin will finally take. Jesus lost all the good that he had before the cross and all sense of his Father's presence and love. He lost all sense of physical, mental, and spiritual well-being. All enjoyment of God and created things, all ease and solace of friendship were taken from him. In their place was nothing but loneliness, pain, a killing sense of human malice and callousness and a horror of great spiritual darkness. The physical pain, though great, was yet only a small part of the story. Jesus' chief sufferings were mental and spiritual and what was compressed into less than 400 minutes was an *eternity of agony*.[4] (italics added)

How could Jesus, one person, die for *all* people? It is because he is God. How could Jesus Christ pay the *full* penalty for sin? It is because he is God. The great Moravian missionary, Count Ludwig von Zinzendorf, captured these two truths when he wrote, "Lord, I believe were sinners more/Than sand upon the ocean shore/Thou hast for *all* a ransom paid/For all a *full atonement* made."[5] (italics added)

One for all: He paid the full penalty for sin. That is why the missionary apostle Paul could write to the Romans, "Everyone who calls on the name of the Lord will be saved" (10:13). "Everyone" includes all people. This is not hyperbole; this is theology. It is because of who Jesus is, what Jesus did, and how those two things go together that Paul could say, "For *everyone* who calls upon the name of the Lord will be saved." (italics added) But Paul follows that sweeping statement with several critical and logical questions: "How, then, can they call on the one they have not believed in? And how can they believe in the one of whom they have not heard? And how can they hear without someone preaching to them?" Paul did not simply ask these questions, he grappled with them and with their implications. Then he did something about it, committing his life to reaching the unreached.

Practical Realities

Remember Sandy, the waitress on the front porch in Chicago, the one who said, "That's not fair!"? A week later at midnight, after we had all gone to bed, a knock came on the front door. I got up and found Sandy and four of her friends on the porch. "What's up?" I asked. Sandy spoke for the group, saying, "After work tonight, instead of going home, we were going to downtown Chicago with some of our friends in their van. We waited and waited, but they never came. Then the phone rang, and we found out that on the way to pick us up they had a terrible accident, and the guy driving the van was killed. The other guy sitting in the front seat lost both of his legs. We just had to talk to somebody. Can we talk with you about it?"

This time, Sandy did not ask me theoretical questions about people who live in far off places. She asked me about the boy in the van. She said, "Where is he right now, the one who died?" Then she asked, "What if I had been in the van when the accident happened and I had died, where would I be right now?" Suddenly, life and death, heaven and hell, and time and eternity were very real issues. Again, I shared with them from my Bible the simple message of the Gospel, and the Holy Spirit was obviously working in their hearts. I said, "I sense that you understand what I have been trying to share with you. I'd like to suggest that we pray. Just talk to God like you talk to each other—be very personal with him. If you don't know what to say, I'll help you." So I led them in a simple prayer of confession and repentance and faith, urging them to thank Jesus personally for dying for them on the cross. Three of them prayed with me, and one of the three was Sandy, who was gloriously saved.

I had a new believer's Bible study each afternoon during that summer outreach and Sandy started coming and reading her Bible, and she just loved it. At the end of the last Bible study she took me aside and said, "I just graduated from high school and have been accepted at the university. But, I've changed my mind. I'm going to a Bible college." Surprised, I asked, "Why do you want to go to a Bible college?" She answered, "I want to go to a Bible college to study God's Word to prepare to be a missionary." I replied, "A missionary? Why do you want to be a missionary?" She responded, "Because I still don't think it's fair!" But then she quickly added, "But, I've suddenly realized that it's not *God* who is unfair, it's *us*. God gave us all that we need for salvation when he gave his precious son Jesus to die on the cross. And God has given us, his children, everything we need to take that message to the ends of the earth. And, if there is anybody living anywhere right now who has never heard about Jesus, it's for one reason and one reason alone, and that's because we have failed to take that message to them!"

Sandy went to the New Tribes Bible Institute in Wisconsin and graduated three years later. Today, Sandy and her husband Ron are the heads of a ministry that touches the lives of ten thousand teenagers a year with the Gospel of Jesus Christ.

Jesus said, "I am the way. No one comes to the Father except through me." How can he make such a claim? He can make this claim because of *who he is* and *what he did* and *how those truths go together*.

One of the things I fear after considering all of this is that we will be orthodox and right in our understanding of Scripture but that it won't make any difference in the way we live and in the way we reach out to lost and unreached people. If these things are really true, it should make all the difference in the world.

Notes

1. McDowell, Josh. *Evidence That Demands a Verdict.* (San Bernardino, Cal.: Here's Life Publishers, 1979), 103-109. See also Lewis, C.S. *Mere Christianity.* (New York: Collier Books, 1960), 55-56.

2. See the January editions of the *International Bulletin of Missionary Research* for the annual statistical analysis report. See also Winter, Ralph D. and Steven C. Hawthorne. *Perspectives on the World Christian Movement.* (Pasadena, Cal.: William Carey Library, 1999), 509-511, 519.

3. Bowring, John. *Hymns by John Bowring*, 1825.

4. Packer, J.I. *Knowing God.* (Downer's Grove, Ill.: InterVarsity Press, 1993), 175-176.

5. Zinzendorf, Nicolaus L. von. (1739) Trans. by John Wesley, *Hymns and Sacred Poems*, 1740.

Chapter Two

The Uniqueness of Christ and Missions

Patrick Cate

The Modern Context

Gerald Anderson, for many years the director of the Overseas Ministry Study Center, says "No issue in missiology is more important, more difficult, more controversial, or more divisive for the days ahead than a theology of religions . . . This is *the* theological issue for missions in the 1990s and into the twenty-first century."[1] At the core of this issue lies the question, "Is Christ the only way of salvation?"

This chapter initially seeks to understand both the importance of this question and a bit more about the cultural values of postmodernism, diversity, and tolerance that generated the question. Thereafter, the reader will find a section on understanding and responding to world religions. This second section draws attention to two major areas which confront the uniqueness of Christ: relativism and tolerance on the one hand and inclusivism on the other. Some suggested responses and answers to these objections follow. This chapter then discusses the related doctrine of the justice and wrath of God, with potential responses. In conclusion it asks, "How should we as mission leaders and professors respond to these central questions of our day?" One must not assume that missionaries, the students whom one teaches and recruits, parishioners or even MKs believe that Christ is the only way of salvation. Dr. Harold Netland provides material for serious thinkers. His two books *Dissonant Voices: Religious Pluralism and the Question of Truth*[2] and *Encountering Religious Pluralism: The Challenge to Christian Faith and Mission*,[3] are among the best scholarly and philosophical works on the subject. Dr. Netland presents an excellent defense against philosophical objections to the biblical position. He thoughtfully proves that propositional truth exists in religion. He carefully paints the relativistic, pluralistic picture and a response to it. This is useful for Christian philosophers who can explain and defend the faith, especially in light of today's religious pluralism and the need for missions to the least-reached peoples. Few readers will enter a debate with John Hick, the leading universalist scholar, yet his kind of thinking influences those in classrooms and pews across the country and even some missionary families. Therefore, every thinking Christian needs to popularize and apply Dr. Netland's well-crafted arguments. One must also understand the objectives and thinking of the religious pluralist. Mixed with prayer for the Holy Spirit's guidance, each individual needs to read, study, write, teach, and preach fresh apologetics related to Jesus Christ as the only way of salvation. This chapter will not restate Dr. Netland's deep philosophical arguments, his answers to religious pluralists, or his response to John Hick. Instead, this chapter will build on Dr. Netland's work in practical ways. The Word of God commands every believer to be ready to give an answer for the hope inside of him (1 Peter 3:15). The Christian must have answers for universalists, for evangelical inclusivists, and for those who deny the existence or eternity of hell.

One of the hallmarks of modern society is choice. Choices have increased exponentially over the last century. Perhaps the clearest illustration is the worldwide web where a person may learn about almost any thing, place, concept, or person with a few clicks of the mouse. The day in which we live is also a day of choice in religions. For example, this author first met a Muslim at the age of twenty three, in Jerusalem. Today, however, many six to ten year olds in Canada or the United States have already met a Muslim in their neighborhood or classroom, and one will find Muslims, Hindus, and Buddhists on almost any secular university campus. This is the context in which Christians must address the question of the uniqueness of Christ. Being a particularist, or an exclusivist—saying that Christ is the only way of salvation—is not popular, and this stance becomes less popular with each passing year. In fact, this exclusivism represents the "single most socially offensive aspect of Christian theology," and the pressure to deny Christ's claim is nothing short of "fantastic," according to James Hunter.[4] As Netland observes, pluralists convincingly argue that "large numbers of sincere, morally good and intelligent people simply cannot be mistaken about their basic religious beliefs."[5] Add to this a connotation of "religion" as rigid, authoritarian, and oppressive while "spirituality" is flexible, creative, and tolerant.[6] Thus a creeping pluralism may easily begin to erase one's focus on Christ, persuading the Christian to tone it down, to mute it.

Postmodernism

Just as people feared the changes of the Reformation and Industrial Revolution, many people today fear postmodernism without understanding it. This failure to understand postmodernism stems in part from the lack of a clear definition for postmodernism. J. I. Packer observes that "the only agreed-upon element is that post-modernism is a negation of modernism."[7] Some have suggested that God may even use postmodernity to undercut the Western church's syncretism with modern culture. In *Post Mission: World Mission by a Post-Modern Generation*, Paula Harris points out, "Postmodernity is not about deconstructing the Gospel. It is about deconstructing modernity. Far from being frightened of postmodernity, we should welcome its questions – they will help us seek ways to enculturate the Gospel for a new generation. Postmodernity does not confront Jesus; it confronts the idols of modern culture that we in the West have failed to renounce."[8]

The missiological community needs to capitalize on some of the wonderful values of postmodernism. Individuals within this community must specialize in being tolerant of people who are different from them, even those who simply come from different generations—both within established mission families and within missionaries' adopted cultures. But this sort of tolerance is different from a tolerance of sin and false beliefs. The reader, therefore, must not think of postmodernity as the anti-Christ. Indeed, postmodernism offers many wonderful advantages for spreading the Gospel. For example, the newest generation of missionaries brings a desire for mentoring, a longing for community and intimate relationships, an interest in holistic ministry, and a concern for the environment, as well as character traits such as transparency, people-centeredness, and spiritual hunger. Many of these new missionaries prefer a meaningful, fulfilling life that counts over status or salary. Thus, postmodernism has shaped them to be excellent cross-cultural missionaries.

The primary area of concern regarding postmodernism lies in the concept of spirituality without truth. Western culture increasingly sinks into pluralism, accepting new age theology and living without absolutes. As previously noted, tolerance and diversity stand among the most important modern-day values in the West, and most missionaries appreciate them. However, when multiculturalism, diversity, and tolerance produce a doctrine that rejects absolutes, the missionary faces significant problems.

This theological drift of relativism without absolutes has infiltrated the media. The media teaches that evangelicals are racists, intolerant, un-American, deceitful, and that they impose their intolerance of diversity on others. In 2002, the magazine *Mother Jones* published a blistering, deceptive article on Columbia International University's Islamics program. The magazine cover blared, "False Prophets: Inside the Evangelical Christian Movement that Aims to Eliminate Islam."[9] The cover article for the June 30, 2003, issue of *TIME* magazine praised Mennonites who give humanitarian aid and no gospel to Muslims, but criticized Christians who also preach Christ to Muslims.[10] The same magazine denounced Franklin Graham as being deceptive and unethical because he presents the gospel message to those who receive relief from Samaritan's Purse.[11] Television programs and many other media sources publicly belittle the basic Christian calling to take light to the least-reached. On April 22, 2003, an AP article read around the world mentioned Christar. The article spoke of an "invasion" of evangelists who "circumvented bans on proselytizing," of Muslim background believers who worship "clandestinely," and of the "crime for Christians to proselytize" in some countries–emotionally biased words to say the least.

Diversity and Tolerance

Westerners live in an environment that elevates diversity and tolerance above all other virtues, carrying them to an ignoble extreme. They are "politically correct," which in itself is an oxymoron.[12] People are taught to be tolerant even of evil and sin. The compromising Christian will sometimes interpret something that is biblically repulsive as just an alternative lifestyle. Homosexuality, mentioned in twelve passages, and gluttony are prime examples.

Arnold Toynbee, a leading British historian of the twentieth century, asserted that modern-day Christians should purge Christianity of the exclusive-mindedness and spirit of intolerance that comes from its belief that Christianity is unique.[13] He argues, "The paramount reason is that exclusive-mindedness is a sinful state of mind. It is the sin of pride . . ."[14] This is intolerance of what he considered intolerance. Netland supplies further insight, saying that Christian exclusivism "is distasteful to many today, for it implies that large numbers of sincere, morally good, intelligent adherents of other religions are mistaken in some of their most fundamental beliefs."[15]

Critics of this exclusivism appear within the Christian community as well, alleging that adherents to exclusivism are intolerant and that exclusivism is merely "a vestige of an immoral religious imperialism."[16] A. T. Pierson (considered by many as the leading spokesman for missions at the end of the 19th century) is credited with saying: "Behind the shameful apathy and lethargy of the church, that allows one thousand million human beings to go to their graves in ignorance of the gospel, there lies a practical doubt, if not denial, of their lost condition." In the century since those words were written, the number has escalated to over three billion, but the cause of the church's apathy has not changed. Too often Christians do not really believe that unevangelized people are lost.

James Hunter, in his 1987 study entitled *Evangelism: The Coming Generation*, documented that one-third of the American evangelical college and seminary students polled held some form of the possibility of salvation for those who have never heard.[17] A number of Bible colleges over many years have found that at least one-fourth of the incoming students from solid churches do not hold that salvation requires belief in Christ for everyone. Ronald Nash declares that more than half of evangelical leaders believe people can be saved by Christ without turning to him personally for forgiveness.[18] Furthermore, one Gallup pole established that 52% of American adults believe that all good people will go to heaven and that 45% of

Americans who claim to be born again say that by good works a person can earn a place in heaven. Therefore, somewhere from 25% to a majority of those in evangelical church pews do not believe Christ is the only answer.

On a variety of levels, Christians need to address Christ as the unique Savior of the world. In mission organizations, sometimes—but certainly not all of the time—missionaries may consciously or unconsciously change or ignore their belief in the uniqueness of Christ and an eternal, real hell. As a result, these missionaries may forget that God can use them to reach people who would not have been reached if they had not proclaimed the good news of Christ's life, death, and resurrection.

Of the potential future missionaries who take mission courses, probably 25% to more than 51% do not believe Christ is the only way of salvation and reject that hell is real and eternal. Therefore, they ask, "Why should I get excited about mission work?" Many—*but thankfully not all*—of the pastors in fellowships where this author speaks are concerned about their community, but the rest of the world is not really lost or else is not on their hearts. Other than a few token mission events each year, they wonder, "Why should I do anything about reaching the world for Christ? There is such a big need here." The church members where missionaries preach may have an even higher level of disbelief in the uniqueness of Christ.

Normally, missionaries deeply love and respect many of their national friends. Sometimes it becomes difficult for the missionaries to believe that God would not save their dear friends. Would God really create many in their country, put them in an environment where—through no fault of their own—they could not hear the gospel, and then send them to hell? Answers for these questions come easily when one is 10,000 miles away, reading about these people without befriending them. So those in support positions must help mission families continue studying these biblical, theological issues.

Harold Netland points out that a large number of evangelicals, including John Piper, Ronald Nash, R. C. Sproul, and Carl F. H. Henry, believe that "only those who hear the gospel and explicitly respond to faith in Jesus in this life can be saved. Explicit knowledge of the gospel of Jesus Christ is thus essential for salvation, and there is not hope for those who pass from this life without having come into contact with the gospel."[19] This is called exclusivism. "According to this view, the importance of missions and evangelism can hardly be exaggerated."[20] In contrast, inclusivism holds to Christian theology except that God's salvation is available through natural revelation to those in non-Christian religions. Universalism, on the other hand, holds that God reveals himself through all religions, and it fully rejects the idea of the uniqueness of Jesus Christ.

Understanding World Religions

As evangelical Christians, how do we understand the religions of other peoples? I resonate with Netland's threefold analysis:

1. There is sin within each religion.
2. Satan is in the business of deceiving, of mixing truth with falsehood and has much to do with stealing the glory of God through substitute religious beliefs.
3. We, and everyone within other religions, are created in the image of God and therefore we need to appreciate the good that is within them and us.[21]

Personally, I believe most of us as evangelicals do fairly well in understanding the sin and the satanic influence of other religions. However, I think many of us could benefit from studying and understanding these religions and appreciating what is noble in world religions and in their adherents who are created in God's image. Hendrik Kraemer emphasized that we should never use the word "superior" for followers of Christ because at the heart a believer is a forgiven sinner. There are no superior sinners, only forgiven ones.[22]

Steven Covey's habit of "seek first to understand and then to be understood"[23] is foundational for missions. Great religions have done some helpful things. That can be a wise place to begin. We can profit from exploring bridges between Christ and those outside of him. Christian colleges, Bible colleges, and seminaries could help their future alumni by requiring a course in world religions for graduation. Within our mission families we need far more MAs and PhDs specializing in the religions of the people we hope to reach. Although we remain outsiders, as much as possible we should work at understanding our friends from within.

I respect the Muslim hatred of formal idolatry, its strong emphasis on the unity and sovereignty of God and the *umma*, or the sociological community which unites Muslims. Their culture of extended family care far outshines the care provided by many of our nuclear and split nuclear families. About 99% of Muslim women are virgins when they marry.

Building bridges begins with understanding the foundations for both ends of the bridge. Our goal is not to be threatened by those of other religions, but to understand them, to love them, to dialogue with them and to share the good news. In many of our circles we tend to think that our only job is to exegete the scriptures, but we also need to exegete the culture and religion where God brings us. We can begin by asking, "What do we have in common?" When Christ was dealing with the Pharisees, he understood their mindset. He did not agree with it, but he did understand it. When our Savior told us to "look" on the harvest fields (John 4:35), out of seventeen words for "look" in Greek, he chose the word which means "carefully contemplate."[24] The apostle Paul quotes pagan philosophers or poets at least four times.²⁵ This meant he had to understand where they were coming from. Because Paul had "carefully observed" their religion in the Athenian Agora, he was able to speak about their unknown god and its monument which he had observed. He said he had "examined the objects" of their worship (Acts 17:23 NASB). One of our responsibilities as mission leaders and professors is to help our people desire to understand the values, theology, and philosophy of their focus group.

Netland challenges us by stating,

> Christian apologists must learn first to listen humbly in silence, cultivating relationships of trust before proceeding into encounters over truth . . . It is a reproach to the cause of Christ that Christians sometimes have been overly aggressive in evangelism and apologetics, subjecting other religions to caricature and ridicule. This is not only ineffective but, more importantly, fundamentally unchristian. One can engage in vigorous apologetics while simultaneously demonstrating genuine respect for opposing views and acceptance of religious others as fellow human beings created in God's image and the object of God's limitless love.²⁶

Relativism and Tolerance

Today's Christian leaders preach Christ in a relativistic and tolerant age. In the past, "tolerance" meant "not saying anything negative about [another] religion's beliefs or practices."²⁷ With this new understanding, however, "any time one disagrees with someone else's sincerely held convictions one is necessarily intolerant."²⁸ In evaluating world religions Netland makes a further important observation:

> Stanley Samartha, for example, makes the curious statement that "The question of truth is indeed important, but God's love is even more important . . . Love takes precedence over truth." Certainly one must not minimize the significance of God's love. But, as it stands, Samartha's statement is confused. Important

as it is, the concept of God's love would have no relevance for anyone apart from the truth of certain basic propositions: that there is in fact a God, that God loves all persons, that God's love is supremely manifested in the Incarnation, and so on. We conclude, then, that the most important basis upon which to evaluate various religions is the question of truth.[29]

If truth is the most important basis for evaluation, how can one deal with the objections of a pluralistic society? Following are a few of the present-day concerns and some potential initial responses. Postmodernism says that absolute truth can be linked to oppression such as seen in the crusades and the inquisition. In answer to this one needs to point out that saying that the crusades and inquisition were wrong is an absolute truth statement. So the question should not be "Does absolute truth exist?" but "Where can we find it?" Christ's claims to absolute truth are part of the fabric holding Christianity together.

When one says, "Absolutes do not exist," he has overlooked the fact that the sentence he just spoke is an absolute sentence and therefore an oxymoron. Or if someone says, "Truth cannot be known," then his own statement cannot be proven true. All believers need to specialize in helping Christians, as well as non-Christians, realize that truth can be known, and truth *is* known in the person of Jesus Christ.

Today's popular theology states that it does not matter what a person believes as long as he is sincere. One need not look far to find fundamental problems with this point of view. For example, suppose in the middle of the night, a man bothered by a cough gets up to take medicine. If, because it is dark, he takes what he sincerely believes to be a bottle of cough medicine but in reality it is Draino, he would be sincerely wrong. If a woman gets on a plane and sincerely believes it will take her home, but in fact it is going in the opposite direction, she will sincerely arrive at the wrong destination.

A few years ago this author flew into a mid-west city to speak at a church. During that weekend this same city also hosted a conference for mathematicians, people with PhDs in mathematics who usually taught at the university level. I happened to be seated next to a Hindu couple—both with PhDs in mathematics—coming for the conference. We began a conversation, and I tried to explain that objective truth does exist. I said opposites can both be wrong, but opposites cannot both be true. Two and two making five, or making fifty five, are opposite answers, and both are wrong. Two and two always make four, never five. When I said this, the lady said that a higher form of mathematics actually exists in which two and two does not always make four. When she said that her husband said, "Oh, be quiet!" He acknowledged that objective truth does exist and that one cannot explain it away by relativism, as Hinduism and the religiously pluralistic world frequently tries to do. For relativists, one needs to point out that murder of your child or spouse is *always* wrong. In other words, absolutes do exist. Every person functions with absolutes throughout life.

If it does not matter what one believe*s* as long as he is sincere, then Judas, Pilate, Nero, Hitler, Stalin, Mao, Osama, and Saddam have an equal place of fellowship in heaven with Paul, Augustine, Luther, Edwards, Wesley, and Billy Graham. All of these leaders were, or are, sincere.

Furthermore, to some degree and in some senses all religions are exclusive. In Islam, only good Muslims will go to paradise. God in the Old Testament is categorically intolerant of idolatry. In the secular world, professors, teachers, salesmen, politicians, and coaches all try to persuade people to their viewpoints, but no one accuses them of being intolerant.

When postmodernists claim that all roads lead up the mountain to God, that all religions teach the same thing, they are simply not connected with reality. Some popular theology teaches that all religions are variations on the same theme with no fundamental differences. However, the facts show the opposite. Biblical faith and other world religions cannot both be true, as the following examples illustrate.

The Bible teaches One God (Deut 6:4). Hinduism, animism, and ancestor worship teach that there are many gods. Both cannot be true. The Bible teaches that believers are to worship only one God, and they are not to make or worship idols (Ex 20:2-5). Hinduism, Buddhism, animism, and ancestor worship teach that people should worship and pray to numerous idols and spirits. Both cannot be true. The Bible teaches that each person will die and face judgment once (Heb 9:27). Hinduism and Buddhism profess that through reincarnation a person can be born and die many times. Both cannot be true. The Bible teaches that salvation comes by grace through faith, not by anyone's works (Eph 2:8-9). Islam, Hinduism, Buddhism, animism, ancestor worship, and Roman Catholicism teach that salvation is through works. Both cannot be true. The Bible teaches that Christ died on the cross for our sins (Rom 3:24-25) and rose from the dead (Luke 24:6-7). Islam says Christ did not die on a cross and did not rise from the dead. Both cannot be true. The Bible teaches Christ is God (John 1:1) and the Son of God (Mark 1:1), and God is a trinity. Islam holds Christ is not God and not the Son of God; God is not a trinity. Both cannot be true. Islam teaches that Christ is not the Savior of the world; there is no assurance of forgiveness of sins, and there is no assurance of eternal life. The Bible teaches the exact opposite. Both cannot be true. Five times the Qur'an says God is a deceiver, two of those times it says that he is the greatest deceiver.[30] The Bible says that God is the truth. Both cannot be true. Some religions and cultures encourage lying, infanticide, widow burning, and cannibalism. The Bible says these are sin (Ex 20:16, for example). Both cannot be true. The Bible teaches Christ is the Messiah. Judaism believes that Christ is not the Messiah. Both cannot be true. Except for Christ, no significant religious leader has ever claimed to be God, including Abraham, Moses, Paul, Buddha, Confucius, or Mohammed.

Humanism characterizes the modern Westerner's life. Wade Roof points out, "The real story of American religious life in this half century is the *rise of a new sovereign self* that defines and sets limits on the very meaning of the divine."³¹ There is, in the heart of every person, a desire to see and hold God, to create God and to make himself into God. To make one's self into God is the ultimate rebuke of the Creator Redeemer God and of his honor. Both this theology and the theology of Scripture cannot be true. The Bible teaches that God and his glory are the ultimate goals of life. Humanism says that man and his happiness, fulfillment, development, and glory are the ultimate goals of life. Both cannot be true.

The Old Testament contains some of the clearest claims to exclusiveness, clarifying God's abhorrent attitude toward idols that steal his glory. The exclusivism taught in the Old Testament reflects an environment of immense Palestinian and Middle Eastern idolatry. In New Testament times Christians faced the worship of the Roman emperor, the cults of Artemis/Diana, the mystery religions, and many versions of Greek philosophies such as cynicism, stoicism, and Epicureanism. Religious pluralism is not a new phenomenon.

Inclusivism versus Exclusivism

For many Christian thinkers the most pressing question involves the debate between inclusivism and exclusivism. Netland issues three cautions concerning Christian exclusivism:

> First, Christian exclusivism does not entail that all of the claims of the other religions must be false . . . Similarly, Christian exclusivism does not entail that other religions are completely without value, or that Christians cannot learn anything from adherents of other faiths. And finally, it should be recognized that Christian exclusivism is but one example of exclusivism in religion . . . An exclusivist religion can be thought of in broad terms as a religion which maintains that its own central affirmations are true, and that if the claims of another religion appear to be incompatible with its own claims, the former are to be rejected as false. ³²

Scripture clearly teaches exclusivism in passages such as John 1:14; John 3:16, 18; John 14:6; Acts 4:12; 2 Thessalonians 1:7-9; 1 Timothy 2:5; and Hebrews 9:12. In order to defend Christian exclusivism, however, one must study the passages which universalists—and especially inclusivists—use in defense of their positions. Some inclusivists use Psalm 19:14; 50:1-6; Joel 2:32; John 1:9; 3:21; 10:16; Acts 10:4, 22, 31; 17:26, 27; Romans 1:18; 2:4, 7; 10:13, 18 and Hebrews 11:6.

Several noted theologians and missionaries advocate an inclusivist perspective. Even the very conservative theologian J. I. Packer says, "We may safely say (i) if any good pagan reached the point of throwing himself on his Maker's mercy for pardon, it was grace that brought him there; (ii) God will surely save anyone he brings thus far; (iii) anyone thus saved would learn in the next world that he was saved through Christ."[33] The inclusivist Millard Erickson, author of a standard systematic theology textbook used in many of our evangelical schools, states "The essential nature of saving faith can be arrived at without the special revelation . . . Perhaps, in other words, it is possible to receive the benefits of Christ's death without conscious knowledge-belief in the name of Jesus."[34] Don Richardson, one of the outstanding missionary statesmen, writers, thinkers, and speakers of our day, yet now an inclusivist, teaches that "Jesus incognito is just as much the Savior as Jesus named!"[35] Each of these inclusivist positions reflects non-biblical theology based on silence, wishful thinking, or both.

Richardson provides an excellent case-in-point when he says that in Acts 11:14, when Peter quoted the angel's instructions to Cornelius, Peter "padded" the angel's actual words.[36] A dictionary definition of "padding" includes "to expand or increase with needless misleading or fraudulent matter." Richardson bases his argument on silence—a very difficult position to prove. Many accounts are not mentioned in every gospel, but this does not mean that the gospel writers who alone included an event of Christ "padded" their account. They still are true, whether the other gospel writers included them or not. By implying that Peter revised what the angel said, Richardson is revising the text of Scripture. If the Corneliuses and Ethiopian eunuchs (Acts 8) around the world are saved apart from the gospel, why take the trouble to tell them they are saved?

The biblical text says sonship comes from believing in his "name" (John 1:12), and there is no other "name . . . by which we must be saved" (Acts 4:12 NIV). Yet Don Richardson teaches that these passages do not really mean "name."[37] This is questionable exegesis. The Savior taught his followers to pray, "Hallowed be thy name" (Matt 6:9). The Greek text uses the word typically translated "name." These passages are written ultimately for all readers, not just Hebrews who esteemed the name of God. The name "Jehovah" in the Old Testament was unique, a different name from the man-made idols. Jehovah and the idols could not both save. If some are going to be saved without hearing the name of Christ, who is to say that most everyone could not be saved without hearing of Christ? Richardson reasons, "If a majority of people created in God's likeness are lost, God has lost an enormous part of a precious commodity–his likeness!"[38] If this argument is true, then if one person is lost, God has lost some of a precious commodity, his likeness. This argument can more readily be used by universalists.

The "wider hope" view, agnosticism, and inclusivism proffer significantly different views of the future awaiting those who have not heard about Christ. However, each of these positions believes that some people may never hear of Christ yet still go to heaven. Thinking on these positions (and those in between) raises a very profound question. Why *should one* go to the mission field since people will reach Heaven regardless of whether or not we tell them about Christ? There are easier ways to make a living than serving as a missionary.

Universalists, inclusivists, and exclusivists agree that those who do not reach the age of accountability will be saved.

The Uniqueness of Christ and Missions 53

The universalists and some inclusivists argue that a large percent of people die in the womb or before their fifth year (before an age of accountability) and some are not mentally competent. Following that line of reasoning, they try to extend God's grace for salvation to others (or to all) who only have general revelation. Such thinking bases doctrine on percentages rather than revelation.

Inclusivists often argue that God saves few people through general revelation alone; most people need special revelation to be saved. Again, this argument springs from silence. If God can and does save some through general revelation, why set up a system where he will not save others? According to the inclusivists, some will be saved by general revelation alone while others need both general and special revelation and, therefore, missionaries are still needed. This theological position still leaves the inclusivist open to the universalist's classic objection: Why would God create so many people and allow them to go to hell?

Inclusivists argue that their position keeps a number of Christians from becoming universalists. This same position, however, will prevent many from going to the mission field. Truth is truth whether it is popular or not.

Furthermore, inclusivists point out that people in the Old Testament were saved by faith without a clear knowledge of Christ. Why should the same opportunity be unavailable for some people today? Progressive revelation is a basic concept of Scripture. Scripture commands Hebrews and other God-fearers to worship on Saturday, offer animal sacrifices for the forgiveness of sin, abstain from certain foods, and go to Jerusalem three times a year to worship. Through the progressive revelation of God and his will, these stipulations have changed.

Some inclusivists will acknowledge that people who have intentionally rejected the gospel are condemned, but they insist that God will not condemn those who have not had an opportunity to hear it. In contrast, notice man's status before belief in Christ according to John 3:18, "Whoever believes in him is not condemned, but whoever does not believe stands condemned already because he has not believed in the name of God's one and only Son."

So some believe the unbiblical premise that the unevangelized are not lost; only those who hear and reject the gospel are lost. If this premise were true, then evangelists and missionaries would bring condemnation to everyone who hears the gospel and then rejects it. The logical course of action then would be *not* to tell the unsaved about Christ for fear they may reject him and become lost. Therefore, if one destroyed or silenced all churches, missionaries, evangelists, Bibles, Christian TV and radio programs, Christian books, literature, schools and hospitals, etc., in one generation, then no one would hear the gospel, no one would be condemned, and everyone would go to heaven.

Some inclusivists suggest that Melchizedek, Job, Jethro, and others were saved apart from direct revelation, thus making a huge assumption that is unproven by the text–another argument from silence. In the first thirty years after Christ's death special revelation was transmitted orally. In the same way, God could have orally transmitted special revelation about himself to Old Testament, non-Jewish believers. All Christians need to be very careful not to build doctrines on assumptions. We do not know how Melchizedek knew, or what he knew, concerning God.

Exclusivists believe that, according to the Bible, people are accountable for how they respond to the information they have about God. Herbert Kane states that the unevangelized person has "the light of creation, providence, and conscience and he will be judged by that light. If he is finally condemned it will not be because he refused to believe the gospel, but because he failed to live up to the little light he had."[39] Sri Lankan Ajith Fernando states that Scripture "also shows that no one lives according to the light he receives, and that no one can be saved without the gospel."[40]

Some Christians believe that everyone has sinned but that the unevangelized are excused because they have not yet received a clear understanding of the gospel. However, Psalm 19:1-6; Acts 14:17, and Romans 1:18-20 clarify that the natural revelation of God is available to everyone—including those who are unreached with the good news of Jesus Christ. Therefore every person is without excuse. Even those without Scripture have the revelation of God through their consciences according to Romans 2:14-15. Furthermore, Romans 1:21-25 declares that the ungodly and unrighteous suppress the truth God provides through natural revelation and one's conscience: they think they know God, but they do not honor him as God or give thanks.

Even as some inclusivists acknowledge that the least-reached have sinned and have not responded to the light of creation which they have received, these inclusivists do not want to believe that the least-reached are completely lost and without hope. However, Romans 2:12 points out that all who have sinned without the Law will also perish without the law. 2 Thessalonians 1:7b-9 also describes the destiny of "those who do not know God and do not obey the gospel" of Christ. Robert E. Speer clarifies, "Men are in this plight, not because they are unevangelized but because they are men."[41] Sin is the destroyer of the soul and the destruction of the knowledge of God, which is life. A failure to hear the gospel does not make someone a sinner. The gospel would save this person if he heard it and accepted it. But it is not the ignorance or rejection of the gospel which destroys him; it is the knowledge of sin.[42]

There is truth and error in all religions, and many people today erroneously believe that adherents who sincerely follow the truth in their religion will find God. They see the various religions as many paths leading up a mountain and one may choose any of these paths as long as he reaches the top. Since many paths lead to God, they suggest, each individual may take the best known and most comfortable path. However, Christ said, "I am the way and the truth and the life. No one comes to the Father except through Me" (John 14:6). As C. S. Lewis persuasively demonstrated, either Christ was telling the truth, he was the Devil, or he was crazy. No one will claim that a great teacher is the Devil, lying, or crazy.[43] The apostle Peter said, "Salvation is found in no one else; for there is no other name under heaven given to men by which we must be saved" (Acts 4:12). Paul also teaches that there is only "one mediator between God and men, the man Christ Jesus" (1 Timothy 2:5).

Undoubtedly, scripture teaches that "You will seek me and find me when you seek me with all your heart" (Jeremiah 29:13). God was addressing Jews who had some written revelation, but to the Athenians Paul preached "that *men* would seek [God] and perhaps *reach out* for him and find him, though he is not far from each one of us" (Acts 17:27, italics added). Exclusivists understand this verse to indicate that God will send special revelation to people who seek God with all of their hearts through the natural revelation and conscience they have. Cornelius exemplifies this principle.

The Justice and Wrath of God

As doctrines, the justice and wrath of God differ from but are related to the uniqueness of Christ. Universalists and some inclusivists tend to disregard all of these.

Clark Pinnock believes that eternal torment in hell is "morally and scripturally flawed" and should be rejected.[44] He states, "Death is the occasion when the unevangelized have an opportunity to make a decision about Jesus Christ."[45] John R. Stott teaches that "the ultimate annihilation of the wicked should at least be accepted as a legitimate, biblically founded alternative to their eternal conscious torment."[46]

In the end, the Word of God must be the final authority, not what one desires or what the contemporary world believes. J. I. Packer has said,

> The modern habit throughout the Christian church is to play this subject down. Those who still believe in the wrath of God (not all do) say little about it; perhaps they do not think much about it. To an age which has unashamedly sold itself to the gods of greed, pride, sex, and self-will, the church mumbles on about God's kindness, but says virtually nothing about His judgment ... The fact is that the subject of divine wrath has become taboo in modern society, and Christians by and large have accepted the taboo and conditioned themselves never to raise the subject.[47]

If individuals believe in heaven because the Bible and Christ taught it, then they must also accept the existence of hell for the same reason. Christ taught more about hell than he did about heaven. D. A. Carson reasons, "It is the Lord Jesus, of all persons in the Bible, who consistently and repeatedly uses the most graphic images of hell. Is it not clear that he does so precisely to warn people against hell, and to encourage them to repent and believe? Should we not, therefore, do the same?"[48]

One of the problems today is that Christians have not emphasized what Christ emphasized: that narrow is the way that leads to salvation and broad is the way that leads to damnation (Matt 7:13-14). God knows that the majority of people will not choose to obey and follow him. This concept connects with the concept of salvation by grace, not one's own merit.

Universalists teach that God does not punish evil. Don Richardson encapsulates their position (which he rejects) very well: "God has no problem breaching his holiness to save the wicked, or perhaps has no holiness to be breached!"[49] Therefore, God is not just. Justice demands payment equal to the wrongs committed. A contemporary trend plays up man's righteousness and goodness and plays down God's holiness and God's standard for holiness in heaven and for those who enter heaven. Joni Eareckson Tada provides thoughtful insight on God's fairness: "It seldom really strikes me that God owes this utterly rebellious and ungrateful planet absolutely *nothing*. In fact, that is an understatement. Actually he does owe us something: hell."[50]

At the root of the thinking Christian's questions about God's justice is his lack of an in-depth understanding of God. He tries to put God in a box, man's box. As Phillip Yancey says about Job, Christians are like spectators watching a drama. They know a little more than Job because of the interaction they observe between God and Satan. However, at the end of the book of Job, God speaks for longer than at any other place in Scripture, and he does not answer Job's questions about his own justice or Job's suffering. Instead, God teaches Job about his power and sovereignty.[51]

Christians know much about God through scripture and Christ, but much remains that is not known. Paul aptly described our perspective: "a poor reflection as in a mirror" (1 Cor 13:12). Compare theology to science: just think what has been learned about God's vast universe in recent years through the Hubble telescope and the Galileo explorations. Or consider the human eye. Over 140 years ago Charles Darwin said, "The eye to this day gives me a cold shudder. To suppose that the eye, with all of its inimitable contrivances for adjusting the focus to different distances, for admitting different amounts of light, and for the correction of spherical and chromatic aberration, could have been formed by natural selection, seems, I freely confess, absurd in the highest possible degree."[52] Darwin wrote these words long before modern science began to understand the deeper chemical and electrical complexities of the eye. The Psalmist reflects, "He that formed the eye, shall he not see?" (Ps 94:9 NASB). This majestic, awe inspiring God is both loving and just, and human beings need to be careful not to squeeze him into man-made boxes of love and justice.

Some people argue that if a person has not heard of Christ, he or she should not be separated from God for eternity. There are two sides to a proper response. First, individuals do not go to hell because they have not heard of Christ. A person goes to hell because of his sin, and everyone has sinned. It is only by grace—by unmerited favor—that anyone has heard of Christ and responded to him in faith. Frequently human beings

The Uniqueness of Christ and Missions 59

have too shallow an appreciation of their sin, God's holiness, and God's grace. Secondly, as previously discussed, the logical conclusion of this argument would require that someone rid the world of all ways of hearing the gospel, then in one generation nobody would have heard the gospel, and therefore everybody would go to heaven.

1 John 5:19 *declares* that the whole world lies in the power of the evil one. One of the clearest passages on the future status of those who do not know God and do not obey the gospel is 2 Thessalonians 1:7b-9 (NIV). It deserves repeating here:

> This will happen when the Lord Jesus is revealed from heaven in blazing fire with his powerful angels. He will punish those who do not know God and do not obey the gospel of our Lord Jesus. They will be punished with everlasting destruction and shut out from the presence of the Lord and from the majesty of his power.

For most readers this is not an enjoyable passage. Truth, however, does not consist solely of concepts that make people feel comfortable. Every Christian needs to be careful not to judge God by his own finite human concepts of fairness and justice.

C. S. Lewis said, "There is no doctrine I would more willingly remove from Christianity than this if it lay in my power. But it has the full support of Scripture, and especially of our Lord's own words; it has also been held by Christendom; and it has the support of reason. If a game is played, it must be possible to lose it. If the happiness of a creature lies in self-surrender, no one can make that surrender but himself, and he may refuse. I would pay any price to be able to say truthfully, 'All will be saved.' But my reason retorts, 'Without their will, or with it?'"[53]

Many, maybe most Christians, *are repulsed by* the doctrine of hell and of Christ being the only way of salvation. However, it is repulsive to this author that 46% of the people in the world have an average income of $326 per year. I do not like the fact that 150 million people have no shelter whatsoever. It is abhorrent to me that many people in our inner cities have neither a home nor enough food to eat. The spiritual decline of North America and the West disgusts me. Yet something's repulsiveness does not determine its truthfulness.

But consideration of this topic must never sink to the level of mere academic exercise or a comfortable in-house theological debate. The implications of this question are staggering. The subject should always be approached in a spirit of genuine humility, sorrow for those who will spend an eternity apart from God, and repentance over one's own sin and lack of compassion that so often prevents the gospel of Jesus Christ from reaching all peoples.

How should Christians respond to these significant biblical doctrines? May each one be moved as Paul was. First, as a result of the fear or terror of God, Paul persuaded men (2 Cor. 5:9-11). Second, Paul felt a personal responsibility to share the gospel, saying, "Woe is me if I do not preach the gospel" (1 Cor 9:16). In Romans 10:13-17 Paul clarifies that Christians are obligated both to preach and to send missionaries.

J. Oswald Sanders concludes, "If this indeed is the present condition and future prospect of the heathen—and Scripture seems to offer no alternative—and if the church of Christ has in her charge the message which alone can transform these tragic 'withouts' into the possession of 'the unsearchable riches of Christ,' then how urgent is the missionary enterprise. And how great the tragedy if we fail to proclaim it."[54]

J. Hudson Taylor is reported to have said, "Would that God would make hell so real to us that we cannot rest; heaven so real that we must have men there; Christ so real that our supreme motive and aim shall be to make the Man of Sorrows, the Man of Joy by the conversion to him of many. . ."

So What?

How should the missiological community respond to this theological decline? First, missionaries need to remember that

Western church members live in a pluralistic world. More and more church members, therefore, desire missions to change from being redemptive to merely offering humanitarian relief. As a result, ministers should not assume that every church member believes that all people need the gospel.

Leaders must emphasize the basic theological and philosophical reasons why everyone needs Christ. All missionaries, whether speaking in a church or on a campus, need to address the uniqueness of Jesus Christ. This world also needs missionary statesmen and missionary theologians who will study the Word, study their world, speak to these issues, write powerfully, and clearly communicate the beauty and uniqueness of Christ along with the lostness of those outside of Christ.

Even if missionaries taught these things clearly in the churches where they speak in the coming year, the total number of people reached would still be much less than if all missionaries clearly taught them in all of their supporting churches and wrote of them in their prayer letters. Christian leaders need to help the missionaries understand these issues so the missionaries can better teach and preach concerning the uniqueness of Christ in a pluralistic world. Furthermore, if these issues were addressed in the main mission publications, hundreds of thousands of mission supporters could be reached.

Again, let neither this author nor his readers forget the foot soldiers. Some missionaries, without saying it, could doubt whether Christ is the only way of salvation. I studied under a professor who went out with an IFMA mission, yet he later gave up evangelism for dialogue and gave up commitment to Christ as the only way of salvation. The same thing can happen to other missionaries. In this author's mission, Christar, all of the missionaries work through an in-depth Bible study called *Through God's Eyes: Biblical Motivations for Missions*.[55] It includes major sections on these subjects. The reader must also consider his influence on MKs, students, pastors, and churches.

Several questions should consistently direct the sincere Christian's thinking: "In the light of his supreme sacrifice, what should my response be to the Lord of my salvation? How do I think Christ feels about this theological drift? How do I think God feels about the creeping acceptance of substitutes for himself and his glory?" Missionaries—indeed, all Christians—must never retreat from Christ as the only way of salvation. Dropping this belief would surely seal the death certificate for missions. There are many other worthy motivations for missions, such as the glory of God, the love of God, and obeying his commands. But Christ as the only way of salvation provides the supreme motivation for missions. If Western culture continues in the direction it is going, there will be fewer people going to the mission field, fewer people praying for missionaries, and fewer people giving to send them. May you and I be culture-changers.

When people from the 10/40 Window immigrate to Canada or the United States, they may be seeking financial gain, freedom, or proximity to family. However, God brings those from other faiths to Canada, the United States, and the West in order for them to hear the gospel from Christians here. Yet only 25% of foreign students are invited into any home—much less an evangelical home—while they are in the United States. Future missionaries may "practice" here with members of the religion where they plan to minister.

Christian leaders must lead missionaries and students to study of both types of biblical passages: those passages which clarify the uniqueness of Christ and the reality of hell, but also those passages which the more liberal contingent would use to justify their viewpoints. These Bible studies should provide guidance in thinking through the philosophical and theological questions and answers facing each person. As a result of this Bible study (of Christ being the only way of salvation and hell being both real and eternal) Christians must recruit, train, send, and support laborers to take the good news of Christ to the least-reached peoples in the world. This is not just an intellectual study, not just one more doctrine or philosophical study. It produces a profound compassion for the lost.

One cannot overstate God's grace. Most of the readers of this chapter were born where they could easily hear the good news and learn of Jesus Christ without persecution, where there are ample resources of prayer and finances to send missionaries. To whom much has been given, much will be required (Luke 12:48). Steven Neill said in his book, *Out of Bondage*, "When a man, by constant contemplation of the Passion and Resurrection of our Lord, finds himself so inflamed with the love of God and man that he cannot bear the thought of any man living and dying without the knowledge of God, he may begin to bear the Cross of Christ. If, as he bears it, this longing for the glory of God and for the salvation of all men becomes so great that it fills all his thoughts and desires, then he has that one thing without which no man can truly be a messenger of Christ."[56]

This author was privileged to visit with a colleague in Tunis and to go to Carthage to observe the church ruins where Monica had prayed and wept all night. She prayed for the conversion of her wayward, rebelling son, Augustine, who was sailing to Italy. We also saw an amphitheater and went to its jail where, in the year A.D. 202, six believers in Christ were kept. When Perpetua came to trial she saw her aged father holding her infant child in his arms. He begged, "Have pity on your baby." The judge took her father's side, saying "Spare your father's white hairs, spare the tender years of your child, offer a sacrifice for the welfare of the emperor." Perpetua answered "I will not sacrifice." The judge asked "Are you a Christian?" Her answer was "I am a Christian." When none of the six would recant, they were put in the arena with a bull who tossed Perpetua in the air, tearing her robe. As soon as she got up, she ran to Felicitas, wounded by the bull, and gently raised her from the ground. When the bull refused to attack again, they were removed from the arena. Saturus was put in the arena one last time and a leopard was let loose and with one bite Saturus was mortally wounded. Finally, those who were still alive were brought back to the arena to be killed by gladiators. Perpetua was given a young, untried gladiator who was not used to the acts of violence. He weakly stabbed her several times between the ribs but did not kill her. So Perpetua guided his wavering hand to her throat.[57]

Perpetua had wealth, a noble birth, a fine family, intelligence, education, beauty and youth, but none of this, including her love for her baby, compared with her love for Jesus. Obeying his will was her first priority. These final words she wrote to her family: "Do not be ashamed by my death. I think it is the greatest honor of my life and thank God for calling me to give my life for his sake and his cause. He gave the same honor to the holy prophets, his dearly beloved apostles, and his blessed, chosen martyrs. I have no doubt that I am dying for God's cause and the cause of truth."[58] May you and I be equally passionate about our Savior.

Recently, at a church of Iranian refugees in Asia, this author visited with a career officer from the Iranian army who had put his faith in Christ. When asked what the marks were all over his arms (larger than the size of a small Band-Aid), he responded that they were brands, burned into his arms and all over his back with red hot metal. They had been burned in him to try to persuade him to return to Islam. He escaped from a hospital where they were intensely drugging him. He refused to deny Christ. May every Christian's commitment to the Savior be just as deep. May no Christian worry about his "comfort zone" but concentrate on the supremacy of Christ and the eternal destiny of those who have not heard of Christ.

Mission families who read this chapter have the highest calling in the world because Christ is the only way of salvation, heaven is real and eternal, and hell is real and eternal. May each person's passion for Christ burn bright. May each one continually share his love, death, and resurrection with others. May thinking Christians continue to pass that vision to the present mission family, the students, and the churches. Netland prescribes, "It is incumbent upon evangelicals not only to proclaim the message of the gospel with humility and sensitivity, but also to demonstrate to a skeptical and relativistic culture why it is that it can claim to have certainty concerning ultimate religious questions."[59]

Historian Jaroslav Pelikan states, "Regardless of what anyone may personally believe about him, Jesus of Nazareth has been the dominant figure in the history of Western culture for almost twenty centuries."[60] The Lausanne Covenant of 1974 clearly stated, "We also regard as derogatory to Christ and the Gospel every kind of syncretism and dialogue which implies that Christ speaks equally through all religions and ideologies. Jesus Christ, being himself the only God-man, who gave himself as the only ransom for sinners, is the only mediator between God and man. There is no other name by which we must be saved."[61] The most crucial questions of life were asked by our Lord when he inquired, "Who do people say that I am?" and "Who do you believe that I am?" (Mark 8:27-29).

Notes

1. Gerald H. Anderson, "Theology of Religions and Missiology: A Time of Testing," in *The Good News of the Kingdom: Mission Theology of the Third Millennium,* ed. Charles Van Engen, Dean S. Gilliland, and Paul Pierson (Maryknoll, NY: Orbis, 1993), 201.

2. Harold A. Netland, *Dissonant Voices: Religious Pluralism and the Question of Truth* (Vancouver, British Columbia: Regent College Publishing, 1991).

3. Harold A. Netland, *Encountering Religious Pluralism: The Challenge to Christian Faith and Mission* (Downers Grove, IL: InterVarsity Press, 2001).

4. James Davison Hunter, *Evangelicalism: The Coming Generation* (Chicago: University of Chicago Press, 1987), 34. Hunter researched Christian students in college or seminary during the 1980s.

5. Netland, *Encountering Religious Pluralism,* 213.

6. Netland, *Encountering Religious Pluralism,* 152.

7. James I. Packer quoted in David Goetz, "The Riddle of Our Postmodern Culture: What is Postmodernism? Should We Even Care?," *Leadership Journal* (Winter 1997): 53.

8. Paula Harris, "Postmodernism is Not the Antichrist," in *Postmission: World Mission by a Postmodern Generation,* ed. Richard Tiplady (Waynesboro, GA: Pasternoster Press, 2002), 68.

9. Barry Yeoman, "The Stealth Crusade," *Mother Jones*, May-June 2002,

10. David van Biema, "Keeping the Faith Without Preaching It," TIME, 30 June 2003.

11. David van Biema, "The Life of Jesus in 830 Languages," TIME, 30 June 2003.

12. The politically correct agenda has two internal fallacies. It implies that absolute truth exists, which contradicts its own philosophy. And politics in a democracy should allow all views to be represented in a free market of ideas. Saddam Hussein practiced his own form of political correctness.

13. Arnold Toynbee, *Christianity Among the Religious of the World* (New York: Charles Scribner's Sons, 1957), 95-100.

14. Toynbee, *Christianity Among the Religions of the World*, 9.

15. Netland, *Encountering Religious Pluralism*, 188.

16. Netland, *Dissonant Voices*, 27.

17. Hunter, *Evangelicalism*, 34. Now these same students are leaders in our churches!

18. Ronald H. Nash, *Is Jesus the Only Savior?* (Grand Rapids: Zondervan Publishing House, 1994), 107.

19. Netland, *Encountering Religious Pluralism*, 320.

20. Ibid., 321.

21. Ibid., 330-377.

22. Hendrik Kraemer, *The Christian Message in a Non-Christian World* (New York: Harper and Brothers, 1938).

23 Stephen R. Covey, *The 7 Habits of Highly Effective People: Powerful Lessons in Personal Change* (New York: Simon and Schuster, 1989), 235-260

24. W. E. Vine, Merril F. Unger and William White, Jr., Vine's Expository Dictionary of Biblical Words (Nashville: Thomas Nelson Publishers, 1985), 377-384.

25 Acts 17:28a quotes a Cretan poet Epimenides (c. 600 B.C.). Acts 17: 28b quotes a Stoic Cilician poet Aratus (c. 315-240 B.C.). I Corinthians 15:33 quotes Athenian Menander (4th century B.C.). Titus 1:12 quotes the Cretan Epimenides.

26. Harold Netland, *Encountering Religious Pluralism*, 283.

27. Netland, *Encountering Religious Pluralism*, 144.

28. Netland, *Encountering Religious Pluralism*, 144.

29. Netland, *Dissonant Voices*, 166. This author resonates with Netland's threefold analysis in *Encountering Religious Pluralism*, 330-377: "(1) There is sin within each religion. (2) Satan is in the business of deceiving, of mixing truth with falsehood and has much to do with stealing the glory of God through substitute religious beliefs. (3) We, and everyone

within other religions, are created in the image of God and therefore we need to appreciate the good that is within them and us."

30. These are located in Surah 10:21, 3:54, and 8:30. In translating the Qur'an, Yusuf Ali-realizes the problem, intentionally and incorrectly substituting "plan" or "plot" for the Arabic "makara." AbdullahYusuf Ali, *The Holy Qur'an: Text, Translation, and Commentary* (Elmhurst, NY: Tahrike Tarsile Qur'an, 1987). Hans Wehr, author of the leading Arabic-English dictionary, defines "makara" as "deceive, delude, cheat, dupe, gull, double-cross." Hans Wehr, *A Dictionary of Modern Written Arabic* (London: MacDonald and Evans LTD, 1974), 917.

31. Wade Clark Roof, *Spiritual Marketplace: Baby Boomers and the Remaking of American Religion* (Newbury Park, CA: Sage, 1992), 155.

32. Netland, *Dissonant Voices*, 35.

33. James I. Packer, *God's Words* (Downer's Grove, IL: InterVarsity Press, 1981), 210.

34. Millard J. Erickson, "Hope for Those Who Haven't Heard? Yes, But . . . ," *Evangelical Missions Quarterly* 11 (April 1975): 122-6.

35. Don Richardson, *Secrets of the Koran: Revealing Insight into Islam's Holy Book* (Ventura, CA: Regal, 2003), 243.

36. Richardson, *Secrets*, 245.

37. Richardson, *Secrets*, 243, 247.

38. Richardson, *Secrets*, 240, 241.

39. J. Herbert Kane, *Christian Missions in Biblical Perspective* (Grand Rapids: Baker Book House, 1976), 162.

40. Ajith Fernando, *The Christian Attitude Toward World Religions* (Wheaton: Tyndale, 1987), 120.

41. Robert E. Speer, "Are the Unevangelized Heathen Lost?" in *Sunday School Times*.

42. Speer, _____.

43. C. S. Lewis, *Mere Christianity* (New York: Macmillan, 1952), 55-6.

44. Clark Pinnock, "Is Jesus the Only Way?," in *Eternity* 27 (December 1976), 34.

45. Pinnock, "Is Jesus the Only Way?," 34.

46. John R. Stott, *Evangelical Essentials: A Liberal-Evangelical Dialogue* (Downer's Grove, IL: InterVarsity Press, 1988), 320.

47. James I. Packer, "The Wrath of God," in *Evangelical Magazine* (1959).

48. D. A. Carson, *The Gagging of God: Christianity Confronts Pluralism* (Grand Rapids: Zondervan, 1996), 530. Christ, however, clearly teaches degrees of judgment or punishment in Matthew 11:20-24, Mark 12:38-40 and Luke 12:47,48.

49. Richardson, *Secrets of the Koran*, 244.

50. Joni Eareckson, *A Step Further* (Glasgow: Pickering and Inglis, 1979), 170.

51. Philip Yancey, *The Bible Jesus Read* (Grand Rapids: Zondervan, 1999), 60-5.

52. Jeremy Rifkin, *Algeny* (New York: Viking, 1983), 139-40.

53. C. S. Lewis, *The Problem of Pain* (London: C. Bles, 1940), 106.

54. J. Oswald Sanders, *What of Those Who Have Never Heard?* (Crowborough, East Sussex: Highland Books, 1986), 104.

55. The William Carey Library will soon print this Bible study, written by this author.

56. Stephen Neill, *Out of Bondage* (Edinburgh: Edinburgh House Press, n.d.), 135-6. Historical examples abound. Consider Monica, who prayed and wept all night at a church in Carthage. She prayed for the conversion of her wayward, rebelling son, Augustine. Or Perpetua, who guided a young gladiator's sword to her throat. dc Talk and The Voice of the Martyrs, *Jesus Freaks: Stories of Those Who Stood for Jesus: The Ultimate Jesus Freaks* (Tulsa, OK: Albury Publishing, 1999), 298-302.

57. dc Talk and The Voice of the Martyrs, *Jesus Freaks: Stories of Those Who Stood for Jesus: The Ultimate Jesus Freaks* (Tulsa, OK: Albury Publishing, 1999), 298-302.

58. dc Talk and The Voice of the Martyrs, *Jesus Freaks*, 302.

59. Netland, *Dissonant Voices*, 314.

60. Jaroslav Pelikan, *Jesus Through the Centuries: His Place in the History of Culture* (New Haven: Yale University Press, 1985), 1.

61. J. D. Douglas, ed., *Let the Earth Hear His Voice: International Congress on World Evangelism, Lausanne, Switzerland* (Minneapolis: World Wide Publications, 1975), 3-4.

Chapter Three

Christ Centered Epistemology: An Alternative to Modern and Postmodern Epistemologies

Michael Pocock

> This chapter was originally presented to the EMS National Meeting, 2003. It appears in a modified form in *The Changing Face of World Missions* (Grand Rapids: Baker Books, 2005). Used by permission.

Standing at the bank of the Yukon River in the old gold rush town of Dawson, the river appears to have two parts. The flow from the shore to twenty yards out is clear. Beyond stretches an immense current of silted, brown water. The clear current comes from the fabled Klondike River, source of so many gilded dreams and from which millions of dollars were mined only a century ago. It joins the Yukon just upstream of Dawson, struggles to retain its identity for some distance, then gradually disperses in the smooth, implacable flow. Which enters which? One cannot tell. Yet there is something in the Klondike and every other tributary that retains a distinct flavor in the larger Yukon. Migrating salmon with imprinted memories of their natal stream can taste it. After several years in the ocean, they enter the big river again, and move inexorably to the waters they departed long before.

Modernity is the silt-laden river in which we have been swimming for so long that we have become accustomed to it. Pragmatically, it seems to be taking us somewhere. It solves so many of our immediate problems in scientific, rational terms. Do the salmon, as young smolt, feel grateful to the huge river that carries them along when they first leave their natal stream? Scientists and fishermen maintain that fish do not feel pain, so presumably they do not have emotions. But are they willing to put up with the silt so long as they get to the sea? Postmodernism is an awakening to the limitations of modernity, or as some would say, its bankruptcy, particularly when it comes to providing any final answers about existence, or to resolving problems of human depravity and intractability. Postmodern people, like salmon in the Yukon, have awoken to the fact that they have been taken for a ride, not in a pristine stream, but in a complex and corrupted river with a mind of its own. The river has flowed on for a long time, the salmon ever hopeful that it would take them to their destination. Some have despaired that they would ever get to the sea. Some are angry that they have allowed themselves to put up with the silt. Others are more furious still that they should have allowed the Yukon to convince them that it was the clear, unambiguous way, when actually it could only deliver them into the frozen wastes of the Arctic.

What do people do when they wake up to the reality of having been fooled, defrauded, or self-deceived? Should they have known better? Should they have fought it all along? There must have been those who knew what was happening, but perhaps they were beguiled by the benefits of modernity, from better transport to better health. And if they got so many benefits from modernity, were they not justified in thinking that modernity could deliver "the whole enchilada"? Could not modernity have provided a totally integrated understanding of reality for all humanity?

Contemporary missions need answers to these questions. Neither modernity nor postmodernity is truly biblical. For Christians, there is actually a faculty of knowing which is more truly Christ centered. It is this approach that holds the most hope of showing the salmon how to get back to clear water, in spite of whatever dams and natural obstructions may be in the way. This is the essence of the discussion in this chapter. The reader will find many references to Paul Hiebert. His *Missiological Implications of Epistemological Shifts* is, to this author's thinking, one of the best attempts to deal with both the shift from modernity to postmodernity and the consequences for missionary ministry.[1]

Identifying the Trend

Like modernity before it, postmodernism is a stream that has gathered momentum over a period of time. Though Hiebert traces its latest and more apparent development to 1979 with the publication of *La Conditione Postmoderne* by Francois Lyotard,[2] he notes that others used the term in the 50's and 60's, but Netland says that the first usage of the term was by Arnold Toynbee in *A Study of History*, published in 1939.[3] Toynbee was describing the period beginning with World War I. This may have signaled Toynbee's recognition that the bright promise of modernity was not going to be realized on its own terms. That is to say, modernity was not producing freedom from the insanity of war, even when those wars were waged by totally modern and, presumably, rational people with the tools of modern technology. There has been a constant stream of influences like Kierkegaard in the 1840s,[4] Schleiermacher in the late nineteenth century, the religious Fundamentalist and the Pentecostal movements of the twentieth century, all of which may be considered either "pre-postmodernist," or "antimodernist" in nature. At any rate, that constant stream reflects criticism and discomfort with the orientation and direction of modernity.

One may characterize postmodernity as a growing awareness of modernity's limitations with regard to knowledge or truth. There is deep disenchantment with a modern epistemology that created the sense that its methods and conclusions were irrefutable while scientists changed their theories and conclusions as often as doctors reverse themselves about issues of health and nutrition. The thinking individual asks, "Can we trust a system of knowledge that speaks with arrogance about what it has discovered and promises yet more, but which cannot resolve inter-tribal genocide whether it occurs in Africa or Europe, crop failures, or the global warming caused by its own technical advances?" Consequently, people, especially in the West, are retreating to a more independent, intuitive, and subjective system of knowing which they hope will be free of the presumptuous absolutism that characterized the heart of modernity: positivism.

When Europeans speak of postmodernism, Americans are helped, because Europeans have a longer history of it and live in postmodern cultures that are manifestly post-Christian. Europeans also are familiar with Bible-based evangelical churches and ministries that flourish in otherwise very religiously apathetic contexts. Britisher Clive Calver, says that to a postmodernist, "true truth," a phrase coined by American Francis Schaeffer while ministering in Europe in the 1960s, is dead. This, to Calver, is the essence of postmodernity. Postmoderns will not accept the superiority or correctness of any religious position beyond its value for the individual.[5]

Hiebert says of the phenomenon:

> Postmodernity focuses on the self and the now—on the concrete in the form of daily life as an alternative to theory. It stresses appearance and image over technical and substance; the unique rather than the general; the unrepeatable rather than the recurring; indeterminacy rather than determinism; diversity rather than synthesis. It is interested in the eccentric, the marginal, the disqualified, and the subjugated. [It is] deeply suspicious of reason. It sees reason as the basis of the Enlightenment, modernity, and Western society, and their domination, oppression,

and rule of the world. It therefore rejects reason as the basis for diversity and tolerance . . . Postmodernists celebrate emotions, intuition, creativity, and imagination . . . [They] have little sense of history. Time is seen as disparate, crisscrossed, and misaligned rather than homogeneous, evolutionary and purposive. It is fascinated with immediate events—with news.[6]

The fragmentary, or "digital" approach of postmodernism is most famously observable on MTV. Rapidly changing scenes, only a few seconds each, generally too fast for old dudes to comprehend, leave a general impression, extrapolated from the sum of the parts. There are words behind the music, or in the music, but the instruments and visual effects carry the day. Music and momentary impressions are what's important. It's not the voices only that communicate; the instruments themselves speak, as Jimmy Hendrix did though his guitar before drugs got the best of him. (Remember, postmodernism has been a long time coming!) After viewing MTV, compare a live concert, and one immediately realizes that almost every sense in the body is simultaneously addressed. Sights, sound, the smell of pyrotechnics, and the feel of music going *through* the viewer. The kinetic energy of the musicians communicates itself to the crowd. This is not music to sit through. It is not an intellectual experience; it is a personal and communal *sensation*.

Postmoderns like to draw on multiple sources, even if they are disparate. They can be from different religions, or cultures, or countries, no problem. This was observable at the World Parliament of Religions in Cape Town, South Africa, in 1999.[7] There, with no judgment on any but acceptance of all in pluralistic harmony, traditional Shamans, Tibetan monks, and Bahais all led in prayers, presentations, and dialogue. This was not only pluralism, it was postmodernity on display. There is no unified field of knowledge. There is no "Grand Unifying Theory," as Hiebert puts it.[8] Paradigms are not mutually exclusive to postmoderns even if they differ from each other, nor can a theory or plan (postmoderns would not like those terms) be rejected if some part of it is proven wrong. With logic out the window, there is nothing like the Law of Contradiction to which one might appeal to prove an assertion right or wrong. In such a situation, one simply agrees to disagree and lets people go their own way. All truth becomes cultural or individual in terms of its claims. It is significant to note that those who attended the World Parliament of Religions were not people younger than, say thirty, but a great many older than that. To the extent that the Parliament was a demonstration of postmodernity, it also showed that older people are included. This fits the idea that postmodernism has been growing for a long while.

Richard Tiplady is an excellent observer of postmodern culture, which has also been termed "Generation X."[9] Tiplady calls the trend toward postmodernity a "massive cultural transformation," which is not simply caused by the media, but reflected in it. For Tiplady, postmodernity and the culture of Generation X are marked by intense individuality and the need to adjust to a shift from mass production to information technology. Consumerism forces producers into "mass customization," so that everyone can have just exactly the car, clothes, or furniture that appeals to them. Lacking a deeper sense of personal identity, or perhaps even worth, individuals find their identity in dress styles and the stuff they own. Because postmoderns have abandoned any "metanarrative" (large scale unifying theories that explain or direct history, like Christianity, Western Civilization, or Marxism), they are marked by individuality, flexibility, and skepticism.[10]

Earlier, this chapter likened modernity to the Yukon River: silty, wide, and unstoppable. But is the picture of modernity so unrelentingly bleak? Why would there be such a reaction to it? Have not all Westerners enjoyed huge benefits with which they would be loath to part company? Do postmoderns not like to board trains that run on time, ride airplanes that get them home for a weekend from university, live in cities with a clean water supply, excellent sanitation, and public safety? Is it better, when charged in court with a crime, to have a judge who references case law (history) or the Constitution, and has access to increasingly accurate tests from DNA to DWI, than to have one who will simply use his intuition? In fact how could there be a just postmodern judge, unless he were Solomonic, or the law became a set of low level communal agreements that postmodernists could somehow collectively grant while rejecting absolutes at a higher level?

Referring to positivism, which is the essence of modernity, Paul Hiebert says:

> Positivism has changed the world for good. It has a strong sense of truth and order, and a high view of nature. By focusing attention on careful empirical research, it gave rise to modern science, which has contributed greatly to our understanding of the world, and to technologies that have benefited life on earth. It is hard for us today to imagine what life was like in the west before modernity.
> But positivism is also flawed. It has divorced knowledge from morality and feelings, and in doing so it has unleashed modern technology with few moral constraints, and power without safeguards. In its materialistic forms it has absolutized scientific knowledge and relegated religion to private opinion, and it reduces humans to robots in a mechanistic world. Today, the certainty of positivism and the optimism that marked its early years, have been undermined from within and from without. Positivism is no longer accepted as universally true.[11]

Obviously modernity and systems management that come with it have brought enormous benefits. What has also come with modernity is what postmoderns perceive as: (1) a crushing intellectual elite, managing education and general thought, (2) the corruption of science, supposedly objective, by businesses that pay for and use its results, often without consideration to environmental or human impacts unless absolutely forced to do so, and (3) political structures of the so-called free world wherein major corporations pay for the election of politicians who will advance and not obstruct their profit-making businesses. Postmoderns rail against the arrogance of modernity that asserts that knowledge is the product of totally objective, empirical research. They simply refuse to believe that so-called rational people actually are completely objective. By giving the impression of finality, modernity has been used to manipulate and control the less powerful or "less connected." This lack of objectivity appears in what is known as the "investigational bias," which says that the act of observing and the presence of the investigator alone actually change the behavior of what is observed. (Are the Osbournes behaving exactly as they would if the camera were not rolling, recording their every move? Is "reality TV" real or simply entertainment?) The observers/interpreters of any phenomenon work from a culturally conditioned point of view; they inadvertently bring subjectivity to their work, but subjectivity may be offset by recognizing the danger, providing multiple tests of results, and consulting in a community of concerned and capable people. This is the view of critical realism that Hiebert proposes.

One cannot place all postmodernists in one basket, but in rough terms, they fall into four large categories:

1. *Reluctant Postmodernists* admit that modernity did not deliver on its implicit or stated promises, but they wish it had. They hold on to a limited faith that human rational processes and the sciences can solve many problems that people face, but that these will still not procure reliable answers to transcendent questions. They are what Jaques Derrida and Rosenau call "Hopeful Postmodernists."[12]
2. *Resentful Postmodernists* are angry that modernity became exploitative, a diversity, culture, and individuality-crushing machine. They are anti-modern and nihilist. They are deconstructivist, believing the only way ahead is to dispense completely with the epistemologies of the past, but they have no replacement and don't believe one will be found. Rosenau would call these "Sceptical Postmodernists."[13]

Christ Centered Epistemology: An Alternative 77

3. *Reconstructive Postmodernists* are hopeful that a new paradigm is out there. They are pluralistic and dialogue-oriented. They are "instrumentalists," in that they are looking for what works. Some, like secular existentialists, believe they must struggle to act responsibly or honorably even though the world as they know it is incomprehensible (Secular existentialists would say "absurd.") in terms of any reliable epistemology of which they presently have knowledge.[14] Hence they need to listen to many and any sources to see what may emerge. There may be no final truth or grand paradigm, but there are helpful insights.

4. *Re-emerging Postmodernists* have been thoroughly immersed in postmodern belief and culture. Like the salmon in the opening story, they went into the Yukon and experienced its muddiness. They looked for clearer currents in postmodernism, but found these waters as muddy as the Yukon after the Klondike merged with it, and decided to get back upstream to clarity as the only possibility for rebirth, life, progress, and meaning. This person may be like Bono of U-2, who is culturally at home with the music and culture of the present generation, but who increasingly sounds like a person of faith, even Christian faith, ready to act on behalf of humanitarian values. Many in the Green movement may also be emerging from postmodernism because it is impossible to sustain passionate concern for anything that is not real. The environment is a reality for which they are ready to die. Unfortunately, for many of them, especially the New Agers among them, the earth and Gaia are a monistic entity, and all of us are part of that single reality.[15]

Evaluating the Trend

As the postmodern consciousness surfaces, the Christian must ask one question: "What is the evangelical's message to the postmodern person?" Is postmodernism something for which its adherents should repent? Should they return to modernism so that on its principles they can prove, presumably with data, that Jesus is God? Evangelicals during the past century first fought modernity as fundamentalists, but then they began to use modernity's methods to refute it. These efforts ranged from Harry Rimmer's "mistake elimination" efforts in the 1920s[16] to Josh McDowell's more sophisticated 1979 work, *Evidence that Demands a Verdict*.[17]

Evaluations of postmodernism by evangelicals range from hostile to empathetic, from critiques of its culture to deeper philosophical responses. All agree that postmodernism is a serious challenge that confronts Christian faith and merits clear and compassionate response. Postmodernism presents an ongoing reality that will continue for some time. It could be the final death throes of modernity itself rather than the beginning of a new era. Modern Western people may believe that it is impossible to sustain a movement that has no foundation in a knowable reality, yet clearly, Buddhism has existed some 2500 years with its central conviction that reality is illusory.[18] Buddhism resonates with postmodernists because Buddhism is essentially atheistic, focusing instead on the self-evident suffering of the world and the process of overcoming it. Postmodernists like processes and pilgrimages, not conclusions and arrivals.

Calver attests to both "the rampant progression of New Age, the spiritual child of postmodernism, and the awful results of its ethical nihilism." Yet, he continues, "I have also seen the spiritual hunger it confesses. I have watched the rejection of the human self-aggrandizement of modernism, and I have listened to the desire to see a faith that works." He adds his belief that "postmodern thinking is totally non-Christian."[19] Elizabeth Tebbe says that postmodernism has become so mainstream that living as an evangelical today constitutes "an alternative lifestyle."[20]

Both Calver and Tebbe express hope for the postmodern's receptivity to a genuine gospel of life and word, but Jonathan Campbell feels they both are too pessimistic about postmodernism and insufficiently critical of modernity. He voices four main concerns about many evangelical responses to postmodernism:

1. The assumption (by evangelicals) that modernity is somehow more biblically sound than its counterpart in postmodernity.
2. The failure to see the hope and positive opportunities to translate the gospel within the cultures of postmodernity.
3. The incognizance of many who do not realize how the church has succumbed to modernity.
4. The refusal to call the church to radical and systemic changes to recover its ecclesial identity and missional purpose in order to engage postmodern cultures. Despite dangers of our current cultural shift, we can still discern and act on distinct opportunities for mission within postmodern cultures.[21]

These concerns, particularly 1 and 3, are valid. One may dispute, however, that the authors Campbell mentions have no hope for ministry to postmoderns. They and other evangelicals have issued calls for the recovery of the evangelical missional identity.[22] But when evangelicals adopted certain modern tools to counter the anti-biblical stance of modernity with its exclusion of religious matters from the bounds of scientific investigation, they may have put too much confidence in those tools. The non-contradictory approach to apologetics, in particular, leaves little room for mystery, or antinomy even though these categories are routinely mentioned in evangelical apologetic and hermeneutics texts. After the Christian has done his best to prove God's existence, he must admit that the fullness of God's nature evades purely rational proofs. God can only be known by special revelation and a subjective grasp (Help me Søren!) of his reality, aided by the illuminating work of the Spirit in a regenerated heart.

In any age or context, Christians, like everyone else, will be creatures of their culture. They want to be "in sync" with their culture because it brings feelings of comfort and belonging. Believers are not immune to this attraction. They need to be cognizant of it. When, years ago, this author sensed God's call into ministry, I gladly chose to attend a Bible College, believing that a solid grasp of the Bible was what I needed and wished to impart to others. In my context, this choice was slightly countercultural. No one in my family had ever been to college, so they did not know how to advise me. Fellow Christian young people were going to University. I scarcely knew anyone who anticipated attending a Bible College. My friends were off to the University of Maryland, Rutgers, Purdue, and MIT, all those venerable educational institutions that regularly visited our High School to recruit new students. Although I was pleased to study the Bible at Washington Bible College, I was relieved to be able to report, when asked, that I was taking courses in Hamartiology, Soteriology, and Eschatology. No one asked me what those branches of science covered, but I felt vaguely pleased that my courses sounded scientific!

Later, as I delved deeper into Hermeneutics, I discovered that the principles for interpreting the Bible were the same as for any other piece of literature, saving that the Scriptures were divinely inspired. In seminary when we progressed to studies in Greek, Hebrew, and biblical exegesis I learned to apply careful grammatical analysis, referring to the historical and literary forms in which Scripture was written. We diagrammed sentences and made flow charts of the Bible. This approach to theology left little room for ambiguity and everything seemed "schematicizable" with neat components that fit together very well. It all seemed so scientific! It was modern instead of archaic or outlandish. People who mastered the system frequently became fine expositors of the Word, and their teaching seemed well grounded. I did not realize that to the extent my Christian studies had a modern feel to them, I felt good too!

In recent years, however, I feel myself bristle whenever a preacher begins to talk about the grammar underlying the teaching of a passage. While it is significant, I wonder if anyone reading Paul's letters for the first time to little groups around the Mediterranean ever stopped in his reading to exclaim: "Did you see that folks? He just used a coordinate conjunction!" They simply read the letter gladly, and having discovered its profundity, someone would have said, "Let's hear that again!" and another would have remarked, "That was pretty convicting!" They would have responded to the story line: the narrative rather than the finely dissected pieces (which belong in the study rather than the pulpit). Perhaps the New Testament believers were pre-postmodernists! Having been influenced by modernity, am I now quietly slipping into postmodernity, with its love of stories, mystery, and subjectivity? I now know that I do not know all about God, and I never will this side of glory. I have no less certainty, but I have more awe. I am glad that God is not completely comprehensible! But he has shown me enough that I can sense him, relate to him, and know through the Scriptures that he is more than my subjective sense and bigger than any humanly rational capacity to comprehend.

The Christian may find it easy to be enamored and actually see the good side of these epistemological trends, both modernity and postmodernity. He may also be unaware and drift, whether to one side or the other, adopting not only epistemologies but the cultures associated with them. Thinking Christians should be deeply troubled that there is so little difference between the general culture in the West and the lives of Christians, as Rose Dowsett has shown.[23]

Paul Hiebert says that Christians need to be critical realists. They need a third path that avoids simply a return to modernity or a submersion in postmodernity. Christians cannot simply move on from one paradigm to another. In the case of postmodernity, Hiebert concludes:

1. It has no agenda of its own to solve the world's problems.
2. It is a reactive rather than a proactive movement.
3. It is opposed to modernity and all its fruits.
4. It offers no criteria for right and wrong, true and false.
5. It is primarily a Western concern and the luxury of those who have plenty.[24]

Reflection on the Trend

In 1988, John Stott reflected on the needs of what he called "modern man" but which had already in the West become "Postmodern Man." He said that people today have three yearnings:

1. For Transcendence: A sense of God or a connection with what is beyond immediate and material things and beings.
2. For Significance: A sense that they are meaningful, have purpose, make a difference.
3. For Community: A sense that in a fragmenting world and society, they belong to a family.[25]

These three yearnings provide an excellent framework for biblical and theological reflection on postmodernity.

The Yearning for Transcendence

Postmoderns demonstrate a profound interest in spirituality. They are skeptical of any unique claims for God, but they are in the market for "spirituality." Recent observers comment that in Europe today, discussions about spiritual matters arise far more often than at any other time in the past twenty years. Students at Dallas Theological Seminary are required to befriend an off-campus international student during the semester in which they take Introduction to Missions. These friendships, frequently pursued far beyond the class requirement, surprise the students in that their counterparts from China, India, and the Middle East are the first to bring up spiritual issues. God and spirituality are of real interest to today's generation, whether they are postmodern Westerners or otherwise.

Babu Pimplekar, an outstanding Indian Christian and student found Christ as a Hindu. When asked how the Christian God captured his interest, Babu replied that he had definitely been a spiritual seeker and had spoken widely with Hindu spiritual leaders. He read the great Hindu scriptures, yet remained unsatisfied. Someone told him that before he gave up his search, he should also read the Judeo-Christian Scriptures. This he did, discovering two things. "The Bible," he said, "seemed like real history to me." In spite of great and wonderful miracles recorded there, it still seemed real rather than fanciful and fantastic. Secondly, he said, "The Scriptures seemed to know me." He found himself in the Bible. And even more importantly, he found Christ.

Though postmoderns may resist one's appeal to authority like Scripture, they may sense God in nature and then find God explained in Scripture. And what a God! This is the God who shows himself in creation, truly transcending all reality, eliciting praise from the psalmists, as in Psalm 19:1-4.

> The heavens declare the glory of God;
> The skies proclaim the work of his hands.
> Day after day they pour forth speech;
> Night after night they display knowledge.
> There is no speech or language
> Where their voice is not heard.
> Their voice goes out to the whole earth,
> Their words to the ends of the world.

Scripture indicates that unregenerate people do not independently draw correct conclusions about what they see in nature. Paul, in Romans chapter one, makes this fact clear (vv.

18-32), but special revelation, that is to say Holy Scripture, is the word of the Spirit (Eph. 6:17, 2 Tim. 3:16-17). In the hands of a believer who is also an agent of the Holy Spirit (John 15:26-27, Acts 1:8), the Scriptures become understandable even to an unregenerate person, as we see in the case of Phillip with the Ethiopian Eunuch in Acts chapter eight.

In distinction from postmodernists, evangelical Christians proclaim God as a cognitive or knowable reality. Although no one would independently "guess" or discover God, knowledge of him is possible through the Spirit (1 Cor. 2:10). Paul's treatment of epistemology in 1 Corinthians 1:18-2:16 reflects a key New Testament teaching. This passage speaks to the Christian as he seeks to communicate in a postmodern context. Paul talks about knowing and communicating God in the context of very diverse philosophies. He declares that God has not been known through pagan philosophy (1:21), even though he addressed philosophers on Mars Hill using the poetry and practices of pagans to illustrate his message (Acts 17). Paradoxically, God is known through the unsophisticated process of preaching—preaching that proclaims Christ, the power and wisdom of God (1 Cor. 1:24). Thus, one finds a point of agreement with postmodernists who claim that no epistemological system has achieved a certain knowledge of absolutes. Scripture says, "You are right. Absolutes, like God as unique Creator and Sustainer of the universe and man, are not learned through any process of deduction, but instead are known only if revealed by that Absolute." Certainly this statement curtails the pride that postmodernists dislike about modern positivist thinkers! In fact God intentionally arranged things this way, using the lowly and despised things of the world (1 Cor. 1:28). "Let him who boasts boast in the Lord" (1:31). There's a certain amount of mystery in biblical epistemology, sure to appeal to postmoderns, but, apart from the Orthodox, Catholics, and some Anglicans, not really capitalized on by many Christians who have spent the modern era minimizing the mystical. This transcendent, triune God prepared to reveal himself in the greatest mystery of all, which Paul says is "Christ, in whom are hid all the treasures of wisdom and knowledge" (Col. 2:2-3). This is indeed transcendent knowledge, because as Paul says in 1 Corinthians 2:9-10, citing Isaiah 64:4, such knowledge has never even entered the ears or eyes of men. The Spirit is the only one who could have revealed it. This wisdom is Christ centered, and leads to a Christocentric epistemology to which the entire epistle of Colossians bears witness.

During the period of modernity, much has been said about the difference between the knowledge of natural things and that of spiritual. This duality goes back to Plato, but positivists conveniently employed it to dismiss spiritual claims from the realm of scientific investigation. This left theologians to work on what materialists held to be unverifiable claims. Modern evangelicals consider this unfair. They believe what they know of God can be demonstrated on the same grounds as any natural claim. They do this either from pure rationality harking back to Aquinas, or from an apologetic that begins by establishing the historicity of New Testament claims about Christ—especially his death and resurrection—as recorded in the historically reliable New Testament documents. Having established that point, these evangelicals then build a case for the truthfulness of all Christ taught and the entire revelation of Holy Scriptures. They make their claim that all Scripture is authoritatively the Word of God because Christ, the self-proclaimed incarnate God, authenticated the existing Jewish Scriptures (Luke 24:25; John 5:46-47) of his day, *and* he promised that the Spirit would bring back to the minds of the Apostles all they had heard him say and do (John 14:25-26, 15:26-27, 16:5-15). By this Jesus meant the Gospels.

Evangelicals typically refer to 2 Timothy 3:15-17 as Paul's claim that Timothy, as a boy, was taught "the holy Scriptures, which are able to make [him] wise for salvation through faith in Jesus Christ." By this Paul surely meant the Jewish Scriptures, or the Old Testament. He continues on to say, "All Scripture is God-breathed and is useful for teaching, rebuking, correcting and training in righteousness." Later, Peter, seeming to refer to all of the Bible, or at least the Epistles, says that Paul's letters "contain some things that are hard to understand, which ignorant and unstable people distort, *as they do the other Scriptures*" (2 Pet. 3:16 emphasis added). By this single statement Peter placed Paul's letters on the same level as the rest of Holy Scripture. If queried about the value of Scripture's internal testimony, evangelicals would add that the *community of God's people* through the Spirit of God, gives universal testimony to the canonicity of the sixty-six books of Holy Scripture, and that they made this clear in several early and important historical consultations such as the Council of Hippo, A.D. 393, and the Third Synod of Carthage, A.D. 397. Earlier discussions by Jewish scholars, centered around Jamnia (Jaffa) about A.D. 90, confirmed the Old Testament Canon of Jewish scriptures as Christians know them today.[26]

Let's return for a moment to the dual level of epistemology noted above. Paul in 1 Corinthians 2:10-12 writes:

> The Spirit searches all things, even the deep things of God. For who among men knows the thoughts of a man except the man's spirit within him? In the same way, no one knows the thoughts of God except the Spirit of God. We have not received the spirit of the world but the Spirit who is from God, that we may understand what God has freely given us.

This sounds like two levels of knowledge, one that relates to people, or at least to the subjective mind, and the other regarding truth about God. Without the Spirit, one can only know one's own mind, or possibly things that relate to human beings. This is reliable knowledge. Therefore, unless the Spirit is in a person, he will not comprehend truth about God. In a few short verses, Paul has said, in effect, "Modern man, you are right. You can only know truth at the level of human beings." But at the same time he has said, "You can access transcendent knowledge through the Spirit of the Living God, but only if you experience his regenerating work."

In contrast to postmodernists, Christians maintain that there is ultimate reality and a real world. This ultimate reality is the God of the Bible. He is knowable, but not by any system devised by man. Instead, he is known by grace through faith in the person of Christ, revealed by the Spirit of God in the Word of God (Eph. 2:8-9; Col. 1:15-23; 1 Cor. 2:6-10). To experience a continuing relationship with the transcendent God, God invites his people to converse with him in prayer (Matt. 6:5-15), walk in his Spirit (Rom. 8:5-17), praise him in adoration (Psalm 148), and enjoy him in the community of Christ's body (Matt. 18:20, "Where two or three are gathered, there am I in the middle of them."). The infinite-personal God of the Bible satisfies the yearning for transcendence that Stott says characterizes this generation, a yearning which everyone who has trusted Christ has found to be true. The catch for postmodern people is that this God, this amazing provision and possibility, is unique. To proclaim this Gospel as the exclusive way of salvation will seem as foolish to postmoderns as it seemed to the Greeks who heard it in the first century. But today's hearers may go beyond laughter to rage that anyone should make a claim for exclusivity. Apart from a very gracious attitude on the Christian's part, Christians will be considered as dangerous as any other idealistic fundamentalist, whether Islamic, Hindu, or Aryan Nation. There may still be a cross to bear by those who follow seriously in His steps. On the brighter side, one reads that postmoderns are "interested in the eccentric, the marginal, the disqualified, and the subjugated."[27] Perhaps Christianity will constitute just the niche postmoderns need!

The Yearning for Significance

This chapter earlier referred to the postmodern's need for personal identity. Tiplady says, "The issues of individuality and identity are at the core of the questions that contemporary culture is asking."[28] Individuality and identity equate to the yearning for significance to which Stott refers. Scripture clearly states that every individual is supremely significant to God.

Why should postmoderns be so concerned with identity, individuality, and significance? Because identity and significance are taking a severe beating in today's world. Impersonal free market forces and globalization move capital from place to place. Both labor and market can be liquidated in a moment. Companies collapse. Super-rich CEOs with inside knowledge of their corporations' weaknesses, suddenly bail out, sell their stock options, and ruin the lives of faithful workers and investors. What does the individual mean anymore? For what does he or she count? Dads leave their children and wives. Wives run away from their husbands. Single moms by the millions are trying to cope with limited time and income, only seeing their children a short time each day. Children are aborted, bartered, and abused. Do little children count? Or only the perceived well-being of adults? What does Scripture say?

According to Scripture, human beings are the acme of God's creation! Appearing at the end of the creation process in Genesis chapter one, man is made in the image of God (1:26-27). So is Eve! She is not only made in the image of God, she is the only living being appropriate as a mate for Adam (2:20-25). Together they have responsibilities and privileges; they walk with God! When they disobey, it is a vastly significant matter. There is no, "Just don't do it again!" or "I told you a hundred times!" This is not a petulant child and a harried parent in a grocery store; this is Adam and Eve. What they do matters supremely. It may seem negative (and who likes negativity in a postmodern world?) to banish the couple from Paradise, and consider the whole ensuing race as a fallen entity, but that is how much the actions of one couple meant to God (Rom. 5:12-20). In every judgment of God, there is also grace and justice procured. Humankind's redemption begins to be spelled out by the third chapter of Genesis (3:15), revealing that brokenness (sin) is fixable (redeemable) in the program of God.

One of the amazing things about God is that he keeps track of so much! He does this because people matter. Their actions can be earth shaking, or earth flooding. God is never indifferent. As people multiply, the Bible reveals that before Israel is ever mentioned, God knows the names of all the nations. A catalog appears in Genesis chapter ten. Later in Acts 17, Paul mentions that God made all people from one man, and also all the nations, moving them around so that each is where he decides. To God, no people group is more superior or less superior. No group is slightly less human than the others, but "all made from the same blood" (Acts 17:26 AV). Does this not answer the postmodern concern that the project of modernity, including the Colonial era, denigrated cultures, exploiting and dehumanizing millions? But the story continues.

Scripture takes pains to focus on individuals and their worth. Abraham may have been a migrant "nobody" to others as he shifted around from Ur to Haran, but God made Abraham a "somebody." He becomes not only the model of faith for Paul (to say nothing of Søren Kierkegaard), but the foundation of a family and nation through whom the whole earth was to be blessed (Gen. 12:1-3). To God, evil people are as much a concern as those who love and serve him. Evil people are the purpose and focus of God's redemptive program. "I take no pleasure in the death of the wicked," declares the Lord (Ezek. 18:32). To a disgruntled Jonah upset that God had spared the wicked city of Nineveh when they repented at his preaching, God said, "Nineveh has more than a hundred and twenty thousand people who cannot tell their right hand from their left, and many cattle as well. Should I not be concerned about that great city?" (Jonah 4:11). Anyone who lives in a huge, depersonalizing urban megalopolis like London, Moscow, Mexico City, or Beijing, or endures the troubles in Belfast or the Kafkaesque chaos of Monrovia, would probably wonder whether he or his city meant anything to God. Scripture says he does.

Whether it is little children hoping for a blessing, women with vaginal bleeding, parents with epileptic children, or demonized mad men in the local cemetery, Jesus had time for them all. This author delights to read the best-known verse of the Bible: "For God so loved the world that he gave his one and only Son, that *whoever* believes in him shall not perish but have everlasting life (John 3:16 emphasis added). But an even greater delight arises in realizing that this is not a generalized statement of humanitarian concern, but a statement about the infinite value of each person, the objects of the life and ministry of Jesus, people for whom he gave his life. That is value! That is significance!

So what does one become if one believes in Jesus? A child of God (John 1:12)! What if a person has a despicable background? Does he still count? Was he sexually immoral, an adulterer, a homosexual prostitute, a thief, a swindler, or an abusive alcoholic? Paul names them all and tells the Corinthians, "And that is what some of you were. But you were washed, you were sanctified, you were justified in the name of the Lord Jesus and by the Spirit of our God" (1 Cor. 6:9-11). How wonderful to "be accepted in the Beloved!" Postmoderns can be accepted too!

The final miracle of significance for the individual is that God includes him or her in his work. Jesus sent out a group of ordinary fellows and put the program of world evangelization in their hands (Matt. 28:19-20). A number of women had helped support Jesus in his ministry (Luke 8:1-3). Later on Paul includes many women in a lengthy list of greetings and thanks to those who had done ministry well in Rome (Rom. 16:1-15). People matter in the program of God, and that is a significant fact to impress on the minds of postmodern people!

The Yearning for Community

As if it were not enough to be a significant individual in the sight of God, believers also become part of a new spiritual family. This is the church, also called "a chosen people, a royal priesthood, a holy nation, a people belonging to God." And Peter adds, "Once you were not a people, but now you are the people of God" (1 Pet. 2:9-10). Christians do not simply have personal identity and significance, they have acceptance in a community as well.

The creation of mankind began with a communal decision. "Then God said, 'Let *us* make man in *our* image, in *our* likeness...and let *them* rule'" (Gen. 1:26 emphasis added). God himself is his own community. As Scripture progresses, one begins to understand what is now termed the Trinity. God himself acted in creation, and the Spirit mentioned in Genesis 1:2 also acted. Later one discovers that the pre-existent Christ was also at work in creation. Jesus claimed his oneness with the Father in being and in working (John 10:25-38), and Paul explicitly recognizes Jesus' presence at creation in Colossians 1:15-18. The communal God created communal man. Humans were never meant to be alone. Man immediately received a partner in Eve. Mankind multiplied. Whatever the plan of God, the multiplication of people made it possible, along with their relationship to each other. When the nations demonstrated the extent of their rebellion against the creation mandate, God created a new nation: Israel, to embody his praises and grow *as a people.* The character of this people as a holy, priestly, and particular nation is stated in Exodus 19:3-6, a passage taken almost verbatim by Peter and applied to the Church in 1 Peter 2:9-10. Even Jesus worked with others (the twelve disciples) and this is the same with Paul who was always working in concert with others.

When people become believers, they become part of the family to which this chapter has already referred, the Church. The church is a worldwide, culturally diverse phenomenon. Its local expressions, especially in communities that are themselves diverse, should reflect that variety. Individual churches certainly did in New Testament times. This community is not present among every culture and community of the world, as this author and many of his readers pray it will be. However, the church is in every country, formally constituting a third of the world's population. It has about a half-billion real believers and is accessible to over two thirds of the world's people.[29]

Henri Nouwen became more and more convinced during his ministry that no Christian work was designed to be done alone. He committed to having others with him in ministry, even when they were one of the severely disabled from his community at Daybreak. None of us who are believers should fail to be in a community of believers.[30] David Howard makes the same point. Arguing for greater cooperation and fellowship among those who do the Lord's work, he says: "The Apostle Paul never conceived of himself as an army of one, even though he was often nearly alone. He fully recognized his need of the strength and help provided by others."[31] As Christians invite the postmodern generation into the community of Christ, it must be evident, even while they are working, that Christians are also part of worshipping, learning, fellowshipping, and fulfilling communities of fellow believers. Hiebert also maintains that theology and missiology must be done in community. There should be no "lone wolves" in either the doing of ministry or the enjoyment of the faith. *Christianity* is a communal venture.

This community love rings clearly through the New Testament, and most beautifully in Acts 2:42-47. Local churches, and even whole denominations, that fail to live out community love are part of the reason many postmoderns remain disinterested in institutional Christianity. Much of their disillusionment with the church, or individual churches, may come more from a general distrust of all institutions than from direct experience. But they read the newspapers and they see the multiplying cases of abuse by clergy. Some have experienced it directly, leading to incredible anger like that expressed by singer Sinead O'Connor. Some years ago she went public with statements against the Pope himself.[32] When a major figure of the postmodern culture explodes like this, her actions should prompt thinking Christians to examine all churches, and repent of ways the church has not been a true community. Sometimes *it has* been a toxic and dysfunctional one. Only when Christians openly admit the failures of the church will they be able to offer the genuine community that postmoderns seek.

This author has had the privilege of serving on the board of an openly Christian NGO in China. The organization works for the well-being of the people of China in the name of Christ and in the spirit of a former missionary who was much appreciated years ago, and who is still remembered by local people and officials in Shanxi. The organization has brought the assistance of many different experts in medicine, public health, police work, and education. This organization also maintains a vibrant staff of committed workers on a long-term basis in China. Local officials are continually amazed by the relationship between members of the expatriate team and local people, as well as by the organization's ability to bring experts in almost any field to address issues affecting the well being of Chinese people. The ability to muster these experts comes from the fact that they are all part of the Body of Christ. In the globalized world of which postmodernism is a major component, NGOs are frequently more effective than nation-states, and there are key roles for the Body of Christ to play—not as an organization or corporation, but as a community linked by spiritual rather than economic or political bonds.

Engaging the Trend

What then are Christians to do with the trend of postmodernity? Reading through this chapter, one may find it difficult to separate recommendations from observations and evaluations. This conclusion, however, will attempt to draw things together under two headings: epistemological recommendations and cultural recommendations. As through this entire chapter, Paul Hiebert's masterful work, *Missiological Implications of Epistemological Shifts*, will continue to be the guide. The repeated references to Hiebert's ideas in many evangelical articles on missionary ministry, cultural anthropology, contextualization, and now the epistemological shift to postmodernism, are a fitting tribute to him and his work.

Epistemological Recommendations

The way forward in the current sociological context is neither insistence on the methods of modernity (positivism), nor the wholesale adoption of postmodern criteria. Hiebert proposes a third way, connected to both modernity and postmodernity, which he calls "critical realism."[33] Because he is quite clear on the matter, read his own description:

> Critical realist epistemology strikes a middle ground between positivism, with its emphasis on objective truth, and instrumentalism, with its stress on the subjective nature of human knowledge. It affirms the presence of objective truth but recognizes that this is subjectively apprehended . . . It challenges the definition of "rationality" in both positivism and instrumentalism that limits rationality to algorithmic logic. In doing so, critical realism offers a third, far more nuanced, epistemic position.[34]

Upon reading this, one will observe that Hiebert has asserted the existence of objective reality, but empirical methods alone will not encompass or produce an exhaustive grasp of it. This squares with his emphasis on the subjectivity that all researchers bring to their task, including their cultural bias. But as he maintains elsewhere, admitted personal and cultural subjectivity does not preclude arriving at real truth.[35] He does not claim that totally objective truth is the result of the investigator's work, but that a reliable *correspondence* between the object observed and its reality is possible. This conclusion implies that, in spite of the presence of subjectivity and cultural differences, truth is not simply "cultural" or relative. Thus, one avoids the relativism of religious pluralism, which is such a hallmark of postmodern thinking and culture.

At the theological level the safety net of critical realism is the hermeneutical community.[36] This approach certainly corresponds to the biblical injunction to establish the truth of any matter through the testimony of multiple witnesses (Matt. 18:16). In Scripture, important decisions—especially interpretive ones—are made in the context of a group. The issue of disputes between widows of diverse cultural backgrounds in Acts 6 presents one such instance. Another occurs in Acts 15, which describes a major conference dealing with the applicability of Mosaic law in the multicultural New Testament community. The checks and balances of theological, anthropological, translational, and church community are the best corrective to the unavoidable subjectivity found in any one person. Multiple witnesses have historically provided the best check on facts, even in the modern scientific community and at law.

Communities are not simply safeguards for correctness or orthodoxy. The Church is a worldwide, culturally diverse community. As such, it not only *corrects*, but it also can and should *contribute* to a more complete understanding of truth. Think of the separate cultures of the world as individuals. Just as no single person may discover all there is to know about the truth, no single culture will either. This principle has many ramifications. It is not an argument for the acceptance of heterodoxy in theological matters based on cultural differences, but for *perspectival enhancement* of understandings growing out of the observation of revealed truth. William Dyrness makes this case well:

> In these and many other areas of thought, our brothers and sisters from non-western settings have a great deal to teach us . . . I think it is safe to say that any renewal that will come to western theology will come by interaction with voices from alternative (i.e. non-Western) traditions.[37]

Cultural Considerations

Rose Dowsett and Hiebert call for "critical contextualization" in ministry among other cultures.[38] This includes the postmodern culture. Western Christians must grasp that without ever leaving Europe or North America, they are in a missionary situation among their own people—a situation that requires intercultural insights and skills. What does "critical contextualization" look like? Essentially it means helping new churches understand that the Bible relates to all areas of life. This concept will be news to postmoderns, who may know nothing of the Bible beyond some biblically inspired movies they may have seen. For Christians to understand this concept, missionaries, incorporating the participation of local lay church members, must teach the whole of Scripture so that believers can grasp its entirety. One of the best ways would be to utilize the approach developed by New Tribes Missions and Trevor McIlwain, namely "Chronological Bible Storying" also known as *Building on Firm Foundations*.[39] The reader may find it strange that this chapter recommends materials developed for traditional tribalists when the subject is ministry to postmoderns, but *Firm Foundations*, having been utilized among tribal peoples the world over, now has an abbreviated version adapted for more urban, educated settings. Another quicker, popular method of achieving a thematic grasp of the sweep of Scripture is the *Walk through the Bible* seminars, developed by Bruce Wilkinson.[40]

Once there is an awareness of the comprehensive nature of Scripture as it relates to life, Hiebert recommends that the church community study particular cultural issues by the church community as they arise, first looking at how their culture has traditionally dealt with each issue. The non-Christian people of the culture should also be consulted to get their perspectives. This helps ensure that no crucial understanding is missed. Lastly, the church examines its own intra-church understanding of the issue and makes a culturally sensitive and biblical decision, either keeping a practice, rejecting it, reinterpreting it, or creating new rituals, if that was the issue, to accomplish the same legitimate ends.[41]

Throughout this process, notice that the community is key. Critical contextualization is not what an outsider *does*, but what he or she *facilitates* from a position of sensitive understanding of cultural dynamics. It presumes that the outsider has a basic framework for understanding culture, and that he enters in the role of a *listener* and *learner*.

Ministry to postmodern people is a bit like zero-based budgeting. Although a company or department knows its last year's budget and closing financial condition, it begins its new budgeting process not with how much it has on hand, but with what it really needs to do in the coming year. Zero-based budgeting does not simply add percentages on to last year's budget; it considers what the most valuable plan for the next year will be. Only then does it consider how to finance that plan. One cannot, as some postmodernists would like, treat history as if it never happened, but neither may one be a prisoner of the past. This is a new, globalized world and it has never been precisely this way before. Realizing that they may already be a bit postmodern themselves, Christians must take the time to sit down, listen, and learn with the very postmoderns they hope to reach. This process has worked with tribal people in Irian Jaya, why not with today's postmodern peoples? God would certainly say of them what he said to Jonah millennia past: "Nineveh has more than a hundred and twenty thousand people who cannot tell their right hand from their left, and many cattle. Should I not be concerned about that great city?" (Jonah 4:11). This author hopes the remaining modernists—myself included—are concerned about postmoderns. I pray we can get past the sometimes strange individuality, embrace or at least tolerate their music, rejoice with their love of the mystical, join in their tremendous diversity, weep about the brokenness all around them, be less judgmental, understand that the generation which has almost broken this planet ought to come back and pick up the trash, and help make it livable in case God gives us another millennia to live on it. One thing is certain: no set of human beings can change anything or help anyone without the One for whom and by whom this planet was created, in whom are hid all the treasures of wisdom and knowledge. For this reason, as always, Christians need a Christ centered way of knowing in the postmodern era. This is the Christ whose promise has more certainty than any attempt to get back to the clear water of the Klondike River: "If any man is thirsty, let him come to me and drink. He who believes in me, as the Scripture has said, out of his innermost being will flow rivers of living water" (John 7:37-38).

Notes

1. Paul Hiebert, *Missiological Implications of Epistemological Shifts: Affirming Truth in a Modern/Postmodern World* (Harrisburg: Trinity Press International, 1999).

2. Ibid., 51. Hiebert is citing Francois Lyotard, *The Postmodern Condition: A Report on Knowledge*, trans. Geoff Bennington and Brian Massouri (Minneapolis: University of Minnesota Press, 1984).

3. Harold Netland, *Encountering Religious Pluralism* (Downers Grove: InterVarsity Press, 2001), 57. Netland cites Margaret Rose, *The Post-Modern and The Post-Industrialist* (Cambridge: Cambridge University Press, 1991), 9.

4. In 1846, Kierkegaard was already upset with the magisterialism, or absolutism of Hegel, who was so certain that all which was real was knowable in terms of rationality. Kierkegaard was equally sure that so great a reality as God could not be known through rational human categories, but only through making Him one's ultimate concern, casting oneself entirely upon him, not because he had been proven, that would not have been faith, but in the very face of nonverifiability. Truth, to Kierkegaard, is subjectivity. It, or God, can only be grasped subjectively and will forever be out of grasp to the one who pursues Him by scientific or objective means. And the issue of God's existence is to Kierkegaard of such immediate significance, that one cannot waste time on either the dialectical approach of Hegel, or any other time-consuming "scientific" pursuit. No wonder Kierkegaard titled the work in which these thoughts appeared, "Concluding Unscientific Postscript to the 'Philosophical Fragments'" to be found in Robert Bretall, ed. *A Kierkegaard Anthology* (New York: The Modern Library, 1946), 190-258. This is why I call him a "pre-postmodernist." He admits his thoughts are philosophical fragments, very much a "digital" approach, he is deeply skeptical of the scientific or dialectical method, and is subjective, or intuitive in his approach. All this is not to say that S.K. was not highly intelligent or less than a Christian. He was passionately both. He is, of course, the father of Existentialism, both used and abused by later thinkers. His subjective senses led him to God, but lacking all objective reference, his method has led others to atheism and despair (Camus, Sarte) became the basis of twentieth century Christian neo-orthodoxy.

5. Clive Calver, "Postmodernism: An Evangelical Blind Spot?" *Evangelical Missions Quarterly* 35, no. 4 (Oct 1999). Accessed online at http://bgc.gospelcom.net/emis/1999/postmodern2.htm.

6. Hiebert, 53.

7. Information on the Parliament of World Religions may be found at www.cpwr.org. Accessed 20 August 2003.

8. Hiebert, 19, 32.

9. Richard Tiplady, "Let X=X," *Global Missiology for the 21st Century: The Iguassu Dialogue*, ed. William D. Taylor (Grand Rapids: Baker, 2000), 463-75. Tiplady does not deal with those born 1980-2000, also known as "Busters" or "Millennials," who now at twenty years old, have their own characteristics which include being postmodern. Tiplady recognizes that it is perilous to categorize the group born between 1965-1980. They don't like labels. He does see them as generally postmodern in outlook, and very much worth dealing with as a special case for Christian outreach. This is because they do not think or value or act in ways that became standard with the Boomer generation before them (those born 1942-65).

10. Ibid., 468-9.

11. Heibert, 29.

12. Jaques Derrida Rosenau, *Postmodernism and the Social Sciences: Insights, Inroads and Intrusions* (Princeton: Princeton University Press, 1992), 14-7. Cited in Heibert, 51.

13. Ibid.

14. Remember Albert Camus' novel *The Plague*. The doctor in the story faces an epidemic in Oran, Algeria. He believes that life is absurd, has no final meaning, yet his training and task compel him to act to restore life. He decides he will act in the face of everything that makes it nonsensical.

15. The Green Movement appears to me as a part of re-emerging postmodernism. It retains parts of postmodern cynicism about modernity, while returning to some form of realism that permits investment of energies in achieving its aims.

16. Harry Rimmer, *The New Testament and the Laws of Evidence* (Grand Rapids: Eerdmans, 1943).

17. Josh McDowell, *Evidence that Demands a Verdict*, vol.1 (San Bernardino, CA.: Here's Life Publishers, 1979).

18. Especially true of Mahayana Buddhism. See David Noss and John Boyer Noss, *A History of the World's Religions*, 9th ed. (New York: Macmillan, 1994), 225. .

19. Calver, 430-1.

20. Elizabeth Tebbe, "Postmodernism, The Western Church and Missions," *Evangelical Missions Quarterly* 35, no. 4 (Oct 1999): 426-9.

21. Jonathan Campbell, "Postmodernism: Ripe for a Global Harvest - But is the Church Ready?" *Evangelical Missions Quarterly* 35, no. 4 (Oct

1999): 432-7. Accessed online at http://bgc.gospelcom.net/emis/1999/postmodern3.htm.

22. Rose Dowsett, "Dry Bones in the West," in *Global Missiology: Reflections from the Iguassu Dialogue*, ed. William D. Taylor (Grand Rapids: Baker, 2000), 447-62.

23. Ibid.

24. Hiebert, 65-6.

25. John Stott, in Griffeth-Thomas Lectureship at Dallas Theological Seminary, 1988. Published as "Christian Ministry in the 21st Century," *Bibliotheca Sacra* 145, no. 578, 1988, 123-32.

26. For an example of this approach, see Josh McDowell's *New Evidence that Demands a Verdict* (Nashville: Thomas Nelson, 1999), 24-26. This volume is a revised update of his earlier work prepared with the postmodern reader in mind.

27. Hiebert, 53.

28. Tiplady, 466.

29. "The State of the World," *Mission Frontiers*, June 2000. <www.missionfrontiers.org> check Archives.

30. Henry Nouwen, *In the Name of Jesus: Reflections on Christian Leadership* (New York: Crossroad, 1996): 6-7.

31. David Howard, "An Army of One," *World Pulse* 38, no. 9 (May 2003): 7. www.worldpulseonline.com.

32. SineadO'Connor, www.sineadoconnor.comAccessed14September2003. On the 3 October 1992 episode of Saturday Night Live, Ms. O'Connor ripped up a picture of the Pope and declared "Fight the real enemy!" See www.tvtome.com/tvtome/servlet/GuidePageServlet/showid-365/epid-104215. Accessed 25 April 2005.

33. Hiebert, 63.

34. Ibid., 69.

35. Ibid., 73-4.

36. Ibid., 102.

37. William A. Dyrness, *Emerging Voices in Global Christian Theology* (Grand Rapids: Zondervan, 1994), 13.

38. Dowsett, 355-6; Hiebert, 111-2.

39. Trevor McIlwain, *Building on Firm Foundations* (Sanford, FL: New Tribes Mission, 1988).

40. Walk Through the Bible offers seminars and Bible studies on a variety of topics, but Walk Thru the Old and New Testaments would be most appropriate in this context. Refer to www.walkthru.org for further information.

41. Hiebert, 112.

Chapter Four

The Relevance of Jesus as the Source of Salvation and Mission for the Twenty-first Century Global Context

William J. Larkin

The socio-economic-political and religio-ideological contours of the radically altered turn of the millennium landscape offer both challenge and opportunity, which Jesus as the source of salvation and mission is more than adequate to meet. With the aid of trend watchers, such as John Naisbitt and Faith Popkorn, Christian missiologists, such as Robert Schreiter, and historians of Global Christianity, such as Philip Jenkins, as well as commentators on the subject of globalization and religion, such as José Casanova and Michael Casey, this chapter traces the socio-economic-political shifts from West to East and North to South and the religio-ideological shifts to increased religious devotion and increased religious conflict. What will, at first, seem alien, hostile landscapes can become important frontiers to traverse when we focus on Jesus' seminal role in salvation and mission.

The Socio-Economic-Political Context: What Rescue Begins with Jesus?

The Global Economic Context of the Twenty-first Century

Though the post-9/11 global economic downturn has meant that the United States must resume its role as "the primary engine of globalization" if a recovery is to proceed apace,[1] the regional shift in the focus of economic power from the Atlantic to the Pacific basin is still in place.[2] Another reality is the increasing severity of the plight of the poor in the southern hemisphere.[3] This is a consistently recognized feature of a world experiencing globalization, according to Joel Kovel of Bard College.[4] Indeed, the gap between the richest and poorest countries has increased from 3-1 at the beginning of the industrial revolution to 30-1 in the mid-twentieth century to 100-1 today.[5] As David Barrett in the 2nd edition of *The World Christian Encyclopedia* chronicles this phenomenon, some 46 percent of the world, 2.8 billion people, eke out a living in 26 countries each with a per capita income of under $235 per annum.[6]

The current demographics of the Christian religion worldwide reflect the same shifts. As Philip Jenkins has ably demonstrated, the center of Global Christianity is now the "global south."[7] Over a little more than a half century (1970 to 2025), Christianity will have gone from a majority Western church (56 percent European and North American) to a two-thirds majority non-Western church (68 percent African, Asian and Latin American). Indeed, the shift has already occurred. Barrett's 2002 Status of Global Mission tables identify the Christian church as currently 38 percent European, Russian, and North American and 59 percent African, Asian, and Latin American.[8]

And such a church exists predominantly among the poor. Some 109 million Christians live in the 26 poorest countries. A look at all the developing countries shows that Christians, living in absolute poverty, number 260 million, i.e., 24 percent of the 1.1 billion absolutely poor. Half of the Christians living in absolute poverty are in Latin America, a third are in Africa, the rest are in South and Southeast Asia.[9]

If the church is to reach that third of the world's population labeled by missiologists as "unevangelized"—those who are unaware of Christianity, Jesus Christ, the Christian message and are without adequate opportunity to hear the gospel and respond to it—it must prosecute its mission among the poor of the "Global South." Since 1989, missions strategists and mobilizers have captured this audience geographically with the phrase the "10/40 Window." Sixty-two countries of Africa, Asia, and a bit of Europe in a swath 10 degrees N Latitude to 40 degrees N Latitude have approximately fifty percent of the world's population, including 55 of the least evangelized countries (but only 8 percent of the global missionary force). Eighty-two percent of the world's poorest live here, i.e., in a region with 23 countries with per capita GNP under $500; a region also containing 29 countries with the lowest quality of life in terms of life expectancy, infant mortality, and literacy.[10]

The Relevance of Jesus, the Source of Salvation

There are two questions that the worsening economic plight of the poor present to the Christian understanding of Jesus, the source of salvation: 1) How can the type of need Jesus as Savior addresses be truly relevant to them? 2) How can the type of hope he offers be truly good news to them? By considering the New Testament's "salvation" vocabulary, clustered around the themes of "redemption" and "reconciliation," this study of the New Testament teaching on Jesus, "the source of salvation" will give us a framework in which to answer these questions.[11]

Salvation, Spiritually-Centered and Holistic in Scope, Meets the Needs of the Poor

Spiritual salvation is consistently the central focus of New Testament teaching concerning the salvation Jesus brings. From the angel's announcement to Joseph concerning his name, "Jesus, because he will save his people from their sins," (Matt 1:21) to Jesus' description of his mission, "to give his life as a ransom for many," (Mk 10:45; cf. 1 Tim 2:6) to Paul's exposition of this redemption work as "through his blood, the forgiveness of sins" (Eph 1:7; cf. Col 1:14), to the writer to the Hebrews' comprehensive picture of Christ's high priestly sacrifice "by his own blood" obtaining "eternal redemption" (Heb 9:12, 14, 15; cf. Rom 3:24) to the final praise of Christ in Revelation, as he who "freed us from our sins by his blood" (Rev 1:5) the message is the same. Whether in deliverance language applied to Jesus' rescue (*exaireō*) of us from "this present evil age" and God's transfer of us into the "kingdom of the Son he loves" (Gal 1:4; Col 1:13) or redemption language applied to Christ's substitutionary atonement in sacrificial context (1 Tim 2:6 [*antilytron*]; Eph 5:2 [*hyper hēmōn prosphoran*]) or salvation language (*sōzō*) applied to Jesus' delivering from the penalty of sin (1 Tim 1:15) and providing a present and future eternal salvation (Heb 5:9; 7:25; Phil. 3:20), the salvation Jesus provides is at its heart spiritual.

At first sight, such a salvation would seem to be irrelevant to those caught in the poverty cycle across the majority world. But it is actually of greatest relevance to them, for it speaks to their greatest need, the need of their spiritual, indeed eternal, release from the guilt, power, and penalty of sin, which has placed them from birth under eternal condemnation. To ignore this need while meeting all others is to relate to humans, reductionistically, only in terms of the material and the here and now. Such thinking misses the true nature of man (a "living" *psychē*—"the seat and center of both earthly and transcendent life"[12]) and his spiritual need and leaves him on the path to certain doom. Jesus put it this way: "For whoever wants to save (*sōzai*) his life (*psychē*) will lose it, but whoever loses his life (*psychē*) for me and for the gospel will save it. What good is it for a man to gain the whole world, yet forfeit his soul (*psychē*)? Or what can a man give in exchange for his soul (*psychē*)?" (Mk 8:35-37).

Yet, the New Testament teaching on Jesus, the source of salvation, does not permit us to be reductionistic in the other direction either, centering on only transcendent, spiritual salvation and forgetting earthly need. Jesus offers a spiritually centered salvation, but with a holistic scope. So, the Gospels' and Acts' use of salvation language, particularly the *sōzō* word group, characterizes Jesus' and the apostles' healing ministry as "saving" people (Mk 6:56; Lk 8:36, 50; 18:42; 17:19). This holistic scope is nicely pictured in the interchange of the Sanhedrin and Peter in Acts four. Peter states the question concerning the power to heal the lame man as "how he was 'saved' (*sesōtai*)" (Acts 4:9). He answers saying it occurred "in the name of Jesus Christ of Nazareth" and that "Salvation (*sōtēria*) is found in no one else, for there is no other name under heaven given to men by which we must be saved (*sōthēnai*)" (4:12).

There are several ways earthly needs are met through Christians who proclaim a holistic gospel. Forgiveness of sin comes to those who repent of their sins, including economic sins of covetousness and injustice (Lk 24:47; 18:22; 19:8). This will bring relief to those economically oppressed, as converted rich oppressors demonstrate their repentance through the practice of restitution. Zaccheus' response to Christ models this: "Look, Lord! Here and now I give half of my possessions to the poor, and if I have cheated anybody out of anything, I will pay back four times the amount" (Lk 19:8). And

Jesus declares, "Today salvation has come to his house . . . For the Son of Man came to seek and to save what was lost" (Lk 19:9-10).

Part of what spiritual saving grace works in a life is graciousness to others. This is modeled first by missionaries. They are concerned for the whole person and model a life of graciousness. So, the early missionaries witnessed in deed through ministries of healing in the name of Jesus (Acts 3:6; 5:12-16; 8:6-8; 9:32-43; 14:8-10; 16:16-18; 19:11-12; 28:7-10). And Paul tells the Ephesian elders, when describing his physical labors among them to support himself and his ministry team, "In everything I did, I showed you that by this kind of hard work we must help the weak" (20:35). The extension of hospitality by Lydia and the Philippian jailer as one of the first acts after conversion is another case in point (16:15, 32-34). They, too, lived out Jesus' dictum: "It is more blessed to give than receive" (20:35).

When the converted poor, particularly those who cannot support themselves, enter a community characterized by "sharing in physical things" (*koinōnia*) and "table fellowship" ("breaking of bread"), they immediately find themselves within a network of caring where physical needs will be met (cf. Acts 2:42-46; 4:32-37). And the grace of God will so work the fruit of the Spirit in lives: "love, joy, peace, patience, kindness, goodness, faithfulness, gentleness and self-control" (Gal 5:22-23) that the working poor will embrace the values and disciplines necessary for "evangelical lift." They will be able to live out Paul's encouragement: "He who has been stealing must steal no longer, but must work, doing something useful with his own hands, that he may have something to share with those in need" (Eph 4:28). And, as the reign of the Lord and Savior Jesus comes into more and more lives, community development, even societal transformation, can blossom as the fruit of a spiritual gospel.

Reconciliation which Brings Hope to the Poor

The cluster of "reconciliation" vocabulary (*apokathistēmi*, "to restore"; *katallassō*, "to reconcile"; *hilaskomai*, "to propitiate") presents Jesus as the source of a salvation which restores sinful man to a right relationship with God (Acts 3:21-26; 2 Cor 5:18-19; Rom 3:25). Again this is accomplished through Christ's death, victorious resurrection and exaltation. God's wrath against man and his sin is propitiated through blood sacrifice (Heb 2:17; 1 Jn 2:2). Christ becomes sin for us, so that we might be reconciled, becoming the righteousness of God through Jesus (2 Cor 5:21). The restoration of all things will come because Jesus died and rose again, now reigns, and will return (Mk 9:12). Right now he is preparing a people for that by turning each one away from his sins by Spirit empowered gospel witness in his name (Acts 3:21-26; 1:6-8).

This reconciliation of man to God also works the reconciliation of man with man. All human divisions are overcome as Christ in his one body reconciles enemies, "both of them to God through the cross, by which he put to death their hostility." (Eph 2:16). In fact, Jesus at his inaugural sermon in Nazareth said he had come to declare "good news" to the poor, a proclaiming of the year of the Lord's favor (Lk 4:18-19/Isa 61:1-2). When understood as a Jubilee Year, this proclamation does involve reconciliation, particularly in the socio-economic sphere. J. Massynbaerde Ford explains,

> Jesus may have been inaugurating or proclaiming a jubilee year, in which, according to Jewish law, debts were cancelled, slaves (and prisoners) were released, and people returned to their own land and the land lay fallow but the poor were allowed to glean the fields and orchards of the crops or fruits which grew naturally.[13]

Among Jesus' contemporaries there were messianic pretenders who used the Jubilee Year concept and the Isaiah passage, especially the phrase "the day of vengeance of our God," to call their fellow countrymen to fight against the Gentiles for political and religious freedom (e.g., Simon Bar Giora reported in Josephus, *Jewish War*, 4.508; cf. 11QMelch). However, as Luke presents it, Jesus consciously concluded his quotation of Isaiah 61 before the declaration of the coming "day of vengeance." When we combine this fact with the rest of Jesus' sermon in which he uses as illustrations God's saving initiatives to Israel's traditional enemies, we begin to see that the kind of "favorable year" Jesus declares is one of reconciliation, healing, forgiveness.[14]

Though the poor may rightly look forward to the future final manifestation of God's kingdom which will be characterized by the great eschatological reversal of blessing for the poor and woe for the oppressing rich (Lk 1:52-55; 6:20-26; 16:25), such reconciliation to God and man now works a present hope in the poor. Indeed, this is what is happening among the poor who are responding to Pentecostalism in Latin America according to Richard Shaull and Waldo Cesar. Pentecostalism is so successful in this context because

> this present globalized economy leaves masses of people uprooted and abandoned on the periphery of ever growing large cities, where they are engaged in a desperate struggle for daily survival. Moreover, all the structures that normally sustain human life in community are breaking down. In this situation they are seeking and finding in Pentecostalism an experience of the Divine which helps them to put their lives together, heals their wounds, and gives them hope for the future . . . Poor Pentecostals often experience a presence and power that turns their lives around and compels them to struggle for a new future . . . [A] Pentecostal experience focused on day-to-day reality may well become a major force for social change."[15]

The Religio-Ideological Context: Prosecuting Mission in a Hostile Environment

Twenty-first Century Religio-Ideological Context: Increased Religious Devotion, Increased Conflict

Before 9/11, future trends scanners had projected religion as a central issue in both East and West. The religiously motivated violence of 9/11 certainly validated those prognostications. In the West, religion has a decidedly tolerant, eclectic, syncretizing face. Popkorn and Marigold in their description of the "anchoring" trend say,

> Whatever it is that Clicks into a deep meaning for your life, one thing is evident: We're at the start of a Great Awakening. A time of spiritual upheaval and religious revival . . . What's different about this Awakening is that there's very little agreement on who or what God is, what constitutes worship, and what this ritualistic outpouring means for the future direction of our civilization.[16]

Simultaneously, there is a clash among religions as some aggressive proponents of world religions use their economic and political clout, not to mention physical force, to accomplish a conversionist agenda.[17] Persecution of other religionists who will not submit is on the rise. Those of a tolerant, eclectic, syncretizing disposition religiously, in a post-9/11 environment, seem increasingly to view any "missionary moves," which proactively commend the Christian faith to others as contributing to a climate conducive to "hate crimes."[18]

In addition to the immediate impact of 9/11, globalization's effect on religion seems to create simultaneously both problems and opportunities. Globalization deterritorializes cultural systems, threatening the intrinsic link between "sacred time, sacred space, and sacred people," common to all world religions, and the essential bonds between histories, peoples and territories, which have defined all civilizations.[19] This deterritorialization occurs as a simultaneous reassertion of the local and the global over the national. What religion may lose at the national level and the fragmentation it faces at the local level is matched by the opportunity for it to break free from the straitjacket of nation-states and regain truly transnational, global dimensions.[20]

Debray[21] sees these twin aspects in a causal nexus: global deculturalization incites local reculturalization. The latter, a mechanism of defensive territorial implantation, necessarily of a sacred nature. "The soil and the sacred" go together. Religion is not the opiate of the people, but the "vitamin of the weak" and among the poorest of the poor, clerical fanaticisms are again prospering. What is needed, says DeBray, is a freely granted "civic religion" with an "agnostic spirituality" and a "credible political and social ethics" annealed to a globalization which currently is a "spiritually empty economism."[22] John Gray in the *New Statesman* actually sees globalization as a religion, a new "modern" secular one which has replaced Marxism. Globalization seen this way, views "religion of the old-fashioned sort . . . [as] peripheral and destined to disappear, or to shrink into the private sphere, where it can no longer convulse politics or inflame war."[23]

The Relevance of Jesus As the Source of Mission

This religio-ideological context poses a number of questions for the Christian missionary: 1) In an increasingly hostile environment, how can one constructively engage an adherent of a non-Christian faith? 2) In a time of globalization's deterritorializing effect on national and local perceptions, how can the Christian missionary prosecute his mission in such a way that the local is transformed? 3) In a day when the secular globalized mindset has no categories for explaining the 9/11 evil done in the name of religion, how can a proper understanding of the relation of religion and evil be found? A consideration of Jesus as the source of mission, as revealed in the Great Commission he gave (Matt 28:18-20; Lk 24:46-49; Jn 20:21-23; Acts 1:4-8), will help us begin to answer these questions.

Components of the Great Commission

The Great Commission contains basically four components.[24] Jesus declares the commission's warrant or authority, its task, its scope, and its power. The authority for a commissioning is very significant, since the basic activity of commissioning (*apostellō*="to dispatch someone for the achievement of some objective"[25]) is investing a person with authority to go and act as a person's agent doing what he would do if he were there himself. The authority Jesus invests in the commission is first the authority of divinely inspired prophetic promises which must come to fulfillment ("This is what is written," Lk 24:46). Those who obey are as much fulfilling Scripture as Jesus did in his obedient death and victorious resurrection. Secondly, the authority is divinely bestowed by the full and final authority of the risen Lord. "All authority in heaven and on earth has been given to me" (Matt 28:18). There is no place in the spiritual or the physical nor is there any creature over which Jesus does not have the "right to control or command."[26] His authority in sending his disciples is of the same nature as the authority with which his Father sent him into the world (Jn 8:42; 17:18; 20:21).

The task to which the risen Lord commissions his disciples, when looked at as a whole, is to be his witnesses, to attest to the good news about Jesus (Acts 1:8). Looking at the task in detail from the activities involved, there is a proclamation about the salvation Jesus accomplished in his atoning death and victorious resurrection and there is a proclamation in the authority of his name about what must be done to apply this salvation to oneself: repent. Then there are salvation blessings which may be embraced: forgiveness of sins (Lk 24:46-47). When the task is viewed in relation to the results which issue from it, we hear Jesus' promise that a divine transaction will take place in the preaching and hearing. For the receptive, "forgiveness," for the unreceptive, "accountability for sins remains" (Jn 20:23). As Jesus commissions his disciples "to make disciples" by "baptizing" them into the name of the Father, Son, and Holy Spirit and "teaching" them to observe everything he has commanded (Matt 28:19-20), we quickly learn that the task is more than evangelism. It is the invitation, introduction, and nurturing of persons in lifelong following after Christ. It involves a new identity as these new disciples take to themselves the name of the Triune God. It involves a new way of thinking and acting as they learn all Christ's commands.

The scope of the mission is worldwide. Jesus presents it cosmically, geographically, and ethnically. He sends his disciples as the Father sent him, i.e., into the world, to any who will hear (Jn 20:21, cf. 17:18). He wants them to bear witness to him "in Jerusalem, in all Judea and Samaria, and to the ends of the earth" (Acts 1:8). Their audience is to be "all the nations, people groups, ethnic groups, cultures" (*ethnē* is "the most general and therefore the weakest of these terms having simply an ethnographical sense and denoting the natural cohesion of a people in general" See Matt 28:19; Lk 24:47).[27] No human being should be beyond the sound of this proclamation. All alike need to hear.

The power of the Triune God is promised to attend the disciples on mission. If these disciples are sent as the Father sent Jesus, then, as they go on mission, they should expect the Father to work: bearing witness and drawing people to faith, just as he did in Jesus' mission (Jn 5:37; 6:44). Indeed, Jesus promises that declaration of forgiveness in witness on earth is a statement of what has already happened in heaven (Jn 21:23). Jesus promises that he himself will empower his disciples on mission. He instructs them to proclaim repentance unto forgiveness "in his name," i.e., by his present reigning authority (Lk 24:47). He says that he will be with them on mission "to the very end of the age" (Matt 28:20). At the very forefront of the promise of enablement is the declaration that the Spirit will empower them. Whether in his proleptic invitation: "he breathed on them and said, 'Receive the Holy Spirit'" (Jn 21:22) or his command to wait until the Spirit comes before embarking on mission (Lk 24:49), Jesus lets his disciples know how indispensable "power from above" is.

Constructively Engaging Others in a Hostile Religious Environment

Jesus, the source of mission, as articulated in his commissioning words works both confident integrity and respectful love in the messenger. The divinely given, full and final authority of the risen Lord, as he commands his disciples to fulfill Scripture through their proclamation, strengthens the messenger to be confident that he has every right, indeed is under divine necessity, to share the good news. The fact that the Triune God is on mission with him—that the Father's work draws people to Christ, that Christ's mighty name saves, that the Spirit's transforming power makes disciples—further buttresses his confidence. Indeed, he is not alone.

Lest such confidence become an "in your face" triumphalism, Jesus' commissioning should also work in us respectful love. We must remind ourselves that the universal scope of the task once included us. We were going the wrong way and needed to hear the call to repentance. So, in humble love, we share this good news with others and ask them to embrace Christ. Again, since the message, the activity, the enablement is not ours, but Christ's, no matter the hostility, we need not be defensive or offended, but can continue humbly to share.

Addressing the Deterritorialization of Religion

Jesus' commission enables us to address this effect of globalization through a gospel message that transforms the local through the global. Jesus, the global savior, who commands all authority, calls us to make disciples, followers of his views. He commands us to place on them a new identity: baptizing them into the name of the Triune God. This identity is at once global. But as we see its embrace in Acts, we understand it is also intended to be lived out locally. At the very first outpouring of the Spirit to empower for witness there was a miracle of hearing, each in his own language, "the mighty saving deeds of God" (Acts 2:8, 11). The author of Acts consistently describes the audience of this commission as *panta ta ethnē* ("all the ethnic or people groups," Matt 28:19; Lk 24:47). So, the Great Commission must ever be fulfilled by crossing cultural thresholds and proclaiming the global message in such a way that it can be rooted in the local context. This understanding of mission alone overcomes globalization's deterritorialization of religion.

Engaging the Secular Globalized Mindset

To the secular globalized mindset's lack of transcendent moral categories for understanding the problem of evil, particularly perpetrated in the name of religion, the Great Commission offers a message which confronts the problem of evil head on. In its salvation accomplished phase, the innocent Jesus suffers an unjust, shameful, excruciating death at the hands of religious authorities. Yet, God conquers this evil by using that death to make atonement for sin and raising Jesus from the dead. Application of that salvation requires that evil be addressed directly since the response called for is to repent of one's sinful ways (Lk 24:47). And the problem of evil begins to be solved one heart at a time as forgiveness is received and persons live a life, following Jesus' teachings, doing deeds worthy of repentance (Matt 28:20; Acts 26:20).

Conclusion

In the globalized context of the early twenty-first century, Jesus as the source of salvation and mission is more and more relevant. Jesus speaks to the socio-economic context of majority world poverty by coming to redeem the poor from their sins. In doing so, he meets their most urgent need—eternal life. But, he also lets loose in their lives and the lives of Christians around them a dynamic repentance and grace, which leads to meeting physical needs through economic repentance, graciousness in the Christian community, and fruit of the Spirit lived out in a transformed and societally transforming life. Jesus gives the poor hope through reconciliation to God and to ones fellowman. This restored relationship with God and others gives the poor strength to deal with their socio-economic marginalization.

Jesus as the source of mission strengthens his witnesses to constructively engage others in a hostile religious environment. By understanding the authority of and power in his Great Commission, they are able to witness with confident integrity. Remembering that they were once in need of repentance and that all they are called to do is from Christ enables them to bear witness in humble love. Through a disciplemaking process which calls persons to follow the global Lord in ones local ethnic context, Jesus' commission constructively addresses globalization's deterritorialization of religion. Both aspects of the gospel—salvation accomplished and salvation applied—deal with evil, including evil perpetrated by religion. By communicating a gospel message which deals with evil and brings salvation to light, the moral quandary of the secular, globalized mindset is addressed. Jesus, Savior and Sender, could not be more relevant to the present global context.

116 CENTRALITY OF CHRIST IN CONTEMPORARY MISSIONS

Notes

1. Joshua Kurlantzick and Jodie T. Allen, "The Trouble with Globalization," *U.S News and World Report* vol. 132, no. 4 (Feb 11, 2002): [OCLC: First Search–Full Text] 2.

2. John Naisbitt, *Megatrends Asia: Eight Asian Megatrends that are Reshaping our World* (New York: Simon & Schuster, 1996) cited by Nancy S. Cheek, Lecture Notes on "Future Trends"(Unpublished; Columbia Biblical Seminary and School of Missions, Columbia, SC: 1997); Robert J. Schreiter, "Mission into the Third Millennium," *Missiology* 18 (1990): 8-9.

3. Schreiter, 8-9; Bruce Nicholls, "Our Theological Task: Preparing for Mission in the 21st Century," *Evangelical Review of Theology* 20 (1996): 373.

4. Joel Kovel, "The Question of the Millennium," *Tikhum* vol. 17, no. 3 (May/June 2002): [OCLC: First Search–Full Text] 1.

5. Georg Sorenson, "Four Futures," *The Bulletin of Atomic Scientists* 51 (July/August 1995): [OCLC: First Search–Full Text] 2-3.

6. David Barrett, *World Christian Encyclopedia*, 2nd ed. (Oxford: Oxford University Press, 2001), 1.

7. Philip Jenkins, *The Next Christendom: The Coming Global Christianity* (Oxford: Oxford University Press, 2002), 2-3.

8. David Barrett and Todd M. Johnson, "Annual Statistical Table on Global Mission," *International Bulletin for Missionary Research* 26 (2002): 23.

9. Barrett, *World Christian Encyclopedia*, 1.

10. Stan Guthrie, *Missions in the Third Millenium: 21 Key Trends for the 21st Century* (Carlisle, U.K.: Paternoster Press, 2000), 58.

11. *New International Dictionary of New Testament Theology*, s.v. "Reconciliation, Restoration, Propitiation, Atonement" and "Redemption, Loose, Ransom, Deliverance, Release, Salvation, Saviour."

12. Frederick W. Danker, ed. *A Greek-English Lexicon of the New Testament and Other Early Christian Literature*, 3rd ed. (Chicago: University of Chicago Press, 2000), s.v. *psychē*.

13. J. Massynbaerde Ford, "Reconciliation and Forgiveness in Luke's Gospel," In *Political Issues in Luke-Acts*, ed. Richard J. Cassidy and Philip J. Scharper (Maryknoll, N.Y.: Orbis, 1983), 82.

14. Ibid.

15. Sara Miller. "Global Gospel." *Christian Century* vol. 119, no. 15 (July 17-30, 2002): [OCLC: First Search–Full Text], 4.

(cited in Miller 2002:4)

16. Faith Popcorn and Lys Marigold, *Clicking: 16 Trends to Future Fit Your Life, Your Work, and Your Business* (New York: HarperCollins, 1996), 143.

17. Schreiter, 10-12.

18. Editorial. "Evangelism Antagonism: Sharing the Good News is not a hate crime," *Christianity Today* vol. 47, no. 2 (February 2003): 32.

19. José Casanova, "Religion in the New Millennium, and Globalization," *Sociology of Religion* 62 (2001): [OCLC: First Search-Full Text] 9.

20. Cassanova (11-13) presents "Global Pentecostalism" as an example of a religion which has made such a move; Jenkins (cited in Sara Miller, "Global Gospel," *Christian Century* vol. 119, no. 15 [July 17-30, 2002]: [OCLC: First Search-Full Text] 1-2) characterizes the new Christendom of the "global south" this way.

21. Régis Debray, "God and the Political Planet," *New Perspectives Quarterly* 19 (2002): [OCLC: First Search-Full Text], 2.

22. Debray, 2; cf. the late Pope John Paul II's contention in *Centesimus Annus* 1991, p. 28 (Accessed 2/1/03 at http://www.vatican.va/holy_father/john_paul_ii/encyclicals) that this deficiency in globalization can only be effectively addressed from a transcendent reference point which places market capitalism at the service of human freedom in its totality.

23. John Gray reported by Michael Casey "How to Think about Globalization." *First Things* 126 [2002]: [OCLC: First Search-Full Text] 1.

24 John Harvey, "Mission in Jesus' Teaching," in *Mission in the New Testament: An Evangelical Approach*, ed. William J. Larkin, Jr. and Joel F. Williams (Maryknoll, NY: Orbis, 1998), 45-48.

25. Danker, s.v. *apostellō*.

26. Danker, s.v. *exousia*.

27. *Theological Dictionary of the New Testament*, s.v. *ethnos, ethnikos*.

II. CHRIST IN CONTEMPORARY MISSIONS

Chapter Five

Mission and Jesus in a Globalizing World: Globalization and the Pluralistic Jesus

Harold Netland

The Gospel of John, chapter 12, records a fascinating encounter between some Greeks, who were in Jerusalem for Passover, and Jesus. The Greeks, probably "God-fearers," approached Philip with a request that should warm the heart of every missionary: "Sir, we would like to see Jesus" (12:21, NIV). Although the text does not explicitly say so, it implies that Philip and Andrew led the Greeks to Jesus, and presumably they engaged in conversation. John does not detail the content of this conversation; rather the gospel writer uses this encounter between Jesus and some Gentiles to indicate the approaching climax of Jesus' ministry. No longer does he belong just to the Jews. He is the Savior of the entire world, Jews and Gentiles alike.

"Sir, we would like to see Jesus." Christian missions has many aspects, but central to everything we do in missions is bringing others, by the grace of God, to the place where they too can see Jesus. To see Jesus means more than merely to observe him with the eyes. The Greeks in John's gospel desired more than merely to gaze upon Jesus; they wished to speak with Jesus, to experience for themselves what they had heard about him from others, to see what Jesus is really like. Similarly, our concern is that others will grasp Jesus for who he really is and will come to acknowledge him as their Lord and Savior.

Unreached Peoples

What is involved today in enabling others to see Jesus, to encounter the living Christ? In many cases this means taking the gospel to those who have no awareness of Jesus, indeed, who have never heard the name of Jesus. And this has certainly been the heartbeat of the modern evangelical missionary movement. Since Lausanne 1974 this emphasis has been reflected in the very significant missiological focus upon "hidden," or "frontier," or "unreached" peoples, with a special priority for "pioneer missions" or "frontier missions." Surely this is appropriate. For regardless of how one defines key categories or how one interprets the statistics, large numbers of people today have never heard the name of Jesus and will never hear unless someone goes to them with the message of the gospel. Reaching these many groups must remain a priority for evangelical missions.

Alternative Jesuses

But contemporary missionaries must also recognize that this rapidly changing world presents multiple contexts and challenges for Christian mission.[1] Some of the more challenging mission frontiers today include cultures in which some awareness of Jesus already exists, but any understanding of Jesus is distorted and incompatible with the picture of Jesus we find in the New Testament. Although Europe and North America, for example, are frequently regarded as heavily Christianized, a closer look reveals multiple perspectives on Jesus in the popular consciousness, many of which have little in common with the New Testament Jesus. The astonishing success of *The Da Vinci Code*, by Dan Brown, demonstrates not only the continuing fascination with Jesus but a widespread willingness to accept revisionist perspectives with no historical support.[2] Moreover, as Stephen Prothero's *American Jesus: How the Son of God Became a National Icon* illustrates, Jesus' enduring symbolic power in popular consciousness often leads to understandings highly at variance with the biblical Jesus.[3]

Alternative understandings of Jesus run rampant not only in the West but also in much of Latin America, Asia, and Africa. And, of course, within the Islamic world, the second largest religious bloc worldwide, there are perspectives on Jesus as a prophet which, while respectful in their own ways, are nevertheless incompatible with orthodox Christian teachings on Jesus.[4] Much of the world, then, has some perspective on Jesus, although these are distorted and incomplete perspectives at best. In such contexts, the missiological challenge is not simply to bring the name of Jesus to those with no prior assumptions about him. Rather, this challenge includes what Bishop Kenneth Cragg, with reference to the Qur'anic understanding of Jesus in Islam, has called the need for retrieval—that is, overcoming the effects of distorted perspectives on Jesus and enabling people to encounter the biblical Jesus, accepting him rather than other alternatives.[5]

There is, of course, enormous variety in these alternative pictures of Jesus. I will focus upon one particular theme or motif in some of these understandings of Jesus as manifested both in the West and in Asia, namely, the pluralistic perspective which sees Jesus as a great religious and moral leader, but not qualitatively different from other great religious figures. This perspective is, of course, increasingly popular in Europe and North America, but it also has parallels in certain traditions in Asia, and its plausibility in the West today is due in part to some of these Asian influences upon the West. I will consider briefly how this perspective is exemplified in late nineteenth and early twentieth-century India, in the contemporary religious pluralism in the West, and finally in modern Japan. Throughout these otherwise rather different contexts one discovers a common theme: the reduction of Jesus to merely one among many great religious leaders. Furthermore, at least in the cases of India and Japan, research reveals significant attempts to domesticate Jesus by adapting the symbolism of Jesus to Asian contexts, thereby giving him a home within indigenous religious frameworks.

These alternative perceptions of Jesus are often deeply embedded within local cultural and religious systems, and are thus reinforced by the relevant "plausibility structures," so that they become normative for those within such frameworks. Plausibility structures encompass the set of institutions, values, and assumptions of a particular culture that support the plausibility of certain beliefs or practices.[6] The gospel of the biblical Christ, then, comes into these contexts not as something totally new and unprecedented, but rather as a rival interpretation of an already familiar symbol, one that maintains a measure of plausibility within those contexts. The question then becomes, "Why should one accept the new, biblical picture of Jesus rather than the perspective already embedded within one's own cultural and religious framework?" Before considering some examples of the pluralistic Jesus, however, we need to give some attention to the concept of globalization, for globalization is partially responsible both for the widespread awareness of Jesus in many cultures and also for the pluralistic nature of such awareness in certain cases.

Globalization and Culture

Remarkably, the past century has witnessed a dramatic shift in Christian presence globally. While much of Europe has been experiencing a decline in Christianity (both in terms of numbers of believers and Christianity's social influence), parts of Asia, Latin America, and Africa have been witnessing extraordinary growth in the Christian church. Dramatic changes in migration patterns worldwide, increasing contact between peoples and cultures, the social and intellectual effects of modernization—all of these work to challenge and transform traditional religious patterns. Philip Jenkins correctly observes, "We are currently living through one of the transforming moments in the history of religion worldwide."[7] The term "globalization" has become widely used to describe the patterns associated with these changes. Interestingly, observers now regard the church—the worldwide body of Christians—both as a product of globalization and, through the success of the modern missionary movement, a significant contributor to the ongoing process of globalization.

Globalization refers to the processes through which patterns of contemporary life are increasingly interconnected worldwide in complex ways that transcend geographical, national, cultural, and religious boundaries. Anthony Giddens defines globalization as "the intensification of worldwide social relations which link distant localities in such a way that local happenings are shaped by events occurring many miles away and vice versa."[8] Events which formerly would demonstrate only local significance now have ramifications on the other side of the globe. Most people are aware of the interrelatedness of globalization in the political and economic dimensions. Astonishing developments in communications technologies both sustain and reflect this political and economic interrelatedness, so that messages and visual images can now be communicated worldwide virtually instantaneously. The symbol of globalization is the World Wide Web, which links people across traditional barriers, thereby extending the influences of modernization to the most remote parts of the earth.

The significance of globalization lies not merely in the fact of growing interrelatedness but in our heightened awareness of this interconnectivity and the reflexive effects of this consciousness upon us; therefore, globalization is so important for understanding cultural dynamics today. Malcolm Waters captures this aspect nicely in his definition of globalization as "a social process in which the constraints of geography on social and cultural arrangements recede and in which people become increasingly aware that they are receding."[9] Such awareness has a reflexive impact upon how people, in their local settings, understand themselves and their relationship with others.

Many have called attention to what seems to be an emerging "global popular culture" resulting from increased contact among peoples worldwide. The increasingly global influences of modern university education, common entertainment media, travel for business and pleasure, and vast linkages provided by telecommunications networks produce certain commonalities worldwide. Thus Waters argues that popular culture has shown a greater tendency toward globalization than either the political or economic sectors.[10] In some ways, an eighteen-year-old in Tokyo is likely to have more in common with eighteen-year-olds in London or Mexico City or Bangalore than with his own grandparents in Tokyo. What they have in common includes tastes in food, music, clothing, and entertainment, as well as educational processes preparing them for a technologically sophisticated world.

One must caution here against two common misunderstandings of globalization. First, globalization does not mean the homogenization of all cultures, so that what were once distinct cultures all blend into one massive commercial theme park—"McCulture." Local cultural distinctives are not eliminated with globalization. Hong Kong is not Nairobi, nor is it identical with Miami or London. Rather, the influences of globalization interact with local social and cultural patterns, resulting not in the disappearance of the local culture but in a fresh expression of that culture—one in which the new coexists with the old, but in altered ways. Globalization means that, for all of the differences between peoples on the local level, there is increased interrelatedness in shared symbolic meanings among groups previously separated by geography, ethnicity, politics, or religion.

Second, globalization is not merely the Westernization of the world or the imposition of Western consumerist culture upon the rest of the world. The simple identification of globalization with Westernization is misleading, since it confuses the origin of modernization and globalization with their current status and effects. It is of course true that globalization has grown out of modernization and that both were initially identified with Western culture. It is also indisputable that the economic and political power of the West, as well as the enormous lure of the Western entertainment industries, result in the spread of Western cultural influences worldwide. One must recognize, however, that the institutions and processes associated with modernization are today genuinely global, and thus the influences from globalization move in all directions simultaneously, including from Asia to the West. Local cultural patterns in Europe and North America are themselves being transformed through globalization, as this chapter shall demonstrate when it considers religious pluralism in the West.

Awareness of the impact of globalization upon local settings affects how one thinks about culture. In particular, the blurring of boundaries that accompanies globalization challenges models which view culture as a clearly defined, static entity tied to a particular group of people living in a set time and place. Historically, cultures have seldom been entirely self-contained systems untouched by other peoples and ways. Cultures have always been, in varying degrees, fluid and unbounded; as groups of people interacted with each other over time, cultural change resulted when elements from other contexts were absorbed. But what distinguishes today is that cultures, languages, and religious traditions have more extensive contact with each other, often resulting in greater "shared space" than at earlier times. The cultural changes brought about by globalization are acutely reflected in religious transformations, as traditional religious understandings adapt to new realities and fresh challenges.

Jesus in Hinduism

One example of a cultural encounter that resulted in changing religious expressions is found in the nineteenth-century engagement of traditional Hindu ways with both British colonialism and the Western missionary movement in India. The presence of Western culture and Christianity challenged traditional Hindu beliefs and practices. Hindu practices such as suttee, caste, and child marriage were strongly criticized as ethically deficient; in addition, religious beliefs and practices were denounced as idolatry and superstition. Jesus, by contrast, became a symbol both of what was wrong with Hinduism and of the superiority of the West and Christianity. To the chagrin of many in the West, however, many Indian social and religious leaders responded by neither converting to Christianity nor rejecting Jesus outright. Rather, these leaders gave Jesus a neo-Hindu identity and embraced him in the nineteenth- and early twentieth-century revitalization movements known as the Hindu renaissance. Jesus became domesticated and indigenized within a neo-Hindu framework. Folk Hinduism presently reflects this syncretism in the widespread practice of including pictures of Jesus inside Hindu shrines or in the *puja* rooms of Hindu homes.

Some Hindu thinkers attempted to combine the best of Western science and the moral precepts of Christianity with a purified and modernized form of Hinduism. Reform movements such as the Brahmo Samaj and the Ramakrishna Mission, and leaders such as Ram Mohan Roy, Sri Ramakrishna,

Swami Vivekananda, Keshub Chandra Sen, Sarvepalli Radhakrishnan, and Sri Aurobindo all advocated modernized versions of Hindu thought in which Jesus occupies an important place.[11] Vivekananda, for example, understood Jesus as a moral and spiritual teacher whose insights were already anticipated, in purer form, in the earlier Hindu mystics. He emphatically rejected the doctrinal formulations of orthodox Christianity and was especially critical of perceived exclusivism.

> [Christianity] is the best for you, but that is no sign that it is the best for others . . . In Christianity . . . when you speak of the Incarnation, of the Trinity, of salvation through Jesus Christ, I am with you. I say, 'Very good, that I also hold true.' But when you go on to say, 'There is no other true religion, there is no other revelation of God,' then I say, 'Stop, I cannot go with you when you shut out, when you deny.' Every religion has a message to deliver, something to teach man; but when it begins to protest, when it tries to disturb others, then it takes up a negative and therefore a dangerous position.[12]

Similarly, Sarvepalli Radhakrishnan, whose distinguished career included positions as professor in both Indian and British universities, ambassador to various countries, and President of the Republic of India, regarded Jesus as a mystic who echoed much of what was already contained in the sacred texts of Hinduism.[13] He reinterpreted Jesus' religious teachings as variations on Advaitin Vedantin themes. Radhakrishnan was willing to speak of Jesus as divine, but not in any exclusive or distinctive sense. In his view, Jesus' divinity and incarnation serve as models for the rest of us in our relationship with God. Radhakrishnan argued that Jesus' teachings were actually shaped by Indian religious and philosophical assumptions, which allegedly influenced the environment in which Jesus grew up. There is, then, little in Jesus' life or teachings that is distinctive or new, and anything of enduring value was actually borrowed from India.

Mohandas Gandhi's interest in Jesus is well known. One of the most influential men of the twentieth century, Gandhi had extensive contact with Christianity and claimed many personal friends who were conservative, orthodox Christians. Gandhi maintained great respect for Jesus, and, although he rejected the orthodox Christian teaching about Christ, he was deeply moved by the moral example he saw in Jesus' life and death. In the cross of Christ Gandhi saw the supreme example of his own principle of *satyagraha*, passive resistance or truth force, and thus he referred to Jesus as "the Prince of *satyagrahis*." In Gandhi's words,

> It was the New Testament which really awakened me to the value of passive resistance. When I read in the Sermon on the Mount such passages as 'Resist not him that is evil; he who smiteth thee on thy right cheek turn to him the other also, and love your enemies, pray for them that persecute you, that ye may be the sons of your Father which is in heaven', I was overjoyed.[14]

Yet Gandhi remained a Hindu and did not become a Christian.

In a perceptive essay entitled "Hindu Views of Christ," Ronald Neufeldt summarizes the understandings of Jesus within the Hindu Renaissance as follows:

> Whether one looks at the issue of Christ as *avatara* or Christ as an ideal, there is a single thread that runs through Hindu views of Christ. This thread is the depiction of Christ as an Oriental or Asiatic. One might even be more specific and say that it is the depiction of Christ as the quintessential Hindu, the one who lives Hindu ideals as they ought to be lived and teaches the essence of Hindu truth as it ought to be taught . . . The purpose of proposing Christ as Oriental is two-fold—to claim Christ and the teachings of Christ, however these may be interpreted, as indigenous to India, and to attack Eurocentric notions of Christ.[15]

Vivekananda, Radhakrishnan, and Gandhi have several things in common. All three were products of the encounter between traditional Hindu patterns and Western culture and Christianity. Each experienced significant exposure to Christianity and upheld positive views about Jesus, yet all three rejected orthodox Christian teachings on Jesus. Each in turn presented an alternative understanding of Jesus in line with Hindu assumptions. And finally, all three had significant influence not only within India but also upon the West. Thus, they each contributed to the pluralistic reshaping of Jesus in the West.

Jesus in the West

Leaving India and turning to Europe and North America, one is struck first by the widespread and dramatic transformations in religious expression and identity found in the West. Observers find, among other things, the social and political disestablishment of Christianity (or the end of Christendom), significant decline in church attendance—at least in much of Europe—popular fascination with the occult and alternative spiritualities, a resurgence of ancient paganism in modernized form, religious eclecticism and an openness to neo-Hindu and Buddhist movements, the growth of extremist religious movements, and the rise of religious violence. Two decades ago the late Lesslie Newbigin placed the Western world squarely upon the missiological agenda by pressing the question, "Can the West be converted? What would a genuine missiological encounter with the West involve?"[16]

One significant development in the West is the growing acceptance of the assumptions and values typically referred to as "religious pluralism."[17] Religious pluralism grows out of the recognition of religious diversity in the world, maintaining that all the major religions are more or less equally legitimate and effective human responses to one divine reality. No single religion can be asserted as distinctively true and normative for all peoples. Within the academic world, the most influential Western pluralist has been the philosopher and theologian John

Hick.[18] But Hick's model of pluralism represents a sophisticated expression of a widespread view in popular culture.

Religious pluralism makes room for Jesus, just not the Jesus of orthodox Christianity. While rejecting the orthodox understanding of Jesus as God incarnate, Hick says "We see in Jesus a human being extraordinarily open to God's influence and thus living to an extraordinary extent as God's agent on earth, 'incarnating' the divine purpose for human life."[19] Hick reinterprets the Incarnation metaphorically, and urges us to recognize that not only Jesus but also Moses, Gautama, Confucius, Zoroaster, Socrates, Mohammed, and Nanak "have in their different ways 'incarnated' the ideal of human life in response to the one divine Reality."[20]

It is no accident that pluralism has become so influential in the West during the past half century.[21] Pluralism thrives in contexts characterized by the loss of confidence in the claims of traditional Christianity and the heightened awareness of religious diversity brought about by globalization. Many factors contribute to current skepticism about orthodox Christian claims. Perhaps most significantly, universities and popular media have legitimized and disseminated the conclusions of two centuries of radical biblical criticism. Furthermore, through globalization, religious influences from the East have become part of the Western cultural fabric. Buddhism, in particular, is growing both in Europe and North America. The beaming face of the Dalai Lama is so familiar in the West that several years ago Apple computers used his portrait in its "Think Different!" advertising campaign—without any identification attached to his portrait. Buddhism, too, acknowledges Jesus. The Dalai Lama states, "As a Buddhist, my attitude toward Jesus Christ is that he was either a fully enlightened being, or a *bodhisattva* of a very high spiritual realization."[22] The various streams of the New Age Movement and the alternative spiritualities, promoted by self-appointed gurus and swamis, also adopt a reinterpreted Jesus. Deepak Chopra, the Indian physician-turned-advocate of an eclectic mix of Vedantin Hindusim and theosophy, asserts, "Christ-consciousness, God-consciousness, Krishna-consciousness, Buddha-consciousness: it's all the same thing. Rather than 'love thy neighbor,' this consciousness says, 'You and I are the same beings.'"[23] The East has come West, and Jesus has been transformed in the process.

Jesus in Japan

The third case this chapter considers is modern Japan. But surely the suggestion that Japan has embraced Jesus in any sense will strike many as odd! After all, missiological circles understand Japan to be distinctively unfriendly to Christianity and resistant to the gospel message—a nation with no place for Jesus Christ. Christians today comprise roughly one percent of the total population of Japan, and the cultural and intellectual dominance of the traditional religions (Shinto and Buddhism) remains intact.[24] Thus, the primary challenge for the church involves those vast numbers of Japanese who have never heard of Jesus. The solution, many declare, is more aggressive and effective evangelism.

Now, to be sure, there is much truth in this assertion. But this picture also misleads the reader. A more careful examination reveals that the introduction of Christianity in the sixteenth and seventeenth centuries, then again in the nineteenth century, forced Japan to come to grips with Christianity. The nation responded by adapting and reinterpreting the meaning of Jesus. While the number of explicit Christians remains very small, the impact of Jesus upon Japanese public consciousness is significant, so that one sometimes finds Jesus in rather surprising places.[25]

Some of the ways in which the Japanese culture has embraced Jesus and Christian symbolism seem trivial and even amusing. For instance, young couples often marry in so-called

Christian wedding chapels, complete with a foreign pastor or priest presiding, even though neither bride nor groom has any real interest in the church as such. Thus, the Japanese adapt and domesticate the symbolism of Western, Christian wedding ceremonies for quite non-religious—even commercial—ends. Similarly, anyone in Japan in December will notice that Christmas is one of the major celebrations of the year. Businesses across Japan organize Christmas parties, complete with Christmas trees, Bing Crosby's "White Christmas," and plenty of alcohol. Christians rightly observe that few of those participating have any idea of the true meaning of Christmas. Anthropologist Richard Shweder graphically illustrates this confusion:

> A few years ago . . . I heard a story from Clifford Geertz about a visitor to Japan who wandered into a department store in Tokyo, at a time when the Japanese had begun to take a great interest in the symbolism of the Christmas season. And what symbol of the Christmas season did the visitor discover prominently on display in the Tokyo department store? Santa Claus nailed to a cross![26]

Having observed many Christmas celebrations in Japan, I have little question about the factuality of the story. While amusing and rather disconcerting, the story poignantly illustrates what happens in globalization when symbols rich with meaning are detached from their traditional settings and adapted in quite different contexts. It is difficult to imagine two symbols more diametrically opposed than Santa Claus and the cross, yet there they were in the department store, together on display, with the store manager apparently unaware of any tension between them.

A fascinating example of local adaptation of Jesus to the Japanese context is the story of Jesus' tomb in northern Japan. Local legend purports that, after growing up in Galilee, Jesus came to Japan before beginning his public ministry. He returned to Galilee at age thirty three and began preaching a heavenly kingdom: namely, Japan. When he encountered trouble with the Jewish leaders, Jesus left Galilee and returned to the town of Shingo, near beautiful Lake Towada. According to the legend, Jesus' brother, Isukiri, was crucified in Jesus' place on the cross. Jesus lived in northern Japan until his death at age 106. Local townsfolk point out the grave where he was supposedly buried.[27] Somehow a distortion of the gospel story long ago embedded itself in local narratives in a remote mountain area, far removed from known centers of Christianity. The origin of the legend remains a mystery, although most scholars believe it is a confused remnant of the Roman Catholic influence in Japan in the sixteenth and seventeenth centuries.

Other more significant factors indicate that Jesus and Christianity have a kind of home in Japan. For example, sales of Bibles in post-WWII Japan demonstrate a surprising interest in the Bible. Average annual Bible sales in the late 1960s were about 400,000. During the period between 1971 and 1990, however, average annual sales of the Bible topped one million, or roughly 2.5 times that of the late 1960s. This is in a country in which the total number of Christians—Protestants, Roman Catholic and Orthodox—is just about one million. Not surprisingly, therefore, many homes have Bibles; Kumazawa Yoshinobu estimates that one in every two or three Japanese homes today has a Bible.[28]

Furthermore, a significant number of Japanese have come into contact with Christians through attending Christian kindergartens or Sunday Schools, studying conversational English with missionaries, or attending one of the many so-called "mission schools," either Roman Catholic or Protestant. Upon meeting a Japanese person, one often discovers that the individual has experienced some contact with Christians or the Church in the past. Unfortunately, such contact with Christianity has rarely resulted in on-going involvement with the institutional church.

One may also consider this phenomenon in terms of the "revolving door" problem in the Japanese church. Typically missionaries and pastors alike present the problem in Japan as one of evangelism: Christians simply need to do more evangelism. During ten years as a missionary in Japan, I became convinced that the Japanese church's difficulties were at least as great in retention as they were in evangelism. Although few reliable statistics exist, one may readily observe that most of those who come into contact with the church, and even participate to some extent within the church, do not remain active but eventually leave. Those who leave become part of the ninety-nine percent considered non-Christian, although they take away varying degrees of understanding about Jesus and the gospel.

Scholars estimate that between ten and thirty percent of the Japanese today participate in some form of new religious movement.[29] Most of the New Religions (or more recently the New New Religions) are products of the complex interplay of Buddhist, Confucian, Taoist and folk religious traditions with Shinto. These new religions emerged in the late nineteenth and twentieth centuries as Japan underwent rapid social changes prompted by modernization and interaction with the West. Observers, however, have yet to define the degree of Christian influence demonstrated by many of these new religious movements, some of which give Jesus a prominent place within their system. Indeed, Richard Fox Young, former Presbyterian missionary to Japan and now professor at Princeton University, argues persuasively that these movements should be understood in part as indigenous attempts to come to grips with the powerful onslaught of Christianity through the missionary presence at the turn of the century. This encounter coincided with the radical social changes of modernization sweeping over Japan.

> Christianity in my view has not just rippled over the surface of Japan but crashed upon it with tremendous force, no matter how

placid the land may look when the waves recede. This, I think, is contrary to the grim outlook of statisticians who measure the magnitude of the Christian impact on Japan in terms of church growth ... The thrust of my argument is that Christianity could hardly be ignored by religiously-minded Japanese of the last century and a half who tried to interpret the tumult around them and drew upon their varied resources, including Christianity, to overcome their sense of dislocation.[30]

Thus, for example, one finds Christian symbolism in the new religion Mahikari. These symbols include the ark-shaped main shrine used for worship, and the floor-to-ceiling cross in its worship sanctuary, said to be a symbol of both the cross of Christ and the internal harmony of water (*yin*) and fire (*yang*) forces. Young claims that there are over eighty allusions to biblical passages in the advanced training textbook of Mahikari. Mahikari claims that Jesus actually came to Japan for religious training in the years before he began his public preaching ministry and that, after running into trouble with the Jewish authorities, Jesus returned to Japan, where he died at the age of 118.[31]

Deguchi Onisaburo (d. 1948), founder of Omotokyo, also gave special attention to Jesus. An off-shoot of Shinto, Omotokyo incorporated Jesus by turning him into a *kami*, and thus he made Jesus—and "authentic Christianity"—something originally Japanese and not foreign at all. Numerous other charismatic leaders of new religions claim either to be reincarnations of Christ or to be inspired by Christ. Shoko Asahara, founder of the infamous Aum Shinrikyo, represents one of the more ominous such cases. He combined Hindu, Buddhist, and Christian elements with an obsession for doomsday scenarios, culminating in the March 1995 sarin gas attacks on the Tokyo underground system, which killed twelve and injured over six thousand. Upon reading through the Bible Asahara stated, "I hereby declare myself to be the Christ." In his mind the similarities between himself and Jesus were simply too close to be explained otherwise.[32]

Japan boasts a literacy rate of almost one hundred percent, and Japanese are among the best educated people in the world. Not surprisingly, literature and literary figures exert enormous cultural influence. In light of this fact, Japan's leading literary figures demonstrate a striking fascination with Jesus. Although not ranked among the top tier of Japanese writers, Ayako Miura is a well known evangelical Christian author widely read by non-Christians today. Many leading writers have also incorporated Christian themes into their work, and some have even written highly personal responses to the person of Jesus.[33] Ryunosuke Akutagawa, for whom the highly prestigious Akutagawa Prize is named, committed suicide in 1927, at the age of thirty-five. A copy of the Bible and a completed manuscript of *Seiho no Hito* (The Man From the West), a highly personal series of reflections upon the person of Jesus, were found by his bed. Akutagawa never professed faith in Christ, but Jesus clearly intrigued him. Rinzo Shiina (d. 1973) became a leading writer in the immediate post-war period; he was also a baptized Protestant Christian. His *Watakushi no Seisho Monogatari* (My Bible Story) reveals his ongoing struggles with faith: his simultaneous attraction to the person of Jesus and incredulity at much of what the New Testament has to say about Jesus.

Perhaps the writer best known for integrating theological themes into his novels is the late Roman Catholic writer, Shusaku Endo. In his later years Endo was probably the most recognized Christian in Japan, and for many Japanese he symbolized Japanese Christianity. In 1973 he gave his interpretation of Jesus in *A Life of Jesus*, a work which quickly sold over 300,000 copies.[34] But Endo is best known for addressing the tension between Japanese culture and Christian faith in such novels as *Silence* and *The Samurai*.[35] In an oft-quoted statement, he said, "Christianity to me was like a Western suit my mother made me wear when I was growing up."[36] Many Christians and non-Christians understood Endo to be advancing the thesis that Japan is a "swamp" which is incompatible with Christianity—for Christianity to take root, either Japan or Christianity must change. The popularity of Endo's writings indicates that many Japanese not only have an interest in these issues but also have some understanding of basic Christian themes.

Endo, however, also illustrates a further dimension of Japan's relationship with Jesus. Whereas Endo's earlier works grappled with questions of the relationship between Christianity and Japanese culture, in his final novel, *Deep River,* published in 1994, Endo explored themes of religious pluralism. With a title that refers to the Ganges (the sacred river of India), this novel depicts the spiritual journey of Otsu, a young Japanese studying for the Catholic priesthood. Otsu is expelled from his order for his excessively sympathetic view of other religions. He eventually finds himself in India serving the lower caste peoples. Reflecting upon his theological transformation, Otsu says,

> I now regret having spoken foolishly in front of the brethren of the Church. But it seems perfectly natural to me that many people select the god in whom they place their faith on the basis of the culture and traditions and climate of the land of their birth. I think that Europeans have chosen Christianity because it was the faith of their forefathers, and because Christian culture dominated their native lands. You can't say that the people of the Middle East chose to become Muslims and many Indians became Hindus after conducting rigorous comparisons of their religions with those of other peoples . . . God has many different faces. I don't think God exists exclusively in the churches and chapels of Europe. I think he is also among the Jews and the Buddhists and the Hindus.[37]

Through the mouth of Otsu, Endo gives expression to a theme deeply embedded within Japanese religious consciousness. In Japanese culture, one frequently encounters the notion that religion is culturally and historically conditioned, and thus various cultures have different—although equally legitimate—religious traditions. As noted earlier, this view has also become influential in the West, expressed persuasively in the work of John Hick. Interestingly, many of Hick's works on religious pluralism have been translated into Japanese (several by Hiromasa Mase, for many years a professor of philosophy at Keio University).

In his journal, published after his death in 1997, Shusaku Endo writes of discovering the Japanese translation of Hick's *Problems of Religious Pluralism* in a book shop:

> It was as if my unconsciousness had summoned it, rather than mere accident . . . This shocking book has been overwhelming me since. And I am now absorbed in reading the same author's *God Has Many Names* . . . I went to my study and read and worked; yet, after Hick's shocking book, any book seemed boring . . . Hick is a Christian. Yet he says world religions are seeking the same God through different paths, cultures, and symbols, and [he] criticizes Christianity for maintaining a tendency toward Christian inclusivism despite its assertion, after the Second Vatican Council, of holding dialogue with other religions. He dares to claim that religious pluralism should give up such a theology as to see Jesus as Messiah, and so should reconsider the problem of Jesus' incarnation and of the Holy Trinity.[38]

In a perceptive essay, Anri Morimoto draws attention to the connections between popular Japanese religious commitments, John Hick's model of religious pluralism, and the later work of Shusaku Endo.

> The pluralistic understanding of religions represented by Hick has a peculiar charm to the Japanese. Japan is a "living museum of religions." Anyone who surveys the religious culture of Japan will be dismayed at the complexity and diversity of religions, both historical and contemporary. Religious pluralism is, as in other regions of Asia, not an ideological construction but a reality in which to live. A traditional Japanese poem captures the atmosphere: "Though there are many paths to climb atop a mountain, we all come to look at the same moon." Hick's pluralism offers an assurance of harmony among religions. It was

this assurance that Endo found with great relief, especially since the idea came from a Western theologian.[39]

Although Endo penned the pluralistic themes in *Deep River* prior to reading Hick's work, Endo clearly found something echoing his own convictions in Hick's pluralism.

Note the considerable irony in these connections. John Hick converted to Christianity while a university student in Scotland. For a time, he was, in his own words, a thoroughly orthodox, even fundamentalist Christian.[40] He is now an influential pluralist. Hiromasa Mase, who translated Hick's works into Japanese, converted to Christianity through the ministry of an evangelical Lutheran missionary in Japan. But Mase is now an outspoken advocate for pluralism in Japan. Endo became a Roman Catholic early on, yet he struggled throughout his life with the relationship between Christianity and Japanese culture. All three, in their own ways, ultimately rejected orthodox Christianity in favor of more pluralistic interpretations of Jesus. All three continue to exert considerable influence upon Japanese people and to shape Japanese understandings of Jesus. Moreover, in the spiritual journeys of John Hick, Hiromasa Mase, and Shusaku Endo, we find struggles, attitudes, and assumptions that unfortunately arise all too frequently among contemporary Japanese.

Conclusion

Thus, the challenge for evangelical missions in contexts like those described in this chapter is to bring those who already have some awareness of Jesus, and indeed are attracted to Jesus in some ways, to the place where they truly do see and encounter the Jesus of Scripture and acknowledge him alone as Lord and Savior.

Notes

1. See Wilbert R. Shenk, *Changing Frontiers of Mission* (Maryknoll, NY: Orbis, 1999).

2. Dan Brown, *The Da Vinci Code* (New York: Doubleday, 2003). At the time of writing, the book had ranked first on the New York Times best seller list for 44 straight weeks and was being translated into 44 languages, ensuring that the revisionist picture of Jesus and Mary Magdalene would have wide circulation globally. See Patrick T. Reardon, "'The Da Vinci Code' Unscrambled," *Chicago Tribune*, 5 February 2004.

3. Stephen Prothero, *American Jesus: How the Son of God Became a National Icon* (New York: Farrar, Straus, and Giroux, 2003).

4. On Islamic understandings of Jesus see Geoffrey Parrinder, *Jesus in the Qur'an* (New York: Oxford University, 1977); Neal Robinson, *Christ in Islam and Christianity* (Albany, NY: State University of New York, 1991); and Kenneth Cragg, *Jesus and the Muslim: An Exploration* (Oxford: Oneworld, 1999 [1985]).

5. Kenneth Cragg, *The Call of the Minaret*, 3rd ed. (Oxford: Oneworld, 2000 [1956]): 218-242.

6. The notion of plausibility structure is associated with Peter Berger's work in the sociology of knowledge. See Peter Berger, *The Sacred Canopy: Elements of a Sociological Theory of Religion* (New York: Anchor Books, 1967).

7. Philip Jenkins, *The Next Christendom: The Coming of Global Christianity* (New York: Oxford University, 2002), 1.

8. Anthony Giddens, *The Consequences of Modernity* (Stanford, CA: Stanford University, 1991), 64.

9. Malcolm Waters, *Globalization* (New York: Routledge, 1995), 3. Emphasis added. Other helpful discussions of globalization include: Arjun Appadurai, ed., *Globalization* (Durham, NC: Duke University 2001) and John Tomlinson, *Globalization and Culture* (Chicago: University of Chicago, 1999).

10. Waters, *Globalization*, 125.

11. See Arvind Sharma, ed., *Neo-Hindu Views of Christianity* (Leiden: E.J. Brill, 1988).

12. Sharma, *Neo-Hindu Views of Christianity*, 94-5.

13. S. Radhakrishnan, *Eastern Religions and Western Thought* (New Delhi: Oxford University, 1989 [1940]), 153-251.

14. Sharma, *Neo-Hindu Views of Christianity*, 149.

15. Ronald Neufeldt, "Hindu Views of Christ," in *Hindu-Christian Dialogue: Perspectives and Encounters*, ed. Harold Coward (Maryknoll, NY: Orbis, 1989), 173.

16. See Lesslie Newbigin, *Foolishness to the Greeks: The Gospel and Western Culture* (Grand Rapids: Eerdmans, 1986); and Lesslie Newbigin, "Can the West Be Converted?" *International Bulletin of Missionary Research* 11, no. 1 (1987): 2-7.

17. See Harold Netland, *Encountering Religious Pluralism: The Challenge to Christian Faith and Mission* (Downers Grove, IL: InterVarsity, 2001).

18. Hick has developed his views on pluralism in many writings. See especially John Hick, *An Interpretation of Religion: Human Responses to the Transcendent* (New Haven: Yale University, 1989); and John Hick, *The Metaphor of God Incarnate: Christology in a Pluralistic Age* (Louisville: Westminster John Knox, 1993). For a critical assessment of Hick's model see Harold Netland, *Encountering Religious Pluralism* (Downers Grove, IL: InterVarsity, 2001), chapters 5-7.

19. Hick, *Metaphor of God Incarnate*, 12.

20. Ibid., 96, 98.

21. I explore some of the factors behind the rise of religious pluralism in *Encountering Religious Pluralism*, chapters 1-5.

22. As quoted in Kenneth Woodward, "The Other Jesus," *Newsweek*, 27 March 2000, 56. See also, The Dalai Lama, *The Good Heart: A Buddhist Perspective on the Teachings of Jesus* (Boston: Wisdom Publications, 1996).

23. Woodward, "The Other Jesus," 58.

24. For a helpful overview of Christianity in Japan in the late 20th century, see *Christianity in Japan, 1971-90*, ed. Kumazawa Yoshinobu and David Swain (Tokyo: Kyo Bun Kwan, 1991).

25. For a fascinating study of non-traditional Christian movements in Japan, see Mark R. Mullins, *Christianity Made In Japan: A Study of Indigenous Movements* (Honolulu: University of Hawaii, 1998). Mullins' careful study shows that Jesus has been reinterpreted and indigenized among many distinct religious movements in Japan, resulting in alternative understandings of Jesus in Japanese popular consciousness.

26. Richard Shweder, "Santa Claus on the Cross," in *The Truth About the Truth: De-confusing and Re-constructing the Postmodern World*, ed. Walter Truett Anderson (New York: G. P. Putnam's Sons, 1995), 73.

27. See John Koedyker, "Another Jesus," *The Japan Christian Quarterly* 52, no. 2 (1986): 167-9.

28. Kumazawa Yoshinobu, "Foreward," in *Christianity in Japan, 1971-90*, xiii-xv.

29. Estimates on membership in New Religious Movements in Japan vary widely, but Robert Ellwood cites a study which put total membership in 1980 at 22% of the Japanese population. Robert S. Ellwood, "New Re-

ligions in Japan," in *The Encyclopedia of Religion*, vol. 10, ed. Mircea Eliade (New York: Macmillan, 1987), 411.

30. Richard Fox Young, "The 'Christ' of the Japanese New Religions," *The Japan Christian Quarterly* 57, no. 1 (1991): 19.

31. Ian Reader, *Religion in Contemporary Japan* (New York: Macmillan, 1991), 28-9, 246.

32. David E. Kaplan and Andrew Marshall, *The Cult at the End of the World* (New York: Crown Books, 1996), 67.

33. See Noah S. Brannen, "Three Japanese Authors Look at Jesus: A Review," *The Japan Christian Quarterly* 54, no. 3 (1988): 132-41.

34. Shusaku Endo, *A Life of Jesus*, translated by Richard A. Schuchert (Tokyo: Charles E. Tuttle, 1978 [1973]).

35. Shusaku Endo, *Silence*, translated by William Johnston (New York: Taplinger, 1969); and idem, *The Samurai*, translated by Van C. Gessel (New York: Harper & Row, 1982).

36. As quoted in Brannen, "Three Japanese Authors Look at Jesus," 139.

37. Shusaku Endo, *Deep River*, translated by Van C. Gessel (New York: New Directions, 1994), 121.

38. As quoted in John Hick, *John Hick: An Autobiography* (Oxford: Oneworld, 2002), 286.

39. Anri Morimoto, "The (More or Less) Same Light but from Different Lamps: The Post-Pluralist Understanding of Religion from a Japanese Perspective," *International Journal for Philosophy of Religion* 53 (2003): 164. The reference to Japan as a "living museum of religions" is from H. Byron Earhart, *Japanese Religion: Unity and Diversity*, 2^d ed., (Belmont, CA: Dickenson, 1974), 1.

40. For Hick's early Christian period see Hick, *John Hick: An Autobiography*, chapters 2-7.

Chapter Six

Mission and Jesus in a Globalizing World: Mission as Retrieval

Harold Netland

"Sir, we would like to see Jesus" (Jn 12:21, NIV). But which Jesus will people see? In the previous chapter I argued that many of the contexts in which Christian missions will be conducted today—both in the West and the non-Western world—already reflect some awareness of Jesus which is embedded within the culture. But these perceptions of Jesus are typically fragmentary or inaccurate and often undermine the plausibility of biblical teachings on Jesus. In particular, this situation occurs with the more pluralistic understandings of Jesus, according to which Jesus is a great spiritual and moral leader but merely one among many such leaders.

The Uniqueness of Jesus

In a recent interview, John Stott stated that the challenge of religious pluralism constitutes the most critical issue confronting the Christian mission community today. He is worth quoting at some length on this:

> Pluralism is not just recognition that there is a plurality of faiths in the world today. That is an obvious fact. No, pluralism is itself an ideology. It affirms the independent validity of all faiths. It therefore rejects as arrogant and wholly unacceptable every attempt to convert anybody (let alone everybody) to our opinions...
>
> The reason we must reject this increasingly popular position is that we are committed to the uniqueness of Jesus (he has no competitors) and his finality (he has no successors). It is not the uniqueness of 'Christianity' as a system that we defend but the uniqueness of Christ. He is unique in his incarnation (which is quite different from the ahistorical and plural 'avatars' of Hinduism); in his atonement (dying once for all of our sins); in his resurrection (breaking the powers of death); in his gift of the Spirit (to indwell and transform us). So, because in no other person but Jesus of Nazareth did God first become human (in his birth), then bear our sins (in his death), then conquer death (in his resurrection) and then enter his people (by his Spirit), he is uniquely able to save sinners.[1]

Stott eloquently encapsulates the distinctiveness of Jesus Christ and the basis for Christian missions even in a religiously diverse world. He rightly calls us to reject pluralism and to hold fast to the uniqueness and finality of Jesus Christ. But pluralism presents an especially problematic challenge to Christian missions. First, to the extent that the church adopts pluralistic assumptions its commitment to Christian missions, traditionally understood, will be undermined. Second, to the extent that the values and assumptions of pluralism shape the contexts within which Christian missions occur, the orthodox teaching on the person of Jesus Christ will be resisted, being perceived as implausible. This chapter will probe some of the factors in the second challenge, examining the implications for doing missions in contexts influenced by religious pluralism.

In particular, Bishop Kenneth Cragg introduces a challenging notion in his superb work, *The Call of the Minaret*. Islam, of course, understands Jesus to be a prophet, but the Qur'anic perspective on Jesus, as understood by Muslims, clearly rejects orthodox Christian teachings on the deity of Jesus Christ. Cragg calls Christians to the task of retrieval; that is, retrieving the true perspective on Jesus from Islamic misconceptions and presenting this perspective to Muslims in a winsome and persuasive manner.[2] His own work marvelously models how this might be accomplished. Many other contexts have lost the biblical Jesus by domesticating him to fit their own religious and cultural frameworks. A similar approach would work in these contexts as well. Here mission as retrieval involves first understanding the alternative perspectives on Jesus within the given context, then correcting misconceptions and recovering the biblical Jesus, and finally answering the question of why the biblical Jesus should be accepted rather than the other perspectives.

Religious pluralism is not the only challenge to Christian missions, and we should not exaggerate the impact of pluralism worldwide. Much of the religious world is anything but pluralistic; the past decades have witnessed an alarming rise of violence among radical religious movements.[3] Some of the most visible forms of religious expression today—at least through the media's eyes—are obstinately anti-pluralist and aggressively exclusivist forms of Islamism. Even the three examples considered in the previous chapter (neo-Hindu movements in India, the contemporary West, and Japan) do not uniformly express their pluralistic tendencies. Despite such cautions, the case remains for identifiable influences of pluralism which shape large numbers of people, and these influences comprise the object of this chapter.

The Challenge of Pluralism

Some general remarks must be made before responding to the challenge posed by pluralism. First, one must note the link, especially in the West, between religious skepticism and religious pluralism.[4] Religious pluralism is a general acceptance of the major religions or of religion in general, which simultaneously rejects any particular religion's claims to distinctive truth. Pluralism thrives in contexts which combine skepticism about specific religions with a vague desire to accept a religious point of view. Religious skepticism of traditional Christianity is widespread in some influential sectors of the West. The idea that one can know religious truth, that fundamental questions about God's existence, nature, and relation to humankind can be answered with any degree of intellectual satisfaction, strikes many today as naive. Religious skepticism most strongly exists in the academy, among the "knowledge sector" connected with the modern university, and among the media. Through the impact of the modern university and the media, such views increasingly influence Asian societies as well. Oddly enough, such skepticism of traditional religion often coexists with a remarkable credulity toward "religion in general" or toward alternative forms of spirituality. Thus, although the particular claims of a specific religion might be rejected, a general sense remains that the religions (plural) are not entirely delusory but are somehow all "in touch" with spiritual realities.

Not that long ago those in the West, even non-Christians, generally accepted that Christianity and Jesus Christ were in some sense privileged and superior to other religious traditions. This is no longer the case. Since the eighteenth century many have deliberately looked to the East for alternatives to Christianity and Western cultural traditions. What was earlier a small but persistent stream of thinkers looking East has today grown into a powerful current which includes not only increasing numbers of academics but also influential leaders in popular culture as well.

Westerners are not the only people attracted to the wisdom of the East: Eastern thinkers are also rediscovering in their own ancient heritage that which they find lacking in the West. Hindus such as Sarvepalli Radhakrishnan, Buddhists such as Gunapala Dharmasiri and Masao Abe, and neo-Confucianists such as Tu Weiming have studied carefully Western thought and Christian theology, rejecting both in favor of traditional Eastern perspectives. These men represent a growing movement, including Eastern and Western intellectuals, that looks to Eastern religious and philosophical traditions for answers not

Mission as Retrieval 149

found in Western paradigms. Thus, they may argue that even if, in principle, one religious tradition supercedes the rest, and one religious figure is universally normative, a person still may not assume that Christianity and Jesus are in this privileged position. After all, why Jesus and not the Buddha? And given the pluralistic understandings of Jesus as just one great religious leader among many, why should one accept the orthodox Christian claims about Jesus?

The effectiveness of Christian witness in pluralistic contexts depends in part upon the Church's response to these issues. Pluralism primarily objects to the Christian insistence upon Jesus as the only Lord and Savior for all people in all cultures. It dismisses this notion as morally and intellectually untenable.

Mahatma Gandhi, the great social and religious leader of modern India essentially concluded the same thing. Gandhi greatly admired Jesus. At one point, during his stay in South Africa in the 1890s, Gandhi actually appeared to consider becoming a Christian. A fellow lawyer and devout Christian, Mr. A.W. Baker, had an especially close relationship with Gandhi. But Gandhi did not become a Christian, and the reasons, given in his autobiography, for rejecting the Jesus of orthodox Christianity are instructive:

> Mr. Baker was getting anxious about my future. He took me to the Wellington Convention. The Protestant Christians organize such gatherings every few years for religious enlightenment or, in other words, self-purification . . . The chairman was the famous divine of the place, the Rev. Andrew Murray . . . But [Mr. Baker's] final hope was in the efficacy of prayer. He had an abiding faith in prayer. It was his firm conviction that God could not but listen to prayer fervently offered. He would cite the instances of men like George Muller of Bristol, who depended entirely on prayer even for his temporal needs. I listened to his discourses on the efficacy of prayer with unbiased attention, and assured him that nothing could prevent me from embracing Christianity, should I feel the call . . . This convention was an assemblage of devout Christians. I was delighted at their faith. I met the Rev. Murray. I saw that many were pray-

ing for me. I liked some of their hymns, they were very sweet. The Convention lasted for three days. I could understand and appreciate the devoutness of those who attended it. But I saw no reason for changing my belief—my religion. It was impossible for me to believe that I could go to heaven or attain salvation only by becoming a Christian. When I frankly said so to some of the good Christian friends, they were shocked. But there was no help for it.

My difficulties lay deeper. It was more than I could believe that Jesus was the only incarnate son of God, and that only he who believed in him would have everlasting life. If God could have sons, all of us were His sons. If Jesus was like God, or God Himself, then all men were like God and could be God Himself. My reason was not ready to believe literally that Jesus by his death and by his blood redeemed the sins of the world. Metaphorically there might be some truth in it. Again, according to Christianity only human beings had souls, and not other living beings, for whom death meant complete extinction; while I held a contrary belief. I could accept Jesus as a martyr, an embodiment of sacrifice, and a divine teacher, but not as the most perfect man ever born. His death on the Cross was a great example to the world, but that there was anything like a mysterious or miraculous virtue in it my heart could not accept. The pious lives of Christians did not give me anything that the lives of men of other faiths had failed to give. I had seen in other lives just the same reformation that I had heard of among Christians.

Philosophically there was nothing extraordinary in Christian principles. From the point of view of sacrifice, it seemed to me that the Hindus greatly surpassed the Christians. It was impossible for me to regard Christianity as the perfect religion or the greatest of all religions . . . Though I took a path my Christian friends had not intended for me, I have remained forever indebted to them for the religious quest that they awakened in me. I shall always cherish the memory of their contact.[5]

While Gandhi had deep appreciation for the moral teachings of Jesus, he was unable to accept the heart of the New Testament picture of Jesus: Jesus as the utterly unique God-man, the only Lord and Savior for all humankind. One finds similar views among leading Indian, Chinese, and Japanese thinkers who struggled with the person of Jesus and, while deeply impressed by him in many ways, rejected the orthodox Christian understanding of Jesus. Moreover, partly through the influence of thinkers such as Gandhi, Radhakrishnan, D.T. Suzuki, and the Dalai Lama in the West, views such as those expressed by Gandhi are increasingly prominent in the West as well.

A Missiological Response

How should the missiological community respond to these issues? Of course, Christians must be faithful to the biblical teachings on Jesus. Christ's disciples must also follow his command to make disciples of all peoples (Mt 28:18-20). Missions and evangelism are not optional; they must be carried out even in today's pluralistic world. The question then is not *whether* but *how* Christians respond to these imperatives. The response must give special attention to three areas.

Plausibility Structures

First, the missionary must understand the relevant social, historical, and cultural factors which undergird the pluralistic understandings of Jesus and thus undermine the acceptability of the orthodox view of Jesus. Peter Berger and others have labeled these factors as "plausibility structures" within a culture. Plausibility structures are those factors which reinforce the reasonableness of certain beliefs or values for a particular group of people.[6] These include social institutions such as the educational system (and the university in particular), inherited tradition, authority figures (parents, teachers and religious leaders), the media and entertainment industries, one's peers, and so on. Plausibility structures vary from culture to culture, with some supporting assumptions and values compatible with Christian theism and others reinforcing perspectives incompatible with Christian faith.

Why are the assumptions and values of religious pluralism so plausible today in the West when they were not so widely accepted even fifty years ago? Answering this question satisfactorily demands that one consider the impact of modernization, secularization, and globalization upon Europe and North America. For example, shifting plausibility structures in the West resulted in skepticism about traditional Christianity. This skepticism combined with greatly increased exposure to other religions to encourage openness to alternative religious perspectives. Furthermore, consumerism encourages choice and pragmatism; this in turn shapes how people approach religious issues. Additional examples abound.

What about pluralistic tendencies in Japan? Here the observer will notice both similarities and differences compared to the situation in the West. For example, Japan has a long tradition of religious syncretism and carefully controlled pluralism—factors which presented obstacles to the gospel from its first introduction in the sixteenth century.[7] Japanese culture has long maintained a rather ambivalent attitude toward exclusivist religious traditions. However, an open pluralism which accepts any and all religious perspectives as equally valid has never taken root in Japan. Although Japanese have been remarkably accommodating of some foreign religious traditions, this openness always exists within certain carefully defined parameters, including acceptance of the ancestral cult and the sense of common religious identity rooted in what it means to be authentically Japanese.

On the other hand, Japanese culture and religion have long accepted the idea that there may be alternative ways of responding to the divine reality. Japanese today generally frown upon strongly exclusivist traditions, from the radically exclusivist sects of Nichiren Buddhism to exclusivist Christianity. Among the Japanese, one finds a strong element of cultural and religious relativism in which they regard Christianity as fine for Europeans and Americans, but Japanese should be Shinto and Buddhist.

The influences of modernization and globalization are deeply entrenched in contemporary Japanese society. Thus, Japan today we have a fascinating blend a highly advanced stage of modernization with spiritual and cultural values rooted in centuries of tradition.[8] The astute observer will discover striking similarities between some themes found in religious expression in the West and contemporary Japanese approaches to religion. For example, in both cases one finds a sense of religious and cultural relativism; emphasis upon personal experience rather than doctrine or belief; suspicion of the exclusivist claims made by any religious tradition; and a highly pragmatic or "this worldly" approach to religious matters; and so on. The presence of these tendencies within Japan today cannot be attributed entirely to the effects of modernization and globalization upon Japan, since these same tendencies have been present in Japanese culture for centuries. Nevertheless, the cumulative effects of the legacy of modernity, combined with centuries of Japanese tradition, reinforce a social and intellectual environment in which the claims of orthodox Christianity appear highly implausible.

In considering the credibility of pluralism in the West and in Asia, one should pay special attention to two factors: the modern university and the legacy of colonialism. The university, despite its roots in European Christendom, reflects an escalating degree of secularization and serves as a major force for the legitimization and dissemination of secularizing influences. Clearly, the university today is especially sympathetic to the ideology of religious pluralism. The institutional structures as well as the educational goals and methodologies associated with the modern university now span the globe and exert increasing influence in Asian societies, where individuals value education so highly. Peter Berger recognizes the secularizing effect of the modern university in non-Western societies:

> There exists an international subculture composed of people with Western-type higher education, especially in the humanities and social sciences, that is indeed secularized. This subculture is the principal 'carrier' of progressive, Enlightenment be-

liefs and values. While its members are relatively thin on the ground, they are very influential, as they control the institutions that provide the 'official' definitions of reality, notably the educational system, the media of mass communication, and the higher reaches of the legal system.[9]

Consequently, Japanese students undergoing a university education will probably be exposed to the person of Jesus and the New Testament as part of their education, but in all likelihood this encounter will come through the filters of those trained in the methods and conclusions of radical biblical criticism.

When one explores the factors that reinforce the plausibility of pluralism today, one cannot exaggerate the impact of Western colonialism and the struggle to live in societies marked by deep ethnic, cultural, and religious diversity. These dynamics, too, develop differently in the West and in non-Western societies. In the West, the dynamics involve massive demographic changes so that people today live near by, go to school with, or work alongside Hindus, Buddhists, Sikhs, and Muslims as well as Mormons, New Age practitioners, and atheists. While perhaps a bit hyperbolic, Diana Eck is nearly correct to state that "The United States has become the most religiously diverse nation on earth."[10] The desire to affirm increasing diversity drives much of the attraction of contemporary pluralism in the West. It provides a means of atoning for Westerners' post-colonial guilt—and surely there is much in colonialism for which to feel guilty.[11] Can people from all cultures indeed learn to live together harmoniously, with such deeply held differences? Clearly everyone must do so. However, separating strictly cultural issues from religious issues remains notoriously difficult. As a result, acceptance of ethnic and cultural diversity becomes largely indistinguishable from endorsement of religious diversity—endorsement not simply in the sense of legally and socially accepting the place of non-Christian religions in American society, but also in the sense of affirming the beliefs of such religions.

The post-colonialist legacy functions rather differently in some non-Western societies. In India, for example, the revitalization and reaffirmation of traditional Hindu ways arose as part of the anti-colonialist, nationalistic agenda; thus the absorption of Jesus into the indigenous religious framework intentionally negated and domesticated foreign influences. Jesus took His place among many great religious leaders—only now the "true" Jesus was discovered to be a Vedantin mystic. A proper response to religious pluralism, whether in the West or the East, must be founded on an adequate appreciation of the complex social and historical factors reinforcing the plausibility of pluralism.

A Responsible Christian Apologetic

Second, a proper response to the multiple challenges of pluralism today must also include the development of a responsible Christian apologetic. Such an apologetic answers the question, "Why should I accept the biblical perspective on Jesus rather than any of the other available options?" This theme has not been particularly popular in missiological circles. Some missions leaders would argue that apologetics has been part of the problem rather than being the solution! This response, while well-meant, misses the point.

Three examples illustrate this point. The first comes from this author's experience in Japan. My wife, Ruth, was expecting our first child. On one of her regular visits to the maternity clinic she happened to meet an American woman, married to a Japanese and living in Tokyo. Since we did not often encounter Americans, Ruth invited the woman to our home. Expecting a casual visit full of small talk about things back home, Ruth was shocked by what followed. After exchanging pleasantries our guest launched into an impressive and moving testimony of how she had "found peace and true meaning to life" in Nichiren Buddhism. The woman, it turned out, was an American convert to Soka Gakkai Buddhism and was now a regional director of Soka Gakkai in Tokyo. In recounting the incident to me later, Ruth said that it was one of the most impressive testimonies she had heard. Change a few key terms here and there and it could have been a beautiful Christian testimony.

This incident illustrates not only some of the new realities in our globalizing world, but also the bankruptcy of any Christian witness that is limited simply to "sharing our story" while refusing to support personal testimony with other corroborating factors. Christian witness based merely upon personal experience or the pragmatic benefits of conversion would have little to say concerning why the woman ought to abandon Buddhism and embrace Christian faith. But that "why" is precisely the question pressed by pluralistic contexts.[12]

The Christian faith includes some profound and controversial claims about the nature of the universe, God, the human predicament, and salvation. Such claims inevitably engender questions about the justification of those claims. Just as a Christian will not blindly accept any claim to truth, the Christian community should not expect others to do so. Those who proclaim the gospel today must prepare themselves to respond appropriately when questions naturally arise.

Skillful argumentation alone will never change hearts and produce conversion, nor will apologetics save a person. No Christian argues another person into the Kingdom. Apologetics, like evangelism or any other activity, is ineffective apart from the power and work of the Holy Spirit on the heart. Saving faith is a gift of God's grace (Eph 2:8-10), and ultimately the Holy Spirit brings about conviction of sin (Jn 16:8-11), liberates the spiritually blind from the grasp of the Adversary, and gives new birth in Christ (Jn 3:5, 1 Cor 2:14-16, Titus 3:5). But, of course, this does not make apologetics unnecessary any more than it renders evangelism optional. Both evangelism and apologetics must be enacted with much prayer and conscious dependence upon the power of God.

In his autobiography, *Unfinished Agenda*, Lesslie Newbigin writes about meeting with Hindu scholars in the Ramakrishna Mission for study alternately of one of the Hindu Upanishads and the Christian Gospel of John. On one particular occasion he spoke of the historical fact of Jesus' resurrection as central to Christian faith:

> I well remember how I astonished the Swami by saying that if it could be shown that Jesus had never lived and died and risen again I would have no alternative but to become a Hindu. He thought only a lunatic would allow his ultimate destiny to hang upon a questionable fact of history which—even if it could be proved—belonged to the world of *maya*.[13]

Behind the incredulity of the Hindu lies a very different worldview in which the space-time world of our experience, including history, is a lower and provisional reality which must be transcended before one may grasp ultimate reality and truth. To the Swami religious truth, which is eternally and universally true, cannot be part of this lower reality, and it certainly cannot be based upon something as flimsy as history.

José Cabezon provides the third illustration. Raised a Cuban Roman Catholic, Cabezon now practices Buddhism and teaches at Iliff School of Theology in Denver, Colorado. In a fascinating essay he reflects, as a Buddhist, upon the significance of Jesus and readily acknowledges the historically factual nature of the New Testament accounts of Jesus' miracles, exorcisms, healings, and even His resurrection from the dead. But, Cabezon claims, these facts do not indicate that Jesus actually was God incarnate.

> That Jesus had these powers—that he could cure the sick, manipulate matter, cast out demons, raise others (and himself be raised) from the dead—most certainly points to the fact that he was an extraordinary individual. None of these events are for Buddhists outside the realm of possibility. At the same time, they are not unique in history, nor is the person possessing these attributes unique. More important, they do not prove that such a person is God or that he or she is enlightened or worthy of worship.[14]

Cabezon appeals to the particular Buddhist understanding of "magic" as an explanation for the extraordinary powers that Jesus had.

The preceding three incidents illustrate two truths. First, while a Christian should include his personal testimony when witnessing to others, occasions will arise in which he must go beyond this personal experience and supply reasons why the listener should accept the Christian gospel over other alternatives. Second, in contexts shaped by, for example, Hindu or Buddhist assumptions, the Christian's appeal to such reasons will necessarily push beyond merely establishing the historicity of Jesus' resurrection. His appeal must address basic worldview assumptions about the nature and significance of history and its relation to religious truth. Philosopher and phenomenologist of religion Ninian Smart has called this approach "worldview analysis:" assessing various religious and non-religious worldviews in terms of truth and rationality. "Worldview analysis" requires not only a sophisticated understanding of the worldviews in question—and the cultural frameworks within which they are embedded—but also competence in epistemology.[15] Although every Christian cannot be an expert in epistemology, such worldview analysis must comprise a central component of theology and missiology in the decades ahead.

The example of Jesuit Matteo Ricci in sixteenth-century China may further inform the missiological applications of apologetics today.[16] One need not agree with Ricci's Roman Catholic soteriology or even with all of his conclusions about Confucianism to benefit from his insights. Ricci clearly saw that the long-term success of Christian missions in China depended upon the expression of the gospel in authentic Chinese idiom and the acceptance of the Christian worldview among the cultural elite, the Confucian literati. In other words, the gospel had to engage the plausibility structures of sixteenth-century Confucian China. Ricci embarked upon an in-depth encounter between Christianity and the Confucian worldview. Andrew Ross observes that Ricci "had become such a master of Chinese and the Confucian Classics that the literati as a class could treat him as if one of themselves."[17] Ricci became convinced that original Confucianism had been monotheistic and that the classical deity, "Tian" (Heaven) or "Shangdi" (Lord on High), was indeed the transcendent Creator God of the Bible. Later generations, he claimed, had corrupted this original monotheism with a more ambiguous metaphysic.

In 1603 Ricci published *On the True Meaning of the Lord of Heaven*, a creative and influential work of Christian apologetics.[18] According to Andrew Ross,

> Ricci was setting out to show that there was a belief in a transcendent God contained in what he insisted was original Confucianism, and that this transcendent Lord of Heaven and the God of the Bible were the same. What is so extraordinary was that in the eyes of a large number of literati he succeeded in proving his point.[19]

Ricci had an enormous impact upon the cultured elite in China, and a number of significant Confucian literati became Christians through his ministry. His achievements were monumental for, as Ross observes, "Ricci's interpretation of Confucius was accepted as a valid form of Confucian discourse by the literati of late Ming China"[20]—whether they ultimately accepted his views or not. The Jesuits could eventually count some 300,000 Chinese Christians before the Rites Controversy resulted in the Jesuit's expulsion from China.

The Right Attitude

The importance of engaging the reigning plausibility structures for the sake of the gospel remains among the enduring lessons from Ricci's experiment. He recognized the need for missionaries to express the Christian message in language and categories that were culturally influential, and to persuade the opinion shapers (the cultural elite) that the Christian faith was a viable and legitimate option. Applying the same lessons to contexts shaped by religious pluralism today will entail engaging the plausibility structures that reinforce pluralism today, in particular, the modern university and the knowledge sector as well as the media and communications elite. Surely these fields represent one of the more challenging frontiers for missions today.

The role of apologetics in modern-day intercultural missions demands special consideration regarding how one engages in apologetics, especially when addressing issues of religious pluralism. This leads to the third component in a missiological response to religious pluralism: Christians must engage in evangelism and apologetics with cultural sensitivity and with attitudes of humility, gentleness, and genuine respect for adherents of other religious traditions.[21] Without question, every Christian must remain firm in his convictions about the truth of the gospel and the Lordship of Jesus Christ. Nevertheless, such commitment must be expressed in ways that are both pleasing to Christ and winsome to those around him.

In considering these issues this author has found guidance in the first little letter of Peter, not least because chapter three, verse fifteen contains every apologist's favorite "proof text" for apologetics. There Peter instructs his readers always to be prepared "to make a defense to anyone who asks [us] for a reason for the hope that is in [us]". As a response to religious pluralism, the context of Peter's admonition instructs the reader on two points.

The entire letter presupposes a context of suffering and persecution (see 2:19-21; 3:14-17; 4:1, 12-19; 5:1, 10). The exact nature of this persecution is uncertain and may have included physical violence, even martyrdom. One may clearly ascertain, however, that at the very least the recipients of the letter were experiencing a kind of social persecution: they were accused of wrong-doing (2:12); they were insulted and spoken against maliciously (3:16; 4:14); they were abused and mistreated in various ways.

The consistent message of the letter calls believers—even in the midst of such suffering and mistreatment— to respond to such evil by doing good. Peter writes, "Dear friends, I urge you as aliens and strangers in the world, to abstain from sinful desires which war against your souls. Live such good lives among the pagans that, though they accuse you of doing wrong, they may see your good deeds and glorify God on the day that he visits us" (2:11-12). Christians today are likewise called to follow the example of Christ, who "when he was reviled, he did not revile in return; when he suffered, he did not threaten, but continued entrusting himself to him who judges justly" (2:23). Indeed, Christ's followers are to be holy in all their conduct (1:15-16).

In other words, the charge to be prepared to give a reason for our hope (3:15) occurs in a context which presupposes that believers are mistreated and suffering. The believers here do not hold a position of social or political power but rather of weakness and apparent insignificance. The shifting social and cultural dynamics in the West today result in the perception, shared by many evangelicals, that Christians are increasingly marginalized or cut off from centers of social and cultural power. Thus Christians, especially in the United States, easily begin to resent the cultural elite and their apparent favor toward religious pluralism, along with their often unfair attacks upon orthodox Christianity. Christians may be tempted to fight back, exerting their limited power to quiet the critics and advance their own agenda. But the principle in 1 Peter applies to modern-day Christians as well: do not return evil for evil; rather, keep one's conduct honorable so that when the pluralists speak against Christians as evil-doers, they may see the individual's good deeds and glorify God (2:12).

Furthermore, a very specific charge follows the call to be ready to give a defense: "do it with gentleness and respect, having a good conscience, so that, when you are slandered, those who revile your good behavior in Christ may be put to shame" (3:16). Verse 15 should never be read without verse 16. Unfortunately, "gentleness" and "respect" do not reflect the typical practice of apologetics. But this is the expectation of 1 Peter. When the apologist employs gentleness and respect—when apologetics is intellectually responsible, culturally sensitive, and conducted in a spirit of humility, gentleness, and respect—it will prove to be an indispensable component of effective missions, especially in contexts shaped by the values and assumptions of religious pluralism.

Conclusion

Globalization implies that increasing numbers of people worldwide will have some understanding of Jesus, but in many cases these understandings will be broadly pluralistic and will domesticate Jesus by giving him a place within existing religious and cultural frameworks. Christian missions in these contexts should involve a retrieval of Jesus: first understanding the social and cultural dynamics supporting pluralistic views on Jesus, then correcting misconceptions and recovering the biblical Jesus, and finally showing in culturally appropriate and respectful ways why the biblical Jesus should be accepted rather than the other perspectives. May God grant us grace so that those around us, like the Greeks in John 12, can be led to a genuine encounter with Jesus the Christ.

Notes

1. As quoted in Gary Barnes, "Why Don't They Listen?" *Christianity Today* (1 September 2003): 50-1.

2. Kenneth Cragg, *The Call of the Minaret*, 3^d ed. (Oxford: Oneworld, 2000 [1956]), ch. 9. See also idem, *Jesus and the Muslim: An Exploration* (Oxford: Oneworld, 1999 [1985]).

3. See Mark Juergensmeyer, *Terror in the Mind of God: The Global Rise of Religious Violence*, 3^d ed., (Berkeley: University of California, 2003); and Jessica Stern, *Terror in the Name of God: Why Religious Militants Kill* (New York: HarperCollins, 2003).

4. On the various influences behind religious pluralism in the West, including skepticism, see Harold Netland, *Encountering Religious Pluralism* (Downers Grove, IL: InterVarsity, 2001), ch. 1-4.

5. M. K. Gandhi, *An Autobiography: Or, The Story of My Experiments With Truth*, translated by Mahadev Desai (New York: Viking Penguin, 1982 [1927]), 134-7.

6. See, for example, Peter Berger, *The Sacred Canopy: The Social Construction of Reality* (New York: Anchor Books, 1967).

7. See especially Hajime Nakamura, *Ways of Thinking of Eastern Peoples: India, China, Tibet, Japan*, ed. Philip P. Wiener (Honolulu: University of Hawaii, 1964), Part IV.

8. On contemporary Japanese religion, see Ian Reader, *Religion in Contemporary Japan* (New York: Macmillan, 1991); and Ian Reader and

Mission as Retrieval 163

George J. Tanabe, *Practically Religious: Worldly Benefits and the Common Religion of Japan* (Honolulu: University of Hawaii, 1998).

9. Peter Berger, "The Desecularization of the World: A Global Overview," in *The Desecularization of the World: Resurgent Religion and World Politics*, ed. Peter Berger (Grand Rapids: Eerdmans, 1999), 10.

10. Diana L. Eck, *A New Religious America: How A "Christian Country" Has Become the World's Most Religiously Diverse Nation* (New York: HarperCollins, 2001), 4. See also William R. Hutchison, *Religious Pluralism in America: The Continuous History of a Founding Ideal* (New Haven: Yale University, 2003).

11. The attraction of pluralism and the rejection of traditional Christian perspectives on other religions are in part due to the widespread popular perception that the modern missionary movement was merely the Christian version of Western imperialism and colonialism among non-Western peoples. The reality is considerably more complex. For helpful discussions of colonialism and missions see Stephen Neill, *Colonialism and Christian Missions* (New York: McGraw-Hill, 1966); and Brian Stanley, *The Bible and the Flag: Protestant Missions and British Imperialism in the Nineteenth and Twentieth Centuries* (Leicester, England: InterVarsity, 1990).

12. On the place of apologetics in Christian missions in contexts of religious pluralism see Netland, *Encountering Religious Pluralism*, ch. 8.

13. Lesslie Newbigin, *Unfinished Agenda* (Grand Rapids: Eerdmans, 1985), 57.

14. José Ignacio Cabezon, "Jesus Christ Through Buddhist Eyes," in *Buddhists Talk About Jesus, Christians Talk About the Buddha*, ed. Rita M. Gross and Terry C. Muck (New York: Continuum, 2000), 20-21.

15. Smart, Ninian. Worldviews: *Cross Cultural Explorations of Human Beliefs*. (Upper Saddle River, NJ: Prentice Hall, 2000), 11-14.

16. For discussions of Ricci and his impact in China, see Ralph Covell, *Confucius, the Buddha, and Christ: A History of the Gospel in Chinese* (Maryknoll, NY: Orbis, 1986), ch. 3; Andrew Ross, *A Vision Betrayed: The Jesuits in Japan and China, 1542-1742* (Maryknoll, NY: Orbis, 1994), ch. 6-7; Charles E. Ronan and Bonnie B. C. Oh, eds., *East Meets West: The Jesuits in China: 1582-1773* (Chicago: Loyola University, 1988); and Jonathan Spence, *The Memory Palace of Matteo Ricci* (New York: Viking Penguin, 1984).

17. Ross, *Vision Betrayed*, 135.

18. See Matteo Ricci, *The True Meaning of the Lord of Heaven*, translated by Douglas Lancashire and Peter Hu Kuo-chen (St. Louis: Institute of Jesuit Sources, 1985).

19. Ross, *Vision Betrayed*, 147.

20. Ibid., 149.

21. For an excellent discussion of the place of apologetics in interreligious contexts, with the need for special sensitivity to those groups who have suffered at the hands of Christendom in the past, see Paul J. Griffiths, *An Apology for Apologetics: A Study in the Logic of Interreligous Dialogue* (Maryknoll: Orbis, 1991), especially chapter 5.

Chapter Seven

Jesus and the Pagan West: Missiological Reflections on Evangelism In Re-Enchanted Europe

Michael T. Cooper

Due to the recent realization that Western society is not as secular as was once believed, a re-enchantment is taking place. As one example of this re-enchantment, Paganism, in its varied expressions, is increasingly considered to be the indigenous religion of Europe. The revival of pre-Christian European native religions has challenged the notion that the West was ever converted suggesting that Christianity was simply a means of social control. This consideration is coupled with the desire to regain what Christianity usurped.

Cultural fragmentation, pluralization and globalization have raised the issue of religious identity in fresh ways. These factors, along with the emergence of postmodernism, have prompted the question: "Who is Jesus?" The increasing popularity of higher criticism's deconstruction of the historical Jesus has fueled an answer: He was in fact a Pagan god seized by Christian theology and propagated as the Christ, and He traveled to southern England and was taught by the Druids.

This chapter will first examine the re-enchantment of Western society in order to understand the contemporary religious landscape. Then, acknowledging the renewed interest in spirituality, the study suggests that the emergence of Pagan religions in Europe indicates it was never completely evangelized. As a result, Jesus can easily be grouped together in the pantheon of Pagan gods. However, the historical attestations of Jesus exhibit his authenticity and uniqueness. Finally, the study will suggest a missiologically informed response in presenting the historical Jesus in the context of re-enchanted Europe.

Disenchantment and Re-enchantment of Western Society

Considering that eighty to ninety percent of early modern Europe was made up of the peasant class,[1] it is not out of the question to suggest a remnant of Pagan belief; especially in light of the church's early struggle with Paganism. These ancient systems of varying beliefs survived in the subconscious of their adherents who called themselves Christians. The medieval historian and practicing Wiccan, Christina Oakley, states, "Those special people who believed in their local spirits, who cultivated psychic or magic powers, who told and retold their ancient myths, who cast spells and performed divinations, who dressed in animal skins – almost all considered themselves Christian once Christianity had arrived and established itself, although in rural areas this may have amounted to no more than a nominal Christianity."[2]

According to Peter Burke, Christians of early modern Europe recognized that missions was needed as much in their own land as in foreign lands. They objected to the many and varied popular customs as Pagan survivals and recognized that many official Christian practices were of pre-Christian origin.[3] Barry Raey describes popular religion in early modern England as, "A coherent popular Catholicism, popular Puritanism, religious apathy, radical sectarianism, a vast amorphous world of syncretistic or folklorised Christianity, a corpus of magical beliefs which helped ordinary people to cope with the vagaries of a harsh and uncertain environment."[4] Prudence Jones and Nigel Pennick illustrate these points: "The use of holy water and incense, solemn processions (the old lustrations), religious rites of passage marking the turning-points of human life, the veneration of local saints, and the great feast of the dead, the annual Christian Parentalia on All Souls' Day, can all be seen as direct imitations of Pagan traditions."[5] Eventually, the Reformers confronted the church and posited personal salvation without the need of ritual. As a result, Christianity (in its Protestant form) was to some degree free from Pagan influence.

Martin Luther, in Gustav Warneck's view, saw the mission field as the re-Paganized church that he so desired to reform.[6] However, Robert Glover stated, "Despite their clear conceptions and statements of fundamental doctrines of evangelical faith, they [reformers] showed a remarkable ignorance of the scope of the divine plan and of Christian duty in relation to the gospel."[7] Nonetheless, Jones and Pennick note, "The reform movements within Catholicism which crystallized into the Protestant Reformation in the early sixteenth century brought about a desire for simplicity of ritual and belief which rejected many of the compromises which the Church had made with Pagan practice."[8]

The Protestant Christianity that emerged and continued into the modern period promoted disenchantment from the world and, combined with the emerging rationalism of the Enlightenment, relied on human ability to solve the problems of the supernatural. Consequently, modern science replaced faith and questions of ultimate meaning were resolved by reason. Concomitantly, the Enlightenment project postulated that knowledge was the key to unlocking the secrets of the universe. Knowledge, to the modern mind, was objective and certain. The ability of the individual to obtain knowledge was limitless and thus the individual could master nature for the benefit of humanity and secure a better world.[9] Lesslie Newbigin asserted that, "While the Catholic Church had attempted to erect barriers against the Enlightenment, the Protestant churches had, in effect, surrendered the public field—politics, education, industry, economics—to the ideology of the Enlightenment and sought refuge in the private world of the home and the soul."[10] The phenomenon of privatized religious faith has been considered a salient feature of secularization.

Secularization and Disenchantment of Western Society

The recently embattled secularization thesis has a long history. Max Weber may have first introduced the thesis when he postulated that the process of industrialization, rationalization and bureaucratization associated with modernity would naturally lead to a decline in religious belief. Thus, modernization would create a society that no longer had the need for the supernatural, mystical and transcendent. The secularization theorists saw this disenchantment from the world as an irreversible fact of society. Taking the place of the supernatural was the meaning that would be created from one's function in society rather than from one's belief.

Peter Berger probes the involvement of the "Western religious tradition" in carrying the seeds of secularization. He asserted that Protestantism stripped itself of mystery, miracle and magic (ancient and powerful ideas of the sacred) which resulted in a radically transcendent God and a radically depraved humanity. Thus, the excluded middle, which once acted in mediation between God and man, was abolished. To Berger, this increased the implausibility of God and ultimately led to His death.[11] "Protestantism served as a historically decisive prelude to secularization, whatever may have been the importance of other factors."[12]

Berger did not stop there. He contended that the force of secularization brought out in Protestantism had its roots in the earlier religion of ancient Israel. To use Weber's phrase, the "disenchantment of the world" began in the Old Testament. The religion of ancient Israel represented the radical transcendence of a God who called His people to a complete break with other mysterious and magical religions. The Catholic Church, according to Berger, successfully constrained the secularizing effects of a radically transcendent God and depraved humanity, thus concealing the practice of ancient Israel and "re-enchanting" the world until the Reformation discovered its roots.[13]

Berger identified that these same secularizing forces in Western society and culture were being exported worldwide through westernization and modernization.[14] Similarly, he saw the manifestation of secularization in the withdrawal of the church's involvement in areas of society and culture that it once influenced. Berger, along with David Martin and Steve Bruce further suggested that the manifestation of secularization was seen in the decline of individual religious consciousness.[15]

Re-enchantment and Postmodernity

More recently, however, Berger and Martin have recognized that the secularization thesis does not adequately describe Western society. The expected decline of the influence of religion on society as a result of modernity has not come to fruition. In fact, the world, and in the case at hand, Europe, is becoming increasingly more religious or re-enchanted. Modernity, in Thomas Oden's words, has spun out in moral decline. The one-time attraction of triumphalistic technological advances, the Enlightenment project, quantifying empiricism and inevitable historical progress has resulted in a moral tailspin of "sexual, interpersonal and familial wreckage."[16] What was once thought to be a natural outcome of modernization, namely a decline in "religious consciousness," has been demonstrated to be inaccurate.[17]

The re-enchantment of the world is a characteristic feature of postmodernity.[18] Oden does not see postmodernity as a rejection of modernity's ideology for "there is no reason to fight something that is already dead."[19] Rather, postmodernity views modernity as "defunct, obsolete, passé, antiquated."[20] He defines postmodernity in light of the failure of modernity to fulfill meaning in life. The postmodern ideology, then, is described as a "hunger for means of social maintenance, continuity, intergenerational traditioning, historical awareness, freedom from the repressions of modernity."[21] Postmodernity is in search of what modernity failed to find. Loren Wilkinson writes, "It is not so surprising, then, that in the contemporary longing for an escape from the modern (which is manifested most dramatically in the cities), many are turning to the ancient religions of the countryside, and arguing that Christianity has little to offer those concerned with the cycle of nature."[22] From this vantage point of the re-enchantment of the world it is easy to understand the resurgence of Paganism.

The postmodern identity can be seen, for example, in the construction of contemporary identity based on the mass-media. Douglas Kellner argued that, "TV myth resolved social contradictions in the way that Levi-Strauss described the function of traditional myth and provide mythologies of the sort described by Barthes which idealize contemporary values and institutions and thus exalt the established way of life."[23] Thus, with the popularity of American television programs in Europe such as *Sabrina, the Teenaged Witch*, *Buffy, the Vampire Slayer*, *Charmed*, *Smallville* and others popular culture is getting a heavy dose of a pre-Christian created reality.

Postmodernism, then, can be understood in Laurence Cahoone's instructive taxonomy of positive postmodernism. Positive postmodernism attempts a positive reinterpretation of fundamental issues regarding humanity, society, art, politics, the self or God in light of postmodernist values. Michael York, retired professor of sociology at Bath Spa University

College and a self-identified shaman, expresses this idea in relationship to new religions:

> The postmodernity of New Age, Human Potential, goddess Spirituality and Neo-Paganism does not deny the utility and validity of legitimate scientific inquiry, but it asserts the spiritual reality encoded within the metaphorical world of myth and religion. It has moved beyond the limits of logical positivism and scientific empiricism to explore what it perceives as a magical-mystical reality only fragmentedly retained or perceived in any given traditional religious belief-system.[24]

While attempting to avoid the inconsistencies of relativism, positive postmodernism stresses the plurality of quests for certainty in knowledge. Cahoone states, "This category refers to writing that applies general postmodern themes to particular subject matters in order to offer a new vision or understanding of them."[25] This "new vision" is looking back to antiquity for meaning and is articulated by a number of Pagan insiders interviewed by the author. For example, one insider states, "My feelings about Druidry is that it offers one of the most direct ways of connecting with those God/Goddess manifestations and through its reverence to Nature offers mankind a stabilizing reconnection with who we really are. This is something that Western civilization is desperately in need of."

This re-enchantment of Western society is not necessarily a recent phenomenon. In fact, the fragmentation of Christianity after the Reformation indicates a desperate search for identity. At times, this search led to exploring the religions of the past whose practices somehow survived within the church in spite of reform. One need only to consider the fascination with the Druids and Stongehenge in 17th and 18th century England. At other times, the search led to new, esoteric notions of religious expression such as that of Swedenborg and later the Theosophical Society. As such, to speak of a Christian Europe is, at best, reading too much into the church's influence on society.

Defining Contemporary Paganism

The literature on Paganism testifies to a general consensus of religious beliefs. Jones and Pennick, thus, define Paganism with three characteristics. First, Paganism is polytheistic. It recognizes a multiplicity of spiritual beings that may or may not act as avatars. Second, Paganism views nature as a theophany. It is a manifestation of divinity rather than a "fallen" creation of the divine. Third, Paganism recognizes the Goddess (with a deliberate use of capital "G") as the principle female divinity. She is distinguished from other geographically particular goddesses. Similarly, Paganism recognizes the God (here not meant to be the Judeo-Christian concept of God) in addition to or in place of the Goddess.[26]

The terms "Pagan" and "neo-Pagan" were once thought of pejoratively; however, they are increasingly looked upon as terms of endearment.[27] Those adherents to pre-Christian European native religions in one form or another are proud to be Pagan or neo-Pagan and do not shy away from using the terms. As understood by them, the term means, "an individual whose interest in the religious sphere lies in patterns of belief which are non-orthodox and non-traditional in Western society and which more specifically pre-date Western society's dominant belief system as represented, for example, by Christianity or Judaism."[28]

The word 'pagan' is etymologically derived from the Latin *paganus*, and referred to one who lives in the country, but the term's original English usage described anyone who worshipped local spirits.[29] Today, Paganism relates its belief systems to pre-Christian mystery religions as well as European native religions. However, the resurgence of Paganism, while reviving the positive aspects of ancient forms, is understood as a contemporary expression of ancient belief systems.[30]

Neo-Paganism, on the other hand, does not necessarily represent a structured belief system. It must be noted that ancient forms of Paganism were polytheistic whereas neo-

Paganism is considered a "theology of polarity"[31] emphasizing the gender of the gods. Furthermore, Jones and Pennick point out that "neo-Pagan" is a term generally used by American commentators for all contemporary practices related to Paganism of any form.[32] Pagan insiders vary on their understanding and use of the terms. For example, one informant states, "Pagan refers to following the ancient ways, neoPaganism is following the old path as we think it was followed."

Nonetheless, to further delimit the terms Paganism and neo-Paganism it must be noted that they are not a part of the New Age movement. While there are similarities between these religious belief systems, Paul Heelas argues that the New Age movement is a product of modernity.[33] Paganism, on the other hand, appears to be a product of postmodernity if postmodernity is understood as the application of the past in the present.[34] York suggests that even though New Age and Paganism are sometimes difficult to distinguish, there are two salient differences. First, New Age pursues a "transcendent metaphysical reality," whereas Paganism pursues an "immanent locus of deity." Second, New Age self-identifies as an innovative religious orientation and Paganism self-identifies as historically continuous with past traditions.[35]

Growth of Contemporary Paganism

In 1996 the Pagan Hospice and Funeral Trust in the UK reported that, "There are at least 25,000 Pagans living, working and practicing in Britain, but this is a conservative estimate, since there is no centralized body. Comparably, the Society of Friends, or Quakers, in Britain number only 20,000."[36] In 1999 the British Broadcasting Corporation (BBC) reported that an undocumented 1997 study indicated there were approximately 100,000 practicing Pagans in the United Kingdom, an increase of 95,000 since 1990. The same report stated that the Pagan Federation, an organization founded in 1971 to provide information about Paganism and to counter misconceptions regarding the religion, received 100 inquiries a month from potential adherents.[37] In 2002 the Pagan Federation estimated the number of adherents in the British Isle to be between 50,000 and 200,000. The BBC reported that on June 21, 2001, 10,000 people gathered at Stonehenge to celebrate the summer solstice, an increase of 2,000 from the year before, and 22,000 celebrated the summer solstice in 2002.[38] In 2003 BBC reported over 30,000 at the event while approximately 21,000 gathered in 2004.

Estimates for other European countries are not readily available. The Order of Bards, Ovates and Druids (OBOD), a UK based Pagan organization, reports the presence of affiliated groups in 12 European countries.[39] The order was revived in 1984 after a hiatus of several years due to the death of its founder and has grown at a 41.5% annual growth rate putting their membership at over 8,000. Similarly, the 1993 creation of the World Congress on Native Religions is predominately European in membership. The congress has the desire to search for authentic native religions and renew their practices in the contemporary religious landscape.

Cultural Congruency between Paganism and Western Religious Beliefs

According to Rodney Stark, a new religious movement's (NRM) success is, to a certain degree, based on the extent to which it retains cultural continuity or what he calls "cultural capital." Cultural capital, according to Stark, results from an individual's socialization and education (capital) in a particular culture.[40] He states, "religious movements will spread more readily to the extent that they build upon the familiar."[41] In other words, they grow to the extent that they utilize acceptable cultural boundaries thus preventing a complete discontinuity between the culture of the movement and that of the potential adherent.

Stark suggests that a favorable environment in which a NRM can grow is one that is religiously unregulated, comprised of weakened conventional faiths, and gives the perception of success to first generation adherents.[42] He suggests that individuals who are no longer active in a religious body will fill the ranks of NRMs more so than those who are active. Thus, where participation by members and attendees of religious groups is low there will be a high incidence of NRMs.[43]

The 1998 International Social Survey Program on religion (ISSP)[44] interviewed 18,523 West Europeans and reported that 85 percent indicated they had not participated in religious or church related volunteer work in the past year while 32 percent never pray.[45] Similarly, 45 percent attend church less than once a year or never, compared to 17 percent who attended once a week or more and 62 percent never take part in religious activities outside of attending services. Interestingly enough, 67 percent claim some affiliation to a traditional Christian church while 23 percent claim no affiliation. Data like this leads Stark to conclude that NRMs are growing at a faster rate in Europe than in the States.

These statistics do not necessarily suggest that Paganism will be successful in the Western spiritual landscape. However, it does point to the potential for success. The very notion that Western society leans as much toward a belief in the sacredness of nature in itself as to its sacredness given by God is congruent with Paganism (Table 1). Not only that, but the belief in astrology as science, horoscopes, fortune tellers and good luck charms is congruent with the beliefs of contemporary Paganism (Tables 2 and 3). With this in mind, the growing numbers of those who would be considered "nature worshippers" should not surprise us. According to Thomas Luckmann, nature religions are one of the most successful purveyors of worldview in the religiously pluralistic marketplace of Europe.[46]

Nation	%Belief in Higher Power other than God		%Belief in Personal God		%Believe Nature is spiritual or sacred in itself		%Believe Nature is sacred because it is created by God	
	2000	1993	2000	1993	2000	1993	2000	1993
Germany (West)	24	21	25	23	24	29	18	20
Germany (East)	12	14	5	9	18	19	6	11
Great Britain	12	13	23	25	21	14	26	24
United States	7	9	66	66	26	23	44	41
Netherlands	21	20	24	23	32	30	12	12
Italy	--	8	--	49	--	36	--	37
Ireland	8	5	49	62	26	22	45	46
Norway	23	23	19	21	31	27	12	12
Austria	24	--	35	--	24	--	19	--
New Zealand	18	18	33	31	31	26	22	20
Australia	--	17	--	31	--	25	--	21
Canada	18	16	47	--	33	32	30	22
Sweden	32	--	11	--	--	--	--	--
Spain	13	14	50	57	13	17	32	33
France	--	--	--	--	--	--	--	--
Portugal	--	--	--	--	--	--	--	--
Denmark	28	--	11	--	--	--	--	--
Switzerland	30	--	32	--	28	--	17	--

Table 1: The Sacredness of Nature[47]

	Good Luck Charms		Fortune Tellers		Faith Healers		Horoscope	
	Definitely True	Probably True	Definitely True	Probably True	Definitely True	Probably True	Definitely True	Probably True
No Doubts about God's existence	42	30.1	36.5	31.9	51.5	36.4	33.2	27.5
Some doubts but still believe in God	14.8	20.1	14.3	19.3	16.9	22.7	19	20.2
Believe in a Higher Power rather than God	20.6	20.3	25.4	22.6	16.6	18.2	24.3	23.6

Table 2: Relationship Between Belief in Pagan Practices and in God[48]

The diversity of religious beliefs is an indicator that religion continues to play an important role in the lives of people living in Western Europe. In general, the data demonstrate that traditional Christian beliefs have declined while non-traditional beliefs have risen. After analysis of the ISSP 1991 data on religion, Andrew Greeley suggested that "the religion and the superstition survive and that indeed we may have a lot more in common with medieval peasants than we had thought."[49]

This is quite a contrast from what Keith Thomas wrote twenty years before Greeley, "Astrology, witchcraft, magical healing, divination, ancient prophecies, ghosts and fairies, are now rightly disdained by intelligent people."[50] He added, "What is certain about the various beliefs discussed in this book is that today they have either disappeared or at least greatly decayed in prestige,"[51] however, the current data suggests otherwise.

Greeley asserts that religion continues to play an important role in the lives of Europeans. At the same time, magic is increasing and growing in situations where religious faith is uncertain.[52] While Greeley provisionally agrees that the belief in magic, fortunetellers, astrology and good luck charms measure New Age attitudes, it is more likely that this continued fascination with what was once considered superstition is a result of the tenacity of European popular religion.[53] According to Peter Beyer, the rise of Pagan religion testifies to "the critique and confirmation of contemporary social normality."[54] He adds, "What makes the rise of contemporary nature religion genuinely intriguing is not simply its counter-structural or even counter-cultural symbolic strategy, but the intricate links between the latter and the values and dominant structures of global society."[55] This increasing belief is coming into the mainstream of popular Western culture.

It is also significant to note that Table 3 suggests astrology is increasingly considered scientific. As an example of this belief, in June 2003 I attended a conference by invitation of Michael York at Bath Spa University College in Bath, England entitled "Astrology and the Academy: The Inaugural Conference of the Sophia Centre." The purpose of the conference was to celebrate "the return of the critical study of astrology's place in the world to the university environment, placed within the context of humanity's perennial use of the sky for religious, artistic, literary, mythological and scientific purposes."[56] The speakers were academics in various fields from the United Kingdom, the United States, Poland, Finland, Brazil, Spain, and France.[57]

In a plenary address, Ronald Hutton, professor of history at the University of Bristol, posited that the Western church fathers left the question of celestial deities open. Citing Augustine, Hutton suggests that his lack of explanation of the planets in effect allowed for the possibility of their recognition as deities. In fact, according to Hutton, by 1320 Western intellectuals considered the planets as deities controlled by God. There was the belief that Christians could legitimately use the planets to gain understanding for their future.[58] However, Augustine clearly had an aversion to astrology. In the *City of God* he notes, "But that all things come to pass by fate, we do not say; nay we affirm that nothing comes to pass by fate; for we demonstrate that the name of fate, as it is wont to be used by those who speak of fate, meaning thereby the position of the stars at the time of each one's conception or birth, is an unmeaning word, for astrology itself is a delusion."[59] While Hutton might exaggerate the level of acceptance of astrology on the part of the church, it is without doubt that the lay people continued in their beliefs. These beliefs in the efficacy of astrology have continued in Western society. Consider for example, the data from International Social Survey Programme (ISSP) Environment I.

All of the data on religious belief in religiously unregulated countries of Western Europe along with the data on the resurgence of Paganism brings me to the conclusion that religious beliefs continue to remain strong. In fact, the data indicates a tenacious holding on to beliefs that were once considered superstitious. There is also an appearance of a legitimizing effect of the folk beliefs due to the attention of the academy. Paganism is positioned in Western society for growth due in part to its continuity with the beliefs of West Europeans. How then should we engage re-enchanted Europe?

Nation	%Believe Astrology – the study of star signs – has some scientific truth	
	Definitely	Probably
Germany (West)	16	41
Germany (East)	15	41
Great Britain	7	39
United States	10	43
Netherlands	7	42
Italy	7	28
Ireland	13	41
Norway	12	44
Austria	--	--
New Zealand	8	40
Australia	4	32
Canada	9	36
Sweden	--	--
Spain	6	41
France	--	--
Portugal	--	--
Denmark	--	--
Switzerland	--	--

Table 3: Belief in Astrology as Scientific truth[60]

Missiological Reflections for Evangelism in Re-Enchanted Europe

It goes without saying that any method of engaging culture with the gospel must begin with what has been called cultural exegesis. This cultural exegesis not only includes a study of socio-religious factors, as discussed in this paper, but also takes into consideration the significance of dialogue when entering conversations with religious others.[61] Given these precursors, there are three important areas that must be considered in relation to evangelism in re-enchanted Europe. These areas are the person of Jesus, the reliability of the New Testament, and the historicity of Jesus.

First, those who would evangelize in re-enchanted Europe must be prepared to answer the question, "Who is Jesus Christ?" It is widely accepted in today's ultramodern/postmodern context that formal religion is open for criticism. As one insider of Paganism stated, "Religions of a book will become increasingly unstable as they try to adhere to what was 'right' at a brief moment 2000 years ago, etc. Where will you find God? In the books of men? Or within His/her creation? If you use the natural world as your text-book, then you will always be [able to find God]."

In the Pagan community there are two common responses to the question of Jesus that build upon the work of Peter Gandy and Timothy Freke as well as Gordon Strachan. Freke and Gandy have been leaders in this criticism and have found wide acceptance of their ideas from the Pagan community. Not uncommon was this insider response to their popular book *The Jesus Mysteries: Was the Original Jesus a Pagan God?*

> There are so many books written to counter others, I try to select what I believe based on what I think sounds most logical to me. The Jesus Mysteries is just the latest book I've read on the subject, that is why I used it. I found it one of the better books on the subject. I found it interesting that they started out trying to prove the existence of Jesus, but in the end could not find the proof in their eyes.

She continues,

> I'm still not convinced that Jesus existed. But if he did, I think he would have been a scholar and a teacher of the old Pagan Mysteries. He would have tried to bring a deeper understanding of life to his people. He would have tried to break away from the traditional stories and teach the truth. From what has been written about him, that is precisely what he tried to do. But people in authority saw him as a threat to their control over the populous. The things Jesus tried to teach are things, we as Druids, are trying to revive, the inner mysteries.

From Freke and Gandy's perspective, "for 2000 years the West has been dominated by the idea that Christianity is sacred and unique while Paganism is primitive and the work of the Devil. To even consider that they could be parts of the same tradition has been simply unthinkable. Therefore, although the true origins of Christianity have been obvious all along, few have been able to see them, because to do so requires a radical break with the conditioning of our culture. Our contribution has been to dare to think the unthinkable and to present our conclusions in a popular book rather than some dry academic tome. This is certainly not the last word on this complex subject, but we hope it may be a significant call for a complete reappraisal of the origins of Christianity."[62]

They began their exploration of the historicity of Jesus from the presupposition that oppressive Christianity of the Middle Ages suppressed the truth of its origin and that in fact Gnosticism came first. "The traditional version of history bequeathed to us by the authorities of the Roman Church is that Christianity developed from the teachings of a Jewish Messiah and that Gnosticism was a later deviation. What would happen, we wondered, if the picture were reversed and Gnosticism viewed as the authentic Christianity, just as the Gnostics themselves claimed? Could it be that orthodox Christianity was a later deviation from Gnosticism and that Gnosticism was a synthesis of Judaism and the Pagan Mystery religion? This was the beginning of the Jesus Mysteries

Jesus and the Pagan West 183

Thesis."[63] Ultimately, they conclude that Jesus was a myth created by an elite group and propagated throughout the world.

Another popular view of Jesus is the belief that he came to England with his uncle, Joseph of Arimathea. One insider from England comments,

> Jesus Christ was a man who had a vision and from an early age built up a following, that was to eventually lead him to his death on a cross. I understand that he traveled to Britain with his Uncle, who was a merchant/carpenter, and they came to the tin mines of the West Country. During these visits, they may have met up with druids.

Gordon Strachan argues that this is indeed the case. Based on a literal understanding of a reference made by Augustine of Canterbury to the construction of the old chapel at Glastonbury Abbey, Strachan has developed an entire theory that Jesus visited the area during the missing years in the Gospels. The claims of Christ's provenance in England are loosely based upon a popular poem "And Did Those Feet in Ancient Time" by English poet William Blake (1757-1827),

> And did those feet in ancient time
> Walk upon England's mountains green?
> And was the holy Lamb of God
> On England's pleasant pastures seen?
>
> And did the Countenance Divine
> Shine forth upon our clouded hills?
> And was Jerusalem builded here
> Among these dark satanic mills?
>
> Bring me my bow of burning gold!
> Bring me my arrows of desire!
> Bring me my spear! O clouds, unfold!
> Bring me my chariot of fire!

> I will not cease from mental fight,
> Nor shall my sword sleep in my hand,
> Till we have built Jerusalem
> In England's green and pleasant land.[64]

Blake was fascinated by the possibility of the Joseph of Arimathea legend and suggested that the Jews themselves were ancient descendents of Druids.[65] However, more elaborate theories, such as Strachan's, suggest that Jesus learned the concept of human sacrifice and atonement from the Druids who regularly practiced such rituals.

Interestingly enough, most Pagans that were interviewed believed in the historicity of Jesus as the founder of Christianity. For example, one insider states,

> As for Jesus Christ [I] believe he did live once and that he was a holy man. But that somewhere in history when man wrote the Bible. That things that were said and things he did were taken out of context and twisted. I believe that man wrote his version of the events and what he wanted the men and women to abide by. That is just my opinion. I could go on but then I would be ranting.

However, the issue of his messianic role, not to mention his deity, remains a question. Consider the following comment, "Of Jesus Christ, I think that his teachings have been distorted over the years, and of course they have been used to justify great cruelty such as the Crusades and the Inquisition. I do not believe he was the Messiah (nor do I necessarily believe there will be a Messiah)." There seemed to be general consensus that "Jesus Christ's teachings were not bad in and of themselves, but were later corrupted by his followers." In fact, Pagans would agree with other pluralists that he is one path of many leading to union with something higher.

> I believe that we all are praying, worshipping, and practicing to the same god/dess, or Spirit or the One. We just all call them a different name. We need different religions and faiths. It's the

diversity of people, culture, environment and belief that makes it so. No one religion is the right one. You have to find the one that makes sense to you and feels right. I may not agree with some of the formal religions but then some of them don't agree with my beliefs. You practice yours and don't bother or look down at me for my beliefs and I'll do the same. We can all tolerate each others' beliefs and faiths.

Based on this data, as well as the decline in traditional Christian beliefs, any approach to evangelism must begin by answering the question "Who is Jesus Christ?" Of course, this must be done while earning respect by understanding people and dialoguing with them cordially.[66]

Reliability of the New Testament

Second, European evangelists must be prepared to make the case for the reliability of the New Testament. Arguments for the reliability of the New Testament are not new. The classical arguments utilize three common tests: bibliographical, internal and external evidence tests. While the arguments for the reliability of the New Testament do not necessarily testify to its veracity, they do point to the fact that what we possess today is a historically reliable document that accurately relates the events of the New Testament period.[67] Not only is the reliability significant, it testifies to early theological beliefs held by the growing Christian community.

The significance of the issue addressing New Testament reliability cannot be underestimated. For one, the pre-A.D. 70 dating of the New Testament synoptic gospels, Acts and the Pauline epistles clearly establish an early belief in the resurrection of Christ and the performance of signs and wonders. These early beliefs were circulated and could be confirmed by eyewitnesses. Not only does the reliability of the New Testament testify to early beliefs, it also testifies to the claims that Christ made about himself. Therefore, it is significant that when Christ claimed to be God, we have a reliable witness to his claim and eyewitnesses could confirm it. While the mystery religions (such as what Freke and Gandy posit[68]) hoped for new birth, signs and wonders and the resurrection of the dead, it is only in Christianity that we see fulfillment. Thus, with the reliability of the New Testament, arguments of Gnostic primacy are dispelled.

Christological Arguments

Third, an ontological and functional argument for the historicity of Jesus is also necessary in a developing encounter with the Pagan West. While there is a general acceptance of the historicity of Jesus among Pagans, there is a growing belief that he could just as easily be incorporated into a mythological pantheon of gods. Obviously, this leads to the notion that there are many paths to God and Jesus is simply one of those. The historicity of Jesus is therefore an important component in contemporary dialogue.[69]

Other literary references outside of the New Testament, while many doubt their authenticity or suggest Christian interpolation, are equally important in the discussion of the historicity of Christ. For example, in the *Testimonium Flavius*, Josephus provides a Jewish attestation to the person of Christ. While many scholars disagree about the extent of Christian interpolation of the three extant Greek manuscripts, the 1971 discovery of a 10th century testimony in Arabic by Shlomo Pines attests to reliable evidence for Christ's historicity:

> At this time there was a wise man who was called Jesus, and his conduct was good, and he was known to be virtuous. And many people from among the Jews and the other nations became his disciples. Pilate condemned him to be crucified and to die. And those who had become his disciples did not abandon their loyalty to him. They reported that he had appeared to them three days after his crucifixion, and that he was alive. Accordingly they believed that he was the Messiah, concerning whom the Prophets have recounted wonders.[70]

Having archeological and literary testimony to Jesus outside of the Gospel accounts only serves to demonstrate his historicity as well as that of the New Testament. In spite of all the modern quests for the historical Jesus, however, we must conclude with Thomas Schreiner that, "The only Jesus of Nazareth we have is the one interpreted by the four Gospel writers, and there are good grounds for trusting their testimony."[71]

The articulation of an ontological Christology was formulated by the early church fathers in the context of competing theologies. In spite of the growing belief that Christian history was written by the victor, those competing theologies were at times a majority. Take for example the Arian controversy. A significant number of eastern Christians, if not the majority, were Arian in their beliefs. Constantine mustered the first council in Nicea (A.D. 325) to discuss the heresy propagated by Arius; namely, that Christ was inferior to the Father. Arius wrote, "Even if He is called God, He is not God truly, but by participation in grace . . . He is God in name only."[72] We see the strength of this movement in the realization that it was very missionary in nature. Similarly, its strength was not simply spiritual, but political as well. It is at the time of Augustine's writing of *The City of God* that the Arian Christian Alaric sacks Rome in A.D. 410 and the beginning of the political fall of Rome ensues.

Other heresies emerged as well and just like Arianism, most dealt with Christological issues. The second council held in Constantinople (A.D. 381) convened to affirm the creed developed at Nicea and to argue for the third person of the Trinity. The third council (Ephesus, A.D. 431), while giving Mary prominence as *theotokos*, denounced the heresy promulgated by followers of Nestorius and Celestius. The fourth council assembled at Chalcedon in A.D. 451 to define the Trinity. At Constantinople in A.D. 553 the fifth council convened to deal with the issue of Monophysitism. The sixth council gathered once more at Constantinople in A.D. 680 to conclude that there are "two natural wills and two natural operations indivisibly, inconvertibly, inseparably, inconfusedly"[73] in Christ.

Thus, it was in an environment of controversy that the great Christological statement of Chalcedon was formulated. While many would object to the "Greekness" of the formulation, it nonetheless remains as a great testimony to the nature of Jesus Christ.

> We, then, following the holy Fathers, all with one consent, teach men to confess one and the same Son, our Lord Jesus Christ, the same perfect in Godhead and also perfect in manhood; truly God and truly man, of a reasonable [rational] soul and body; consubstantial [coessential] with the Father according to the Godhead, and consubstantial with us according to the Manhood; in all things like unto us without sin; begotten before all ages of the Father according to the Godhead, and in these latter days for us and for our salvation, born of the Virgin Mary, the Mother of God, according to the Manhood; one and the same Christ, Son Lord, Only-begotten, to be acknowledged in two natures, inconfusedly, unchangeably, indivisibly, inseparably; the distinction of natures being by no means taken away by the union, but rather the property of each nature being preserved, and concurring in one Person and one Substance, not parted or divided into two persons, but one and the same Son, and only begotten, God the Word, the Lord Jesus Christ, as the prophets from the beginning [have declared] concerning him, and the Lord Jesus Christ himself has taught us, and the Creed of the holy Fathers has handed down to us.[74]

While ontological Christology states Christ's nature as God, it is functional Christology that connects him with us.[75] It is this connection with us that helps us understand God's heart for humanity.

Conclusion

The growth of Pagan religions testifies to the notion set forth in this paper: Western Europe is not as secular as once believed. If we are to engage Western Europe evangelistically, the starting point must be the person of Christ and the reliability of the New Testament. And because one fundamental characteristic of postmodernism is looking back to antiquity for meaning, engaging the Pagan West with the gospel of Jesus Christ must include a clear articulation of his historicity. He is not simply another Pagan god. His historicity cannot be questioned. What was spoken of metaphorically in the mystery religions and early Christian Gnosticism was accomplished in Christ.[76] Given the reliability of the New Testament gospels and the historicity of the person of Jesus, what he has said about himself as well as what others have said (ontological Christology) in addition to what he did (functional Christology) provides the foundation to the message we proclaim.

Notes

1. Peter Burke, *Popular Culture in Early Modern Europe* (London: Temple Smith, 1978), 29.

2. Christina Oakley, "Druids and Witches: History, Archetype and Identity," in *The Druid Renaissance: The Voice of Druidry Today*, ed. Philip Carr-Gomm (London: Thorsons, 1996), 278.

3. Burke, *Popular Culture in Early Modern Europe*, 208-209.

4. Barry Raey, "Popular Religion," in *Popular Culture in Seventeenth Century England*, ed. Barry Raey (New York: St. Martin's, 1985), 117.

5. Prudence Jones and Nigel Pennick, *A History of Pagan Europe* (London: Routledge, 1995), 75.

6. Gustav Warneck, in Hans Kasdorf, "The Reformation and Mission: A Bibliographical Survey of Secondary Literature," *Occasional Bulletin of Missionary Research*, 4, no. 4 (1980): 170.

7. Robert Glover, *The Progress of World-Wide Missions*, rev. ed. Herbert Kane (New York: Harper Brothers, 1960), 40.

8. Jones and Pennick, *A History of Pagan Europe*, 203.

9. Stanley J. Grenz, *A Primer on Postmodernism* (Grand Rapids: Eerdmans, 1996), 3-4.

10. Lesslie Newbigin, *A Word in Season: Perspectives on Christian World Missions* (Grand Rapids: Eerdmans, 1994), 69.

11. Peter L. Berger, *The Sacred Canopy: Elements of a Sociological Theory of Religion* (New York: Anchor, 1969), 112.

12. Ibid., 113.

13. Ibid., 113-125.

14. Ibid., 108.

15. Ibid., 107; cf. David Martin, David Martin, *The Religious and the Secular* (New York: Schocken, 1969); David Martin, *A General Theory of*

Secularization (New York: Harper & Row, 1978); Steve Bruce, *Religion in the Modern World: From Cathedrals to Cults* (New York: Oxford, 1996).

16. Thomas C. Oden, "The Death of Modernity and Postmodern Evangelical Spirituality" in *The Challenge of Postmodernism: An Evangelical Engagement* 2 ed., ed. David S. Dockery (Grand Rapids: Baker, 2001), 24-25.

17. See Grace Davie, "Believing without Belonging: Is This the Future of Religion in Britain?," *Social Compass* 37, no. 4 (1990); Rodney Stark, "Secularization R. I. P.," *Sociology of Religion* 60, no. 3 (1999); Peter Berger, ed., *The Desecularization of the World: Resurgent Religion and World Politics* (Grand Rapids: Eerdmans, 1999).

18. See Christopher Partridge, "The Disenchantment and Re-enchantment of the West: The Religio-Cultural Context of Contemporary Western Christianity," *Evangelical Quarterly* 74, 3 (2002):235-256.

19. Oden, "The Death of Modernity," 21.

20. Ibid.

21. Thomas C. Oden, *Agenda for Theology: Recovering Christian Roots* (San Francisco: Harper and Row, 1979), 38.

22. Wilkinson, "Circles and the Cross," 30.

23. Douglas Kellner, "Popular Culture and the Construction of Postmodern Identities," in *Modernity and Identity*, eds. Scott Lash and Jonathan Friedman, 141-177 (Oxford: Blackwell, 1992), 148.

24. Michael York, "Postmodernity, Architecture, Society and Religion: 'A Heap of Broken Images' or 'A Change of Heart,'" in *Postmodernity, Sociology and Religion*, eds. Kieran Flanagan and Peter C. Jupp, 48-63 (London: MacMillan, 1996), 58.

25. Lawrence Cahoone, "Introduction," in *From Modernism to Postmodernism: An Anthology*, ed. Lawrence E. Cahoone, 1-23 (Oxford: Blackwell, 1996), 17.

26. Jones and Pennick, *A History of Pagan Europe*, 2.

27. Wilkinson, "Circles and the Cross," 30-31.

28. Quoted in Wilkinson, "Circles and the Cross," 31.

29. Jones and Pennick, *A History of Pagan Europe*, 1.

30. Ibid. "Followers of specific paths within it such as Druidry, Wicca, and Ásatrú aim to live a contemporary form of those older religions which are described or hinted at in ancient writings . . . ."

31. Ibid., 3.

32. Jones and Pennick, *A History of Pagan Europe*, 216. Cf. Carl E. Braaten, "The Gospel for a NeoPagan Culture," in *Either/Or: The Gospel or NeoPaganism*, eds. Carl E. Braaten and Robert W. Jenson (Grand Rapids: Eerdmans, 1996), 7-8.

33. Heelas, *The New Age Movement*, 3.

34. See Wilkinson, "Circles and the Cross" and Oden, "The Death of Modernity."

35. Michael York, *The Emerging Network: A Sociology of the New Age and Neo-Pagan Movements* (London: Rowman and Littlefield, 1995), 2.

36. Information from www.demon.co.uk/charities/PHFT/what_is_pag.html. Accessed 26 April, 2002.

37. The BBC News, "UK Pagans celebrate as numbers soar," Sunday, 31 October, 1999.

38. The BBC News, "Solstice dawns over Stonehenge," Thursday, 21 June, 2001; The BBC News, "Crowds gather for the solstice," Friday 21 June, 2002.

39. Information from http://druidry.org/obod/maps/europe.html. Accessed 26 April 2002.

40. Rodney Stark, "Why Religious Movements Succeed or Fail: A Revised General Model," *Journal of Contemporary Religion* 11, no. 2 (1996): 135.

41. Rodney Stark, "How New Religious Movements Succeed: A Theoretical Model," in *The Future of New Religious Movements*, eds. David G. Bromley and Phillip Hammond (Macon, Georgia: Mercer University Press, 1987), 13.

42. Ibid., 19.

43. Stark, "Why Religious Movements Succeed or Fail," 141.

44. The data utilized in this chapter were documented and made available by the Zentralarchiv Fuer Empirische Sozialforschung, Koeln. The data for the ISSP were collected by independent institutions in each country. Neither the original collectors nor the Zentralarchiv bear any responsibility for the analyses or interpretation presented here.

45. Sample size by country as follows: Germany – 2006; Great Britain – 1616; Austria – 1002; Italy – 1008; Ireland – 1010; Netherlands 2020; Norway – 1532; Sweden – 1189; Spain – 2488; France – 1133; Portugal – 1201; Denmark – 1114; Switzerland – 1204.

46. Thomas Luckmann, "The Religious Situation in Europe: The Background to Contemporary Conversion," *Social Compass* 46, no. 3 (1999): 254.

47. Data from variable 18 Environment II and variable 23 Environment I, International Social Survey Programme, (Cologne, Germany: Zentralarchiv Fuer Empirische Sozialforschung, 2000). Sample size for Environment I distributed as follows: Germany (West) – 1014; Germany (East) 1092; Great Britain – 1261; United States – 1557; the Netherlands – 1852; Italy – 1000; Ireland – 957; Norway – 1414; New Zealand – 1271; Australia

– 1779. Sample size for Environment II distributed as follows: Germany (West) – 974; Germany (East) 527; Great Britain – 972; United States – 1276; the Netherlands – 1609; Ireland – 1232; Norway – 1452; Austria – 1011; New Zealand – 1112.

48. Based on East Germany, West Germany, Austria, Portugal, Netherlands, Switzerland, Ireland and France.

49. Andrew Greeley, "Magic in the Age of Faith," *America* 169, no. 10 (1993): 7.

50. Keith Thomas, *Religion and the Decline of Magic* (New York: Charles Scribner's Sons, 1971), ix.

51. Ibid., 668.

52. Andrew Greeley, *Religion in Europe at the End of the Second Millennium: A Sociological Profile* (New Brunswick, N.J.: Transaction, 2003), 39-53.

53. In a personal communication with the author, Greeley agrees with this suggestion stating "I agree that your explanation is more likely." See J. Gordon Melton, "The Future of the New Age Movement," in Eileen Barker and Margit Warburg (eds.), *New Religions and New Religiosity* (Aarhus-London: Aarhus University Press, 1998), 133-149 and David Spangler and William Irwin Thompson, *Reimagination of the World: A Critic of the New Age, Science, and Popular Culture* (Santa Fe, N.M.: Bear & Company, 1991) for discussions on the decline of New Age.

54. Beyer, "Globalisation and the Religion of Nature," 18.

55. Ibid., 19. Nature religion, according to Beyer, is defined as "any religious belief or practice in which devotees consider nature to be the embodiment of divinity, sacredness, transcendence, spiritual power, or whatever cognate term one wishes to use" (11).

56. From the conference brochure, "Astrology and the Academy: The Inaugural Conference of the Sophia Centre."

57. For example: History (Ronald Hutton, University of Bristol; Anna Marie Roos, University of Minnesota); Religious Studies (Angela Voss, University of Kent; Joanne Pearson, Cardiff University).

58. Ronald Hutton, "Astral Magic: The Acceptable Face of Paganism," Lecture given at the inaugural conference of the Sophia Centre, Bath Spa University College "Astrology and the Academy," 13 June 2003. Notably, as phrased, this is an argument from silence, but it demonstrates an attempt to legitimize the practice of astrology. While it seems likely that nominal Christians continued the practices, it was clearly thought of as absurd by the Church Fathers and Apologists.

59. Augustine, *City of God* (Book V, Chapter 2). Augustine is consistent with others e.g. Hippolytus states, "But since, estimating the astrologi-

cal art as a powerful one, and availing themselves of the testimonies adduced by its patrons, they wish to gain reliance for their own attempted conclusions, we shall at present, as it has seemed expedient, prove the astrological art to be untenable, as our intention next is to invalidate also the Peratic system, as a branch growing out of an unstable root." (*The Refutation of All Heresies*, Book IV, 2). St. Basil declares, "You who are sound in yourselves have no need to hear more, and time does not allow us to make attacks without limit against these unhappy men." (*Homily* VI, 7).

60. Data from variable 31 Environment I, International Social Survey Programme, (Cologne, Germany: Zentralarchiv Fuer Empirische Sozialforschung, 2000). Sample size for Environment I distributed as follows: Germany (West) – 1014; Germany (East) 1092; Great Britain – 1261; United States – 1557; the Netherlands – 1852; Italy – 1000; Ireland – 957; Norway – 1414; New Zealand – 1271; Australia – 1779.

61. See Michael T. Cooper, "Early Christian Proselytism: Implications for Interreligious Dialogue Between Christians and Pagans." Paper presented at the Center for Studies on New Religions annual conference, Baylor University (2004).

62. Timothy Freke and Peter Gandy, *The Jesus Mysteries: Was the "Original Jesus" a Pagan God?* (New York: Harmony Books, 1999), 2.

63. Ibid., 8-9.

64. William Blake, "And Did Those Feet in Ancient Time."

65. Strachan, "And Did Those Feet?," 237.

66. See Michael T. Cooper, "Prolegomena To A Christian Encounter With Contemporary Druidry: An Etic Perspective of a European Native Religion and Its Relationship to the Western Religious Landscape" (Ph.D. diss., Trinity Evangelical Divinity School, 2004), 223-230.

67. Two recent discussions concerning the reliability of the New Testament should here be mentioned: P64 and 7Q5. Both of these papyri fragments might provide evidence for an early dating of the New Testament gospels. In fact, the German papyriologist, Carsten Peter Thiede, has championed a call to include 7Q5 in the textual apparatus of the Greek New Testament, "It is thus highly likely that 7Q5=Mark 6,52-53 will have to be added to the official list of New Testament papyri sooner or later" (in "Greek Qumran Fragment 7Q5: Possibilities and Impossibilities," *Biblica* 75, no. 3 [1994]: 394). All of these recent discussions have come under criticism by both liberal and conservative scholars in the field of New Testament studies. However, as missiologists and missionaries, we should be aware of these debates (see Carsten Peter Thiede and Matthew d' Ancona, *The Jesus Papyrus* [New York: Galilee, 1996]).

68. Timothy Freke and Peter Gandy, *The Jesus Mysteries: Was the "Original Jesus" a Pagan God?* (New York: Harmony Books, 1999).

69. The discovery of the James Ossuary might be the only non-literary archaeological testimony to the person of Jesus. While there is as much debate regarding its authenticity as there is for P64 and 7Q5, if it does hold up to scrutiny then it will be a remarkable testimony to Christ.

70. Available from http://www.uncc.edu/jdtabor/josephus-jesus.html. Accessed 1 September 2003.

71. Thomas A. Schreiner, "New Dimensions in New Testament Theology," in *New Dimensions in Evangelical Thought: Essays in Honor of Millard Erickson*, ed. David Dockery (Downers Grove, Ill.: Intervarsity, 1998), 60.

72. Leo Davis, *The First Seven Ecumenical Councils* (325-787): Their History and Theology (Wilmington, Del.: Michael Glazier, 1987), 52.

73. Ibid., 283.

74. Carl F. H. Henry, "New Dimensions in Christology," in *New Dimensions in Evangelical Thought: Essays in Honor of Millard Erickson*, ed. David Dockery (Downers Grove, Ill.: Intervarsity, 1998), 306-311.

75. Ibid., 301.

76. See Elaine Pagels, *The Gnostic Gospels* (New York: Vintage, 1989), 3-27; cf. N. T. Wright, *The Resurrection of the Son of God* (Minneapolis: Fortress, 2003), 32-84.

Chapter Eight

WDJS—What Does Jesus Say . . . About Receptivity?

Cecil Stalnaker

When posed the question: "Why is your church growing?" the church planter replied: "Because I preach the Word!" Another was asked, "Why is your church not growing? His response: "Because I preach the Word!" Indeed, responsiveness and receptivity are a mystery. Why do some willingly follow Christ while others move away from him? Why are certain people receptive while others resist? What are the reasons for their resistance? What would Jesus say about receptivity? Although church growth experts, missiologists, and field workers provide various answers to these questions, it would seem logical that the first source to consult would be the Scriptures themselves. They should be the "integrating center of the meta-discipline: missiology."[1] In light of the fact that missions is rooted in both the Old and New Testaments, revealed from Genesis to Revelation, the Scriptures should be the point of departure as well as the final grid for missionary methodology.

It is, thus, the intent of the writer to examine the words of Jesus regarding responsiveness. To put it simply, WWJS:

"What Would Jesus Say . . . about receptivity?" Better yet, what does Jesus say? Since this study will only be limited to his sayings, the reader is invited to read through a red-letter edition of the gospels.[2]

Defining Receptivity According to Jesus

Some church growth experts define receptivity as follows: "those who are most likely to hear the gospel message positively,"[3] the "state of being open to evangelism, the gospel and the communicator of the message,"[4] and "open to hearing and obeying the gospel of Jesus Christ."[5] Wagner for one has implied that receptive mission fields are those where there are a growing number of churches.[6] Many church growth experts view receptivity in terms of openness, willingness to listen, approval, or favorable responses to the gospel.

Jesus uses the word "receive" in various ways but only a few times does he actually use it in relation to the gospel. The first of these times he refers to "receiving" himself (Mt. 10:40); the second, to "receiving" the word (Mt. 13:20; Mk. 4:16; Lk. 8:13); and the third, to "receiving" the kingdom of God (Mk. 10:15; Lk. 18:17). The first and third usages employ the Greek word *lambano*, while the second uses *dechomai*. The New Testament expression *ton logon dechesthai*,[7] signifying to receive the word, was in essence a technical expression for acceptance by faith of the gospel.[8] There appears to be a parallelism between the concept of receiving and believing.[9] Although *lambano* has a wide range of meanings, it too may refer to God's giving of Himself in Christ and his kingdom, meaning that Jesus himself is to be the object of believing and acceptance.[10] In receiving Jesus, the individual knows and believes God, for knowing him is knowing God (Jn. 8:19), and believing him is believing God (Jn. 12:44, 14:1). When theologically related to the gospel, true receptivity implies an acceptance of the gospel by faith: putting one's faith in Jesus as the object of this faith and as the means of entry into the kingdom of God. Jesus thinks of it more in terms of taking in, possessing, and entering into the kingdom, and putting one's faith into himself as the object of this faith. True receptivity involves receiving Jesus.

It is important to know that Jesus also speaks of another type of receptivity that does not put one into the kingdom of God. For the time being, one must know simply that receptivity occurs in varying degrees, even making a distinction between superficial receptivity and "true" receptivity.[11]

Missiological Causes for Receptivity

Missiologists, church growth experts, and church planters provide varying explanations for the causes of receptivity. The father of church growth, Donald McGavran, declared that many people become receptive to the gospel due in part to new settlements, travel, being conquered, nationalism, religious change, and freedom from control.[12] John Wimber maintained that "power evangelism," displayed through miraculous signs and wonders "produces dramatic results" and "can make all other approaches to evangelism more effective."[13] C. Peter Wagner postulates that receptivity could change overnight if the breaking of territorial spirits would be considered as a missiological approach.[14] Others say that general unresponsiveness is due to a lack of contextualization. Glasser and McGavran maintain that missionaries should concentrate on the contextualization process for it plays a significant role in the spread of the gospel.[15] Within a North American context, church growth advocate Rick Warren states very bluntly that "anyone can be won to Christ if you discover the key to his or her heart," for this was the approach of Jesus.[16] But what does Jesus say?

Lessons on Receptivity from Jesus: WWJS

Although those mentioned above provide the missionary and pastor with some helpful information, we must ask what Jesus thinks of all of this. What lessons can we learn from our Lord and Master about receptivity?

Lesson One: Everyone is potentially receptive to the gospel

Jesus clearly teaches that the gospel is for everyone. Throughout Scripture, Jesus employs expressions suggesting that all people have a chance to put their faith in Him. Such words as "whoever" (Jn. 3:16, 4:14), "he who" (Jn. 5:24, 6:47, 7:38, 11:25) and "everyone" (Mt. 7:24, 26; Lk. 6:47; Jn. 6:40, 11:26, 12:46) are indicative of a universal offer of the gospel. These words agree with the command of the Lord himself to "make disciples of all the nations" (Mt. 28:19). The gospel is not restricted to a few but universally offered to everyone without any exclusions or discrimination. Such phrases imply that all humans can potentially place their faith in the Lord Jesus Christ for salvation. Without entering into the polemic concerning the sovereignty of God and the human will, one should not forget that every "person who will come to Jesus Christ can come to Jesus Christ."[17] Although man suppresses the truth in unrighteousness (Rom. 1:18), is hostile toward God (Rom. 8:7), and walks in disobedience to Him due to sinfulness (Eph. 2:2), every human heart is redeemable.

Jesus purposes to show that the Father intends to offer redemption to all peoples—even to the Gentiles. Why? Because it is the Father's will that no one experience eternal damnation (2 Pet. 3:9). However, a word of caution is in order. A universal offer of the gospel is not synonymous with universalism. There is a unique distinction between universality and universalism, for the two are not to be considered equals in any way. Universality attempts to proclaim the gospel to all of humanity, but universalism attempts to provide salvation for all. Universalism alters the message of Jesus and is unworthy to be considered His teaching.[18] Additionally, universalism "forces" people into the kingdom of God, eliminating their personal choice. John MacArthur reminds Christians that

> not everyone wants God, and many who claim to want Him do not want Him on His terms. Those who are saved enter God's kingdom because of their willing acceptance of His sovereign,

gracious provision. Those who are lost are excluded from the kingdom because of their willing rejection of that same sovereign grace.[19]

In such an offer, Jesus clearly says to "repent and believe in the gospel" (Mk. 1:15). Although the literal notion of repentance, *metanoeo*, signifies "change of mind," it takes on a greater meaning in the New Testament because it stresses a decision encompassing the whole being—the will, the mind, and heart. Jesus demands much more than mere external or intellectual change.[20] He demands a new direction—a turning away from sin and a turning to righteousness and the will of God. This is the first step toward understanding true receptivity.

The parallel to repentance is belief in the gospel, which directs one's attention to the good news as the basis of faith. Of course, true receptivity demands more than mere intellectual credence to the message; it requires personally committing oneself to, and relying upon that which is believed. In essence, "genuine repentance prepares the heart for true faith in the gospel."[21] There is no true receptivity without the dual actions of repentance and faith. Repentance without faith or faith without repentance is nothing more than reformation, but together, they lead to true transformation.

Lesson Two: Ultimate receptivity is the unique work of God, not human effort

Pivotal to this discussion concerning receptivity is the work of God through the ministry of the Holy Spirit. Jesus clearly teaches that understanding, revelation, and responsiveness are not due to "flesh and blood," but to the Father. Specifically, the book of John sheds great light on the thoughts of Jesus and receptivity. He says: "All that the Father gives me will come to me" (6:37); "No one can come to Me unless the Father who sent Me draws him" (6:44); "It is the Spirit that gives life" (6:63); and "no one can come to Me unless it has been granted him from the Father" (6:65). The "sheep" have been given to the Son by the Father (10:29). In essence, receptivity occurs only at the invitation of the Father. Humans do not make their way into eternity without the drawing power of the Father through the convicting ministry of the Holy Spirit (16:8). However, such sayings of Jesus do not exclude evangelistic responsibility on the part of the believer. The drawing power of God does not reduce or eliminate the necessity and the urgency to evangelize, the genuineness of inviting people to follow Jesus, nor the responsibility of the unbeliever to respond to the gospel.[22] Without the drawing power of God—without His sovereign work—there is no hope for truly successful results in evangelism. Only this power "creates the possibility—indeed, the certainty—that evangelism will be fruitful."[23] Van Engen's comment should be taken seriously by any missionary or evangelist.

> Any theology of conversion in Evangelical missiology must begin by speaking of the miraculous work of the Holy Spirit by grace through faith in Jesus Christ. No amount of the effectiveness in relation to contextualization can promise that humans will say *yes* to God. Quite the contrary. Even if—or precisely *when*—humans come to understand the gospel being offered to them—even if they understand it in very appropriate cultural, relational, and social forms—humans will still say *no* to God, apart from the working of the Holy Spirit.[24]

Put briefly, there is no method, no approach, no strategy, and no contextualization that will guarantee true receptivity. Finding the "key" to the culture or to the individual's heart will not assure anyone's entrance into the kingdom. Based on Jesus' sayings, one would also find it difficult to hold to the teaching that the audience is sovereign, as some have claimed, when it comes to accepting the message of the gospel.

Even the working of miracles and healings will not guarantee entry into the Kingdom of God. The Gospels testify that Jesus performed more than forty miraculous healings with varied intended purposes, of which one was to call people to believe that Jesus is the Messiah (Jn. 20:30-31).[25] Indeed, the miraculous work of Christ opened the hearts of some people, leading them to favorableness toward him, which resulted in glorifying God (Mt. 15:29-31; Lk. 7:11-17). However, this was not always the case. Although his healings were instantaneous,[26] abundant, varied in method,[27] unique, accomplished both when faith was manifested and even without faith on the part of the person healed,[28] many did not believe. Even though they were amazing, spectacular, fantastic, and undeniable, they were not always convincing and did not assuredly lead to receptivity. Interestingly but sadly, in Chorazin, Bethsaida, and Capernaum, where he had done most of his early miracles, the people still remained faithless (Mt.11:20-30).[29] This may be the case for many of the crowds who observed the miraculous working of Christ in other areas as well. They saw but remained unconvinced. In some cases he specifically refused to do miracles because there was no belief (Mt. 13:58). In reading the Gospels, one clear*ly* sees that even though Jesus healed multitudes of people and worked miracles among them, the majority eventually resisted him. Few seemed to be following him by the time of the crucifixion. Thus, miraculous workings were no guarantee of evangelistic success.

In summary, if missionaries and Christian workers take the authoritative words of Jesus earnestly, receptivity is not dependent upon human effort. Although there are many unanswered questions in reference to human planning in evangelism, Jesus says that the Father is the one who brings people into the kingdom. The missionary and evangelist are called to humility regarding strategy.

> The Holy Spirit brings a response that we can never produce by artful communication skills. We may stimulate the reality of manipulative use of stimulus-and-response in religion, but the reality of beginning a new life in Jesus Christ, of being born again, is a result of the Holy Spirit's transmuting mental understanding into spirit life.[30]

Yes, there is a human role of rational thinking and planning for evangelism.[31] Every farmer knows that he has to plant, water, hoe, and harvest, but he also surely knows that he does not cause the crops to grow.

Some inherent dangers exist when one thinks of evangelism in merely human terms. First, the human role can move one away from acknowledging God as the "drawer" of men. Maintaining that one has the secret to responsiveness manifests arrogance and presumption. This is dangerous thinking, for the human side of evangelism can tempt one to view method and technique as the sole solutions to the problem. Second, one may replace faith with method or strategy. Missionaries and church workers are fooling themselves if they think that their strategy has been the element that draws people to Christ for it is God and God only. Third, human-based puts a tremendous burden on the missionary and evangelists. J.I. Packer observes,

> If we forget that it is God's prerogative to give results when the gospel is preached, we shall start to think that it is our responsibility to secure them. And if we forget that only God can give faith, we shall start to think that the making of converts depends, in the last analysis, not on God, but on us, and that the decisive factor is the way in which we evangelize. And this line of thought, consistently followed through, will lead us far astray.[32]

Jesus teaches the missionary that apart from the work of the Father through the Spirit, people will remain—and some very happily so—in their sin. Without the work of the Holy Spirit, the gospel is disruptive, disagreeable, and disgusting for many people. For people to come to faith, it is necessary for the Father, through the Spirit, to touch people's hearts. Leon Morris summarizes this point by saying, "Unbelief is to be expected apart from a divine miracle . . . Conversion is always the work of grace."[33] Christians must never forget that Jesus builds the church.

Lesson Three: Receptivity is impossible with a hard heart

The parables of Matthew 13 provide a great amount of information concerning receptivity. Large crowds, even from other cities, gathered by the seashore as Jesus began to speak to them from a nearby boat (Mt. 13:1-2; Mk. 4:1; Lk. 8:4). For the first time, Jesus began to address them in parables, framed as "mysteries of the kingdom of heaven" (Mt. 13:11).[34] For some scholars, these parables represent the thematic "central point of the Gospel."[35] Within this context we find the parable of the sower (Mt. 13:3-9; Mk. 4:1-9; Lk. 8:4-10). Many missiologists have stated that this parable teaches much about missiological methodology. For instance, C. Peter Wagner maintains,

> The obvious lesson for missionary strategy is that the seed of the Word must be concentrated on fertile soil if fruit is to be expected . . . The world's soils must be tested. Concentrating, come what may on rocky soil, whether or not any disciples are made, is foolish strategy. Farmers who have the vision of the fruit do not make that mistake too often, but some missiologists unfortunately do.[36]

Contextually, the parable of the sower speaks of Israel's receptivity and how Israel will respond to the preaching of Jesus and the disciples in the near future.[37] Van Engen correctly states that "the parable of the sower is in fact about the sower, about Jesus' mission, and by extension the mission of the disciples."[38] In doing this, the parable shows that the same sower, sowing the same seed, produces varied responses on various soils. In other words, "The parable addresses the failure and success of seed in the goal of fruit bearing."[39]

Briefly stated, Jesus describes the "seed" as "the word of the kingdom" according to Matthew, "the word" in Mark, and "the word of God" in Luke.[40] The expression used by Matthew is one of a kind in his gospel and is identical to "gospel of the kingdom," which he uses elsewhere.[41] One must not gloss over the importance of the word "kingdom" for it implies rule or sovereignty. "When Jesus came preaching the kingdom of God, He came preaching God's right to rule over the minds and hearts of all people. But that is precisely what the people involved did not want."[42] Ultimately the parable refers to the reception or non-reception of Jesus himself," [43] and to the following of him in discipleship.

Specifically, when the farmer sows seed, it falls on four different locations. The soils identify different hearers who have varying spiritual heart conditions. Selective targeting does not appear to be a teaching of the parable as the seed was sown everywhere. Both Luke and Matthew refer to the soil as a reference to the "heart" (Lk 8:12; Mt 13:19). Being a Hebraic concept, the heart was understood to be "the locus of reasoning and decision making"[44] or "the center of the personality" where spiritual decisions are made or not made, kept or not kept.[45]

What does Jesus say about receptivity? His instruction is that people are unreceptive because of the hardness of their heart. Seed falls "beside the road" (Mt 13:4; Mk 4:4; Lk 8:5) which, in the context of Palestine, was most likely a path for walking between fields. The ground is impenetrable. Although the birds, who are identified with Satan or demons,[46] ate the seed, Jesus attributes unresponsiveness to the hardness of the heart and not to Satan. Because the heart is so hard and resistant, the gospel message is then snatched away. Interestingly, these hearers did hear the message, even having it sown in their hearts, but they did "not understand it" (Mt. 13:19). Although elsewhere Scripture indicates that Satan is a factor in receptivity (2 Cor. 4:4), Jesus attributes it here to the sinfulness of the heart. In this context such resistance permits the evil one to take away the word.[47]

In any case, the result of resistance was unbelief. Salvation was not experienced (Lk. 8:12).[48] The lack of understanding was not due to poor communication or the lack of contextualization, but to the hardness of the heart. Such hardness of heart fits well within the context of speaking in parables because the Lord Jesus had previously explained to the disciples that He would teach them in this way so that the general audience would not see, hear, or understand (Mt. 13:13). He even cited the words of Isaiah (6:9-10) who said that Israel "will not understand," "will not perceive," had become "dull," having inadequate hearing and eyesight. Just as Isaiah found people resistant to the truth, Jesus did too. Thus, unresponsiveness is due to the hardness of the hearers, not the messenger or Satan. The sinful condition of the heart, without the intervention of the Holy Spirit, naturally causes one to reject God and His truth.[49] Those with hardened hearts have "never been softened by remorse, never broken up by conviction of sin, never cultivated by the smallest desire for anything good, pure, and holy."[50] The soil of the listener's heart has become trampled down, making it impenetrable.

Lesson Four: All receptivity is not necessarily "true" receptivity, for not everyone who receives is "truly" receptive

Receptivity of the Word is no guarantee of entry into the kingdom of God. The second soil is described as initially responsive, but eventually unfruitful. The seed falls on "rocky places" (Mt 13:5), which is characteristic of the limestone bedrock in Palestine. Here too, the unproductiveness of the seed is not attributed to the work of Satan but to the type of soil. The individual "immediately receives it with joy" (Mt 13:20), but because there is no firm root, the response is only temporary. The text indicates that there is a positive response to the seed; a profession of faith is elicited. The individual may have even jumped to accept the message. Hendriksen proposes that "He is thrilled and enthused, may even be sufficiently affected to shed a tear."[51] Yet, lurking behind such emotion is a failure to continue. In time, this positive response is threatened by "affliction or persecution" (Mt. 13:21; Mk. 4:17), or as Luke records "temptation" (8:13). The scorching sun of affliction, persecution, and temptation come "because of the word". This follower of the Lord heard the Word, but eventually "falls away." This later verb signifies "to ensnare, lure into sin, lead astray,"[52] and literally means to be "tripped up," meaning that the professing follower of Christ "collapses under pressure."[53] What pressure? Most likely the pressure placed by family, friends, and co-workers on the professing believer because of receiving the Word of God. Because there was no deep root, the emotions were only touched by the message. The mind and will remained untouched. The change is only superficial.

True understanding of the gospel of the kingdom includes understanding the cost factor—that of discipleship. Jesus teaches that testing exposes the authenticity of the faith commitment. The passage possibly indicates that the acceptance of the message was highly influenced by the personal benefits of receiving the gospel of the kingdom. In fact, the notion of falling away may even indicate that there was a sudden shock when it was discovered that affliction or persecution followed.[54] The result, of course, was unfruitfulness. Referring to the Matthew passage, MacArthur states:

> Sometimes shallow acceptance of the gospel is encouraged by shallow evangelism that holds out the blessings of salvation but hides the costs—such as repenting from sin, dying to self, and turning from the old life. When people are encouraged to walk down an isle, raise their hand, or sign a card without coming to grips with the full claims of Christ, they are in danger of becoming further from Christ than they were before they heard the message. They may become insulated from true salvation by a false profession of faith.[55]

Jesus teaches that some people will respond positively to the gospel of the kingdom but that this receptivity will not be authentic.

Referring to the third soil, the seed is sown or falls "among the thorns" (Mt. 13:7, 22; Mk. 4:7, 18; Lk. 8:7, 14), resulting in unfruitfulness. Jesus describes the thorns as the "worry of the world," and "the deceitfulness of wealth" (Matt. 13: 22).[56] There is a type of thorn, *silybum merianum*, which, if only cut down rather than de-rooted, will display a dense growth around roads in Palestine, rapidly reaching a height of more than three feet in the month of April.[57] Such thorns strangle the Word. The world (*aion*) or "present kingdom, the secular concerns as opposed to the kingdom of God,"[58] includes both the cares and the material things of the world. Understanding "the cares of the world" as "the distractions of the age," Hiebert reflects that such cares "leave little time for spiritual and eternal concerns."[59] Once again, the choking of the seed is not instantaneous.[60] Shifting one's focus from the Lord to the world and its riches leads away from the path of discipleship. Thus, the text implies that there is initial reception of the message, but resistance sets in. Why? Because the unrighteous person eventually allows worldly concerns and wealth to gain the rule in his heart. This plant of false receptivity produces no fruit. In contrast, true receptivity liberates people from the cares of the age and the deceitfulness of wealth.

To summarize, only the first soil or heart was impenetrable. However, Jesus says that the second and third individuals were receptive, yet not "truly" receptive. In both cases, falling away occurred. So, people who appear receptive are not necessary true followers of Jesus. The extent, and therefore truthfulness, of receptivity is determined by continuing with the Lord.

Lesson Five: Both initially "professing" and "following" him does not necessarily indicate true receptivity

In the context of the narrow gate section (Mt. 7:13-14), Jesus reveals that some people are deceived regarding their own entrance into the kingdom. Jesus says, "Not everyone who says to me, 'Lord, Lord,' will enter the kingdom of heaven, but he who does the will of My Father who is in heaven will enter" (Mt. 7:21). Amazingly, lack of entry through the narrow gate may even apply to those who prophesy, exorcise demons, and do miracles (Mt. 7:22). Outwardly, it appears that the individual is headed for the narrow gate because he is doing religious things—even good things; yet he inwardly resists God and his words and actions are empty. He professes, does "signs and wonders," but does not live lawfully. Such individuals are resistant, not receptive. Appearing to hold to a form of spirituality, they actually follow the broad path to destruction. The Scriptures are clear: even an emphatic profession of faith does not prove true receptivity if not accompanied by righteous living. Yes, there is faith, but it is not a transforming faith.

> Not only the profession of discipleship, but even miraculous activity in the name of Jesus, is not enough to prove a genuine disciple . . . Prophecy, exorcism and miracles can be counterfeited. 'Charismatic' activity is not a substitute for obedience and a personal relationship with Jesus.[61]

Thus, profession of faith and the performing of miraculous works are no guaranteed indication of a truthful response to the gospel.[62]

One of Jesus' most striking, authoritative, and repetitive statements is "follow me." He speaks such words to Simon, Andrew, James, John, Matthew, Phillip, Peter, the rich young ruler, another of his disciples, and to all people.[63] The verb that he uses, "to follow" (*akolouthein*), and its participle form, "those who follow" (*hoi akolouthountes*), are employed in two distinctive manners, indicating the general crowd who gathered around him or those who actually pursued him as his disciples.[64] In the latter sense these terms are an equivalent metaphor for discipleship.[65] True receptivity demands following Jesus, which is indicative of one's heart condition. Of course, Jesus meant for some to actually follow him physically, but for the most part the sense is figurative, referring to putting one's faith commitment in action and "drawing upon his life to become more like him."[66] Although believers experience lapses in the pursuit of the Lord from time to time, as with Peter when he denied Jesus, following the Lord is to be central in the life of a disciple and is to be continuous. It is indicative of true receptivity.

Not all initial followers continue to the end. By reading the gospels one can see that "the crowds flocked to Jesus in ever increasing numbers. This was not a surprising response in a day with little effective medicine and in an era that believed strongly that demons could possess a person."[67] Some followers of Jesus pursued him for material reasons in order to have their hunger satisfied (Jn. 6:26), and not because he was the true Messiah. Although they had seen him perform signs, they were unable to connect those signs with Jesus being the Son of God. Their stomachs were receptive, but not their hearts. Later, when these followers realized what was demanded of them by Jesus they ceased to follow him (Jn. 6:66) and went back to what they had left behind, which included not only their lives but also their thinking patterns.[68] Their resistance to Jesus' Lordship resulted in abandoning Him and proved that their receptivity was not authentic.

Lesson Six: True receptivity includes understanding, which brings repentance and belief, and produces fruitfulness

Interestingly, among the four types of people represented in the parable of the sower, only the fourth recipient actually understands. Jesus says: "This is the man who hears the word and understands it" (Mt. 13:23). Understanding is directly related to authentic conversion.

> If people do not understand, they will not (cannot) turn. Understanding is the key to conversion. If people do not understand, they will not (cannot) decide to turn around in terms of their view of God and their response to Jesus (i.e. repent). Without repentance, faith becomes irrelevant. Faith has no focus, context, direction, or motivation without understanding. There is no will to turn . . . Insight (understanding) is the first step in conversion.[69]

Because understanding is essential in moving people toward conversion it is very important in the proclamation of the gospel. Without it "there is no motivation for turning."[70]

When considering the concept of understanding, one must know that understanding involves much more than an intellectual assent to the gospel. Understanding extends to implications. Without violating the ministry of the Holy Spirit, it "is our task and responsibility to make sure that they (unbelievers) are clear what the gospel is, how it affects them, and why and how they should respond to it; and until we are sure that a person has grasped these things, we are hardly in a position to press him to commit himself to Christ, for it is not yet clear that he is in a position really and responsibly to do so."[71] The human element of helping and teaching others to understand is significant.

Included in this understanding is a clear comprehension of Jesus: who he is and what he did. He is central to the gospel for he is the gospel. Richard Peace has said, "So many presentations seem to portray a Jesus who is a product of our own making: one who gives gifts we desire, who demands nothing, and who is what we want to make him. I suspect that if we were to make the Jesus of the New Testament the core of the message, fewer might respond but more would stay on with Jesus."[72] True receptivity demands thorough teaching, not just a presentation of the gospel. Someone has said, "In order for someone to truly reject the gospel, you have to give him enough of it."

Amazingly, some individuals have a basic intellectual understanding of the elements of the gospel—sinfulness, the death, burial, and resurrection of Jesus Christ—yet, they do not grasp its personal implications, especially that of sinfulness. They may know something about sin, but they do not truly realize their own personal sin, understanding that they are truly separated from God, being His enemy and that they can do absolutely nothing to merit His favor. The cross may be a historical fact for them, but they really do not know how the cross applies to them and their dreadful, alienated, and sinful condition. They have not yet, for some reason, understood. They have head knowledge, but no heart grasp. In other words, they understand neither how the gospel personally applies to them nor what it demands. One often finds this situation in countries and cultures where there is a long traditional history of Christianity, such as in Roman Catholic and Eastern Orthodox contexts.

Referring once again to the parable of the sower, it is only in this fourth soil that the listener "understands" (*sunoni*)[73] Using different Greek words Mark wrote "accepts" (4:20) while Luke says "holds fast" (8:15). Otherwise stated, with this audience there is true acceptance of the gospel of the kingdom. Finding a base in the good heart, the seed produces fruit, "some a hundredfold, some sixty, and some thirty" (Matt. 13:23). "Matthew employed the word *poiei* ("brings forth" or "produces") to convey the idea of fruit being produced by the one who is rightly related to the Father through Jesus' message and is thus assured of entrance into the kingdom."[74] The order of the verbs helps one to understand the concept of true receptivity. Frederick Bruner observes,

> But the seed sown on the good earth is the person who *listening* to the Word *understands* it; this person of course bears fruit and *does* things (v. 23). Hearing comes first ("faith comes by *hearing*," Rom 10:17), understanding comes next (Matthew's special way of describing true faith), and the doing of fruitbearing then naturally (*de* "of course"!) follows.[75]

Fruit-bearing is an important concept in the gospels for it is generally related to authentic spirituality and discipleship.[76] In other words, Jesus is teaching that true regeneration results in doing good works, including transformed attitudes and behavior, and more specifically a pattern of conduct described in the Sermon on the Mount where the true disciple attempts to live out the kingdom of God on a daily basis.[77] Of course, the cause of this growth is always attributed to God as is implied by the context of Matthew, a context of kingdom growth. It is God, and God only who can produce fruit.

Also related to the fourth soil, Luke records Jesus saying that these people "hold it fast, and bear fruit with perseverance" (Lk. 8:15). Marshall adds, "It represents people who hear the word and hold fast to it," that is, people who "maintain their faith with steadfastness."[78] Truly receptive people will not only follow Jesus, but will do so in a fairly consistent and continual manner, even when the road with him is quite bumpy. In another passage Jesus forcefully states, "The one who endures to the end, he will be saved" (Mk. 13:13).[79] Continuing with Jesus is a sign of true receptivity, especially when one faces opposition to the gospel, and those who cease to follow demonstrate, in essence, a form of resistance.[80] Truly responsive mission fields bring lasting fruit. Appropriate to the concept of "receptivity and true receptivity" is the statement of J. I. Packer: "It must be said that what the Bible looks for in Christians is not the consciousness of a conversion-experience, but the evidence of a converted state."[81]

Although some would say that the parable of the sower teaches the "Harvest Principle," concentrating the maximum amount of resources to reaching the most receptive people,[82] others would disagree. "The parable speaks of the fact that Jesus presented his message to everyone alike, but that some were willing to hear and others *were not*. The difference in soils may have significance in relation to receptivity. But even so, this passage will *not* tell missionaries to concentrate on the good soil. That may be good farming, but it is totally extraneous to the text of the parable."[83]

Based on the words of Jesus, it may be premature for the missionary to present glowing reports concerning converts immediately after evangelistic efforts, for only time will tell if those who follow continue to follow and produce fruit. Truly receptive mission fields are those where people repent and believe based on a good understanding of the gospel, resulting in fruitfulness and continuance in following Jesus.

Lesson Seven: Unreceptive people should not be rejected or abandoned

After equipping the twelve disciples with power and authority in order to face demons and human diseases according to Lk. 9:1, Jesus sent them to proclaim the kingdom of God and heal. In carrying out this ministry they were to go "missionary light," without staff, bag, bread, or money. Further, if they faced resistance, they were to "shake the dust off" their feet as a testimony against the people in that town (Lk. 9:5; cf. Mt. 10:14; Mk. 6:11). Because of this passage as well as various "harvest" passages, some missiologists have maintained that workers must be redeployed according to receptivity. In other words, the most responsive areas should receive more workers, while the less the response areas receive fewer workers.[84]

For many missionaries, shaking the dust off of one's feet is a puzzling instruction, especially for those who minister in "resistant belts." History is replete with many examples of deeply committed missionaries who have seen little visible fruit—sometimes seeing one or two converts during an entire missionary career. Can it be said that David Livingstone and Samuel Zwemer ignored the advice of Jesus? Should those ministering among Muslims or secular, post-modern Europeans pack up their belongings and leave, shaking the dust off of their feet?

Shaking the dust off of one's feet, according to R. T. France, was a symbol, shown through a shocking gesture, for repudiation.[85] Possibly, this action arose from scribal and rabbinical thought when referring to heathen territory. Even the dust of heathen Gentile dirt was considered to be defiling. Strict Jewish sects even forbade the entry of plants and herbs from heathen lands because even the dirt and dust could defile them.[86] "The action of shaking off the dust of a gentile city was practiced by the Jews for they removed what was ceremonially unclean before returning to their own land, lest they should defile it."[87] The Lord Jesus was in essence saying that those Jews who reject the disciples and the message of the Kingdom are to be considered "outside of the people of God,"[88] that is, unbelieving, pagan, sinfully impure, and liable for eternal judgment.[89] If, and when, rejection occurs of the kingdom of God, the disciples were to consider the Jews as pagan, that is, no better than the Gentiles. Contrary to some, this does not signify a last witness or abandonment.[90] Interestingly, after Paul and Barnabas, on the first missionary journey, visited Pisidian Antioch they "shook the dust off" of their sandals and departed for Iconium (Ac. 13:51).[91] However, they later passed back through the same city (Ac. 14:24). One cannot forget that even though the Jews were resistant to the Gospel, they had to be a priority in salvation history in light of the Abrahamic covenant (Gen. 12:1-3). Jesus clearly taught that "salvation is from the Jews" (Jn. 4:22). The Jews could not have been abandoned according to the will of God. This explains why Paul, the apostle to the Gentiles, gives priority to the synagogue and the Jews.[92] Even though he was rejected and harshly treated by the Jews, time and time again he returned to evangelize them. Abandonment would be contrary to the will and purposes of God at that time. Of course, in due time, the gospel spread toward the Gentiles; yet, the Jews were never totally abandoned.[93] Historically, there are many cases where missionaries have laid a gospel foundation with few or no conversion results and have refused to "shake the dust off of their feet." In some of these cases, years later (sometimes a generation or more later) multitudes of people entered the kingdom of God. The apostles did shake the dust off their feet and, in some cases, departed in other directions. This symbolic act was merely "a testimony against them," indicating that the Jews were no better off than the pagan Gentiles who did not belong to the kingdom of God.[94] But it does not mean abandonment. Perseverance and patience is called for, not total rejection of the people merely because they refuse the gospel. Salvation may not be for that time because the Father may not have drawn them to Himself yet. It would seem that missionaries need to follow the example of the Lord who is patient, not willing that any perish (2 Pe 3:9).

Lesson Eight: There will be great growth of the kingdom of God; yet the truly receptive will be limited in number

What does such a seemingly contradictory statement mean? In two parables Jesus says: "The kingdom of heaven is like a mustard seed . . . but when it becomes full grown, it is larger than the garden plants and becomes a tree, so the birds of the air come and nest in its branches" (Mt. 13:31-32); and "The kingdom of heaven is like leaven, which a woman took and hid in three pecks of flour until it was all leavened" (Mt. 13:33).

From small beginnings, Jesus teaches that the kingdom of heaven will grow in power, might, and glory, pointing to the ultimate success of his mission.[95] It will "grow to great proportions and provide blessing and bounty for the many people who would come into it."[96] This "many" will be composed of "every tribe and tongue and people and nation" (Rev. 5:9; 7:9). Jesus says that "many will come from east and west" into the kingdom of God (Mt. 8:11),[97] with the word "many" (*polus*) referring to a great number.

This lesson, however, provides a good reminder not to equate the growth of the kingdom with the church or growth in numbers of believers. An increase in the size of the church may be part of the growth of the kingdom, but it is just one aspect. There will be tares among the wheat and bad among the good fish within the kingdom sphere, but at the time of eschatological judgment a separation of the true from the false will take place.[98] "At that time only the righteous—those who have received the kingdom with appropriate response in the form of discipleship— [will] survive; the evil [will] go to their punishment."[99] Thus, authentic receptivity and discipleship are of extreme significance. But just how many will enter into the kingdom?

Jesus' teaching on "fewness" may confuse and puzzle some, especially in light of Jesus' teaching about the increasing growth of the kingdom. Having just taught on prayer and the "Golden Rule" in the Sermon on the Mount, Jesus particularly addresses the listening Jews in his epilogue: "Enter through the narrow gate; for the gate is wide and the way is broad that leads to destruction, and there are many who enter through it. For the gate is small and the way is narrow that leads to life, and there are few who find it" (Mt. 7:13-14). Due to the Jews' physical heritage, having Abraham as their father, most of them believed that they would be saved for eternity. However, Jesus knew that such thinking was faulty and deceptive . In order to challenge their thinking he employs contrasting images: the narrow and wide gates.[100] Although many Jews of the day were indeed religious, they were personally disillusioned. Jesus considered them lost and in a minority.[101]

Jesus clearly states that "the way is narrow that leads to life" (Mt. 7:14). Such wording corresponds with many other statements in the gospels, for the messengers of the Pharisees and Herodians recognized that Jesus taught "the way of God" (Mk. 12:14). When Jesus responded to Thomas's question, "How do we know the way?" (John 14:5) he pointed to himself, "I am the way" (John 14:6).

With the narrow gate language Jesus is calling for a following, a moving toward the proper gate for entry into the kingdom of God. MacArthur observes, "Here the Lord focuses on the inevitable decision that every person must make, the crossroads where he must decide on the gate he will enter and way he will go."[102] And Gundry remarks, "Many will try to enter but fail, initially not because the door is already closed, but because the door is too narrow for vast throngs to crowd through. In other words, few will be saved."[103] The "fewness" of Jesus, or maybe better stated, the "narrowness" of Jesus is directly opposed to the "wideness" of Pinnock, who denies the exclusivity of Jesus in this passage by attempting to make it non-applicable today.[104] Pinnock bases this "wideness" on an extremely doubtful hermeneutic.[105] As the context of the Sermon on the Mount indicates, those who enter this narrow gate must have surpassing righteousness (Mt. 5:20). Jesus says that these will be few. This word "few" (*oligos*) signifies "few, little, small, slight in reference to number, quantity, size,"[106] indicating that the number is not great. "True discipleship is a minority religion."[107]

But just how many? No one can say, but entry has nothing to do with gate size. Even though the gate size is narrow, all can be accommodated. Paradise can hold everyone. God wishes that all will enter, but only if the condition is met: repentance and belief in the Son of God. Those beyond the few are headed down the wrong path: to destruction.[108]

All will not enter the kingdom of God, for Scripture indicates that rejection of some, if not many, will occur, resulting in judgment of those rejected.[109] Two of the "rejection" parables provide some information concerning the number. In one the parable of the "Narrow Door," someone asks Jesus frankly, "Lord, are there just a few who are being saved?" (Lk. 13:23). Such a question was often debated within Judaism.[110] Although Jesus places the emphasis on "who" shall enter the kingdom of God rather than on "how many," he gives the impression that the number is not great.[111] His reply is indirect and negative in its tone because he speaks of how many will not be saved. He says that many will seek and strive to enter through the narrow door but will not be able to enter (v. 24). Jesus' response, however, does not indicate "that there are many who strive in vain to enter, but that there *will be* many who will seek in vain to enter, after the time of salvation is past. Those who continue to strive now, succeed."[112] The verb "strive" (*agonizomai*) takes on the sense of struggle or of making every effort, reflecting difficulty, which is found in Hellenistic, Jewish, and early Christian thinking.[113] Jesus clearly excluded the notion that those who had the right bloodline would pass into the kingdom. While many may seek entry, genuinely wanting to be inside, the element of the narrow door suggests criteria other than "wanting" are necessary.[114]

This human responsibility of striving, which merely emphasizes earnestness rather than salvation by merit,[115] must be tempered with Luke 14:15-24, which shows God's grace initiative. Nolland summarizes the Luke 13 passage as follows:

> Will those who are saved be few? Jesus is quite sure that there are many who are experiencing his ministry but will not be present at the final kingdom of God banquet. But whether those who are saved will be few or not depends upon the response to be made to his challenge to strain to make every effort to gain entry through the narrow door.[116]

Even though certain ones will eat and drink in the Lord's presence, they are considered but "evildoers" (v. 27), indicating that he was familiar with them and their lack of righteousness. The poser of the question employs the term "few" (*mikros*) in reference to the number saved. Jesus merely responds by saying that "many . . . will not be able to enter." The number appears to be small.

Thus, the Scriptures give the impression that only a minority has been truly receptive. They will come from the east, west, north, and south, entering into true communion with the Lord at the eschatological banquet table. Some have concluded that the Gentiles may be well represented.[117] In reality the Jews thought that the Gentiles would be excluded from the kingdom and that the Jews, due to their heritage and spirituality, would be more receptive to the kingdom of God. But in fact, the Jews who were to be first, but will now be last (Lk. 13:30).

In the second parable, a "Wedding Banquet" occurs (Mt. 22:1-14). Some understand this parable as a picture of "the blessings of God's salvation."[118] It is also instructive in relation to receptivity. For basically three years Jesus had been offering the kingdom of God to his own people, but he met resistance for the most part. At this time there were really just a handful of faithful followers. Many followed for they liked his refreshing teaching, were amazed by his miracles, admired his sterling example of living, and sought to emulate his obedience to God. But one learns later that such receptivity is merely superficial. In reality, Jesus' true followers were not in great in numbers.

In this parable, Jesus tells how slaves were sent out to call all those who had been invited to the feast, but they were unwilling to come. In fact, the slaves went a second time, but the invited were still unwilling. The Master then sent the slaves out a third time to invite others from the highways and streets. They, good and bad, came, and the wedding banquet room was filled with guests.

The notion of "fewness" and "chosenness" puzzles many. Jesus says, "For many are called, but few are chosen" (Mt. 22:14). The first expression, "many are called," should be taken as a Semitism, meaning everyone.[119] This is an open invitation to all. Deciding not to come to the feast was a personal choice of those who had been invited—it was their personal decision to reject the invitation even though they had been called to the feast. Correspondingly, responsibility falls on the invited one's shoulders to show the true repentance necessary for entry into the kingdom of God (Mt. 3:2, 4:17). Regarding "fewness," Hagner recommends taking this term *oligoi* as a Semitism signifying "fewer than" in the sense of "not all." Thus, the term does not really indicate a number but only a proportion, contrasting those that came with those that were called.[120] However, the term "chosen" strikes the reader in that "their fate depended on someone else's (God's) choice."[121] In other words, receptivity is due to the work of God. Yet, the passage also speaks of man's willingness to accept the call to come to the wedding. This, of course, raises the complex issue of man's will and God's sovereignty. Although this issue has been debated over the centuries, Jesus does not suffer the tension between God's sovereignty and man's responsibility that normal humans tend to experience. In fact, there seems to be a well-balanced emphasis here. MacArthur states: "The invitations to the wedding feast went out to many, representative of everyone to whom the gospel message is sent. But few of those who heard the call were willing to accept it and thereby be among the chosen."[122] In the final analysis, even though man has great personal responsibility regarding resistance and acceptance, salvation is the free gift of God.

To summarize, it would be impossible to know how many are receptive to the gospel. What one knows, however, is that the kingdom will manifest great growth, including many actually entering into an authentic relationship with Jesus Christ. However, one also knows that "fewness" will also be descriptive of the group entering the kingdom. Such teaching by Jesus reminds missionaries and evangelists to take great caution crunching numbers when it concerns people entering the kingdom of God. In light of Jesus' words it appears somewhat presumptuous to name conversion number goals. Questions regarding goal-setting such as, "How many will be won to Christ during this next five years?" should be discarded, for only the Lord knows. The Lord calls Christians to proclaim and teach the gospel, with the intent of making disciples. Thus, all numbering should be left to his discretion.

Implications for Evangelism and Missions

Based upon the Gospels, particularly the parables, Jesus' "receptivity/resistance axis"[123] might be described as follows. Immediate receptivity is not necessarily equivalent to true regeneration, but it can include both the truly believing and nonbelieving. In other words, it is possible for people to be responsive to the gospel, even receiving and following Jesus; yet, in time fully abandon him. If there is no "holding to" or fruit, there is no true receptivity. True receptivity arises from good soil, which is due to the work of the Father. People may respond to the gospel, but their response may be superficial. In many cases, only time will indicate their true condition.

What are the implications of Jesus' sayings for missions and evangelism?

First, missionaries and evangelists should be doing missions according to Jesus. Although the gospels do not contain all revelation concerning receptivity, it is essential to consider the sayings of Jesus regarding receptivity. After all, he is the Lord and Savior who came in truth. Should missionaries not be asking if their missiological approach is biblical? Is it according to Jesus? Would he encourage them to pursue their plan of evangelism? Larkin has recently stated, "Mission strategy needs to constantly face the question, 'But is it biblical?'"[124] To this one may add, "Is it according to Jesus?"

Second, the missionary enterprise will be successful. All humans are spiritually resistant to the things of God. They are not just indifferent or neutral. They are all naturally hardened, rebellious, and resistant to the gospel due to their sinful nature. However, the sayings of Jesus provide the missionary with hope and encouragement regarding evangelistic success. Even though people will resist the gospel, missionaries and evangelists can be assured that some people will positively respond to it. There will be fruit; in some cases small portions, in others large. This assurance comes from the fact that the Holy Spirit is continuing to convict people of sin, and the Father is drawing them to Himself.

Third, seed-sowing should imply meaningful personal evangelism. Sometimes missiologists talk about seed sowing as if it is a matter of tract distribution or radio waves, but this is only one small aspect. For the most part, it concerns meeting people face to face. Jesus sowed seed both by preaching to the crowds and by conversing and meeting with people. Although there may be some value to mass gospel proclamations, this should not be viewed as the essence of sowing the seed. Would Jesus have indiscriminately placed portions of Scripture in the mail-boxes of the citizens of Narareth? Possibly, but it is certain that he sowed seed through personal contact and involvement with people. Dialogue, discussion, and questioning were crucial parts of his seed-sowing approach.

Fourth, there are degrees of receptivity. Some who "receive Jesus" really do not. "True" receptivity is a positive faith response to the conviction ministry of the Holy Spirit and the Father's invitation to salvation, which results in continual following and God-produced fruit. True receptivity is truly the work of God.

Five, faithfulness in sowing seed is essential to successful evangelism. God does not call the missionary to be a success regarding the results of his ministry, but to be faithful in seed-sowing. Seed must be sown everywhere: to all peoples, cultures, and nations. This is simply because God is the cause of all growth. Growth is humanly uncontrollable, according to Jesus. But, "Where there is no seed sowing there will be little harvest."[125] Although inexplicable, the harvest is dependent to some extent upon a human who sows the seed and God who produces the fruit. The Lord could have chosen to go it alone, but he has chosen the human instrument as co-laborer.

Sixth, one's view of receptivity determines one's evangelistic approach. If receptivity is merely seen as a "decision" for Jesus, then the missionary or evangelist will emphasize invitations "to receive Jesus," simple sinner's prayers, evangelistic events, and encounter approaches. True, the approach has and continues to have its effectiveness due to the power and pull of God. However, its weaknesses are serious, including a "huge falloff" between those that merely "received" Jesus and those that bear fruit and continue to follow the Lord.[126]

Seventh, prudent follow-up is necessary in reference to receptivity. Because of different levels of receptivity, it is important for missionaries to take caution when welcoming people into the kingdom of God. Unfortunately, some well-meaning missionaries and evangelists have sometimes assured people of entry into the kingdom of God, when this may not have been the case at all. Such cases often lack a discipleship emphasis. If one emphasizes "true" receptivity, one views evangelism more as a process in its disciple-making. True receptivity is marked by obedience and fruitfulness.

Eighth, an emphasis on understanding the gospel is of great essence. True receptivity places a large emphasis on trying to give understanding to the unbeliever: understanding sin, who God is, who Jesus is and what he did, what is involved in true faith, obedience, and commitment to Jesus. Teaching the gospel is essential, rather than merely "presenting" it. For this reason missionaries must be well-grounded in biblical and theological truth for they are responsible for correctly and effectively teaching the gospel. This has great implications for missiological training. Unfortunately, in an effort people to get to the field as fast as possible, some missionaries, and even mission training institutions, take short cuts regarding theological preparation. Often, little emphasis and preparation on the theological foundations of the missionary message takes place. The missionary should be able to explain the theological themes of regeneration, justification, and sanctification.

> For Jesus "who is blessed and only Sovereign, the King of kings and Lord of lords, who alone possesses immortality and dwells in unapproachable light, whom no man has seen or can see, To Him be honor and eternal dominion! Amen" (1 Tim. 6:15-16).

Notes

1. William J. Larkin, "The Role of Biblical-Theological Methods in Missiological Research," *The Occasional Bulletin* 16, Evangelical Missiological Society (Winter, 2003): 1.

2. The writer, of course, admits that the words of Jesus are not the complete revelation concerning receptivity because other ideas can be found in the Old Testament as well as the New Testament. However, what Jesus does say must be heeded. Additionally, all Scripture citations will be from the *New American Standard Bible* (Anaheim, CA: Foundation Publications, Inc., 1995), unless otherwise stated.

3. Thom S. Rainer, *The Book of Church Growth: History, Theology, and Principles* (Nashville, TN: Broadman & Holman, 1993), 30.

4. Elmer Towns, ed., *Evangelism and Church Growth* (Ventura, CA: Regal, 1995), 331.

5. C. Peter Wagner, ed., *Church Growth: The State of the Art* (Wheaton, IL: Tyndale House, 1986), 298.

6. C. Peter Wagner, *Strategies for Church Growth: Tools for Effective Mission and Evangelism* (Ventura, CA: Regal, 1987), 78.

7. This latter Greek term is of the same family of *dechomai*.

8. Colin Brown, ed., *The New International Dictionary of New Testament Theology*, vol. 3 (Grand Rapids: Zondervan, 1978), 746. See Lk. 8:13; Acts 8:14; 11:1; 17:11; 1 Thess. 1:6; 2:13.

9. Ibid. See Jn. 1:12; Acts 2:41.

10. Ibid., 749.

11. This author intends to show this later in the chapter.

12. Donald A. McGavran, *Understanding Church Growth*, 3rd ed., ed. C. Peter Wagner (Grand Rapids: Eerdmans, 1990), 182-6.

13. John Wimber, "Power Evangelism: Definitions and Directions," in *Wrestling with Dark Angels*, ed. C. Peter Wagner and F. Douglas Pennoyer (Ventura, CA: Regal, 1990), 28-9.

14. C. Peter Wagner, "Territorial Spirits," in *Wrestling with Dark Angels*, ed. C. Peter Wagner and F. Douglas Pennoyer (Ventura, CA: Regal, 1990), 77.

15. Arthur F. Glasser and Donald A. McGavran, *Contemporary Theologies of Mission* (Grand Rapids: Baker, 1983), 148-9.

16. Rick Warren, *The Purpose Driven Church* (Grand Rapids: Zondervan, 1995), 219.

17. John F. MacArthur, *The MacArthur New Testament Commentary: Matthew 1-7* (Chicago: Moody, 1985), 458.

18. Jesus does state that he will "draw all men to Myself" (Jn. 12:32), but let the reader remember that it is one thing to draw people to himself and another to save all men. The expression "all men" signifies that Christ draws people to himself without thought of race, nationality, and social status. Merrill C. Tenney, *The Gospel of John*, The Expositor's Bible Commentary, ed. Frank E. Gaebelein, vol. 9 (Grand Rapids: Zondervan, 1981), 131.

19. John F. MacArthur, *The MacArthur New Testament Commentary: Matthew 16-23* (Chicago: Moody Press, 1988), 313.

20. Colin Brown, ed., *The New International Dictionary of New Testament Theology*, vol. 1 (Grand Rapids: Zondervan, 1975), 358.

21. D. Edmond Hiebert, *Mark: A Portrait of the Servant* (Chicago: Moody, 1974), 48.

22. J. I. Packer, *Evangelism and the Sovereignty of God* (Downers Grove, IL: InterVarsity, 1961), 97-115.

23. Ibid., 106.

24. Charles Van Engen, "Reflecting Theologically About the Resistant," in *Reaching the Resistant*, ed. J. Dudley Woodberry (Pasadena: William Carey, 1998), 52.

25. Other purposes include: (1) to fulfill messianic prophecy (Mt. 8:17, 12:15-21), (2) to show that Jesus had the authority to forgive sins (Mt. 9:6), (3) to provide confirmation of Christ's messianic ministry for John the Baptist while in prison (Mt. 11:2-19), (4) to show people the works of God manifested in Christ (Jn. 9:3), (5) to show the glory of God in Christ (Jn. 11:4), (6) to show God's confirmation of the ministry of Christ.

26. The exception being three cases (Mt. 8:22-26; Lk. 17:11-19; Jn. 9:1-7).

27. Healings came through touch (Mt. 8:15), spoken word (Jn. 5:8-9), spittle (Mk. 8:22-26), spittled-clay (Jn. 9:6), and by touching the cloak of Christ (Mt. 9:20-22).

28. Jairus's daughter (Matthew 9), the widow's son (Luke 7), and Lazarus (John 11) were all dead, incapable of displaying personal faith in the healer.

29. Matthew 11:20 contains the Greek phrase *hai pleistai dynameis autou*, literally signifying "his very many miracles," but also correctly translated "most of his miracles." D.A. Carson, *Matthew*, The Expositor's

Bible Commentary, ed. Frank E. Gaebelein, vol. 8 (Grand Rapids: Zondervan, 1984), 272.

30. Donald K. Smith, *Creating Understanding* (Grand Rapids: Zondervan, 1992), 21.

31. Although there seems to be a general absence of specific plans and strategies regarding outreach in the New Testament, one can observe that the Apostle Paul did have some sort of strategy because he went first to the synagogue when he entered a particular city. In another case, during the second missionary journey Paul was headed in one direction (indicating some sort of plan), but God intervened and directed him to go to another—Macedonia (Acts 16:9-10).

32. Packer, *Evangelism*, 27-8.

33. Leon Morris, *The Gospel According to John*, The New International Commentary on the New Testament (Grand Rapids: Eerdmans, 1971), 387.

34. Recent biblical scholarship maintains that different parts or details of a parable may at times be interpreted separately, rather than just one main thought or point. See Craig S. Keener, *A Commentary on the Gospel of Matthew* (Grand Rapids: Eerdmans, 1999), 384; R. T. France, *The Gospel According to Matthew*, Tyndale New Testament Commentaries, ed. Leon Morris (Leicester, England: InterVarsity Press and Grand Rapids: Eerdmans, 1985), 217.

35. Observation made by Keener, *Matthew*, 371.

36. C. Peter Wagner, *Stop the World I Want to Get On* (Glendale, CA: Regal, 1974), 82.

37. Donald A. Hagner, *Matthew 1-13*, Word Biblical Commentary, vol. 33a, (Dallas: Word, 1993), 380-81.

38. Van Engen, "Reflecting Theologically," 54.

39. Hagner, *Matthew 1-13*, 369.

40. The Word of God is also referred to as the "seed" in 1 Peter 1:23.

41. *See* Matthew 9:35, 24:14.

42 James Montgomery Boice, *The Parables of Jesus* (Chicago: Moody, 1983), 17.

43. Hagner, *Matthew 1-13*, 379.

44. C. S. Mann, *Mark: A New Translation with Introduction and Commentary* (Garden City, NY: Doubleday, 1986), 224. Quoted in Richard V. Peace, *Conversion in the New Testament: Paul and the Twelve* (Grand Rapids: Eerdmans, 1999), 234.

45. Carson, *Matthew*, 313.

46. Matthew 13:19; Mark 4:15; Luke 8:12. Birds regularly symbolize evil, including demons and Satan. Carson, *Matthew*, 313; Hagner, *Matthew 1-13*, 379.

47. Lenski maintains that Satan snatches away the Word while the sower is sowing. R. C. H. Lenski, *The Interpretation of St. Matthew's Gospel* (Minneapolis: Augsburg, 1943; reprint, 1964), 517. However, since the

word was already sown in the heart it seems that Satan came after the sowing.

48. This is contrary to the teaching of Kingsbury who maintains that those who hear the message became Christians. Jack Dean Kingsbury, *The Parables of Jesus in Matthew 13: A Study in Redaction-Criticism* (London: SPCK, 1969), 55. Quoted in Carson, *Matthew*, 313.

49. Romans 1:18-19 speaks of men who "suppress the truth in unrighteousness," even though that they have some revelation of God.

50. John F. MacArthur, *The MacArthur New Testament Commentary: Matthew 8-15* (Chicago: Moody, 1987), 357.

51. William Hendriksen, *Exposition of the Gospel According to Matthew* (Grand Rapids: Baker, 1973), 560.

52. Hendriksen, *Matthew*, 561.

53. France, *Matthew*, 219.

54. R. V. G. Tasker, *The Gospel According to Matthew* (Grand Rapids: Eerdmans, 1979), 139.

55. MacArthur, *Matthew 8-15*, 358.

56. Mark 4:19 adds "the desires for other things enter in" and Lk. 8:14 employs the expression "worries and riches and pleasures of this life."

57. Keener, *Matthew*, 374, cites the work of Hepper and Argyle.

58. France, *Matthew*, 219.

59. Hiebert, *Mark*, 104.

60. Alfred Plummer, *The Gospel According to S. Luke*, The International Critical Commentary (Edinburgh: T. & T. Clark, 1896; reprint, 1975), 221.

61. France, *Matthew*, 148-9.

62. Philip Edgcumbe Hughes, "Hebrews 6:4-6 and the Peril of Apostasy," *Westminster Theological Journal* 35 (Winter 1973): 148.

63. Mt. 4:19, 21(implied); 9:9; 16:24; 19:21; Mk. 1:17; 2:14; 8:34; 10:21; Lk. 5:27; 9:23; 18:22; Jn. 1:43; 21:19, 22.

64. Richard N. Longenecker, ed., *Patterns of Discipleship in the New Testament* (Grand Rapids: Eerdmans, 1996), 4.

65. Michael J. Wilkins, *Following The Master: Discipleship in the Steps of Jesus* (Grand Rapids: Zondervan, 1992), 320.

66. Ibid., 131-2.

67. Peace, *Conversion in the New Testament*, 234.

68. William Hendriksen, *Exposition of the Gospel According to John*, New Testament Commentary (Grand Rapids: Baker, 1972), 247.

69. Peace, *Conversion in the New Testament*, 236.

70. Ibid., 279.

71. James I. Packer, "What is Evangelism?" in *Theological Perspectives on Church Growth*, ed. Harvie M. Conn (Nutley, NJ: Presbyterian and Reformed, 1977), 102.

72. Peace, *Conversion in the New Testament*, 299.

73. Understanding is only attributed to the good soil, that is, truly receptive heart.

74. Mark L. Bailey, "The Parable of the Sower and the Soils," *Bibliotheca Sacra*, 155 (April 1998): 184.

75. Frederick D. Bruner, *Matthew: A Commentary* (Waco, TX: Word, 1990), 495.

76. Robert H. Gundry, *Matthew: A Commentary on His Handbook for Mixed Church Under Persecution*, 2^d ed. (Grand Rapids: Zondervan, 1994), 261. See Matthew 3:10, 7:17-20, 12:33-35; Luke 3:8; John 15:8.

77. Ibid., 259. MacArthur, *Matthew 8-15*, 361. Hagner, *Matthew 1-13*, 380.

78. I. Howard Marshall, *The Gospel of Luke*, The International Greek Testament Commentary (Grand Rapids: Eerdmans, 1978), 327.

79. See also Mt. 10:22, 24:13; Jn. 8:31; 1 Cor. 15:1-2; Col. 1:23.

80. For the sake of clarification, Jesus is not presenting salvation by works, but merely emphasizing that true receptivity results in faithful following and obedience.

81. Packer, "What is Evangelism?" 104.

82. Described by Towns, *Evangelism*, 257.

83. Van Engen, "Reflecting Theologically," 54.

84. Vergil Gerber, *God's Way to Keep a Church Going & Growing* (South Pasadena, CA: William Carey and Glendale, CA: Regal, 1973), 26-27. C. Peter Wagner implies the same thought in *Strategies*, 67.

85. France, *Matthew*, 181.

86. James M. Freeman, *Manners and Customs of the Bible* (Plainfield, NJ: Logos International, reprint 1972 from Nelson and Phillips, NY), 346.

87. Marshall, *Luke*, 354. See also Joel B. Green, *The Gospel of Luke* (Grand Rapids: Eerdmans, 1997), 360.

88. Green, *Luke*, 360.

89. Carson, *Matthew*, 246.

90. Opposing views include: Brown, *NIDNT*, vol. 3, 560; John Nolland, *Luke 1-9:20, Word Biblical Commentary,* vol. 35a (Dallas: Word, 1989), 428.

91. In this passage, the Gentiles positively responded to the gospel, but the Jews resisted. As a result, Paul and Barnabus shook the dust off of their feet in protest to this negative response, which signified that the Jews were outside of the kingdom of God, but the Gentiles had entered it.

92. Upon entry into each city Paul first went to the Jews in the synagogue (Acts 14:1; 17:1, 10, 17; 18:4, 19, 26; 19:8).

93. See Acts 13:46-47; 18:6. Cf. Romans 11:1-2, 17, 19-22.

94. Leon Morris, *The Gospel According to St Luke*, Tyndale New Testament Commentaries (Grand Rapids: Eerdmans, 1980), 164.

95. Carson, *Matthew*, 318. Donald Guthrie, *New Testament Theology* (Downers Grove, IL: InterVarsity, 1981), 423.

96. J. Dwight Pentecost, *The Parables of Jesus* (Grand Rapids: Zondervan, 1982), 57.

97. Lk. 13:29 employs a similar expression but does not use the term "many."

98. France, *Matthew*, 225, 230.

99. Hagner, *Matthew 1-13*, 400.

100. The image of two paths or ways was often employed among Greek, Roman, Jewish, and Christian writers. Keener, *Matthew*, 250.

101. Ibid., 251.

102. MacArthur, *Matthew 1-7*, 449.

103. Gundry, *Matthew*, 126.

104. Clark Pinnock, *A Wideness in God's Mercy* (Grand Rapids: Zondervan, 1992).

105. W. Gary Phillips, "Evangelical Pluralism A Singular Problem," *Bibliotheca Sacra* 151 (April 1994): 150.

106. G. Abbott-Smith, *A Manual Greek Lexicon of the New Testament* (Edinburgh: T & T Clark, 1921; reprint 1968), 315.

107. France, *Matthew*, 146. For a discussion on "fewness," the reader is encouraged to view the works of Abraham Kuyper, *De Gemeen Gratie*, II (Kampen: J.H. Kok, n.d.), 91-92, and B. B. Warfield, "Are They Few That Be Saved?" *Biblical and Theological Studies* (Philadelphia: Presbyterian and Reformed, 1962), 344.

108. Hagner, *Matthew 1-13*, 179. The term "destruction" is not a reference to annihilation, but everlasting damnation (Mt. 18:8; 25:41, 46).

109. Several parables appear to deal with this rejection theme: Tares and Wheat (Mt. 13:24-30, 36-43; Dragnet (Mt. 13:47-50); Wedding Banquet (Mt. 22:1-14); Narrow Door (Lk. 13:22-30); Good and Bad Servants (Mt. 24:45-51; Lk. 12:41-48); Ten Virgins (Mt. 25:1-13; Talents (Mt. 25:14-30); Minas (Lk. 19:11-27); Sheep and Goats (Mt. 25:31-46).

110. Marshall, *Luke*, 564; Morris, 1974, 225.

111. Fewness appears to be a recurring respnse of Jesus in Luke. See Lk. 4:25-27, 7:9, 8:9-15.

112. Plummer, *Luke*, 346. Italics mine.

113. John Nolland, *Luke 9:21-18:34, Word Biblical Commentary*, vol. 35b (Dallas: Word, 1993), 733.

114. Karl E. Pagenkemper, "Rejection Imagery in the Synoptic Parables," *Bibliotheca Sacra* 153 (July 1996): 317.

115. Walter L. Liefeld, *Luke, The Expositor's Bible Commentary*, vol. 8 (Grand Rapids: Zondervan, 1984), 973.

116. Nolland, *Luke 9:21-18:34*, 733.

117. Plummer, *Luke*, 348. See Is. 49:12; Mt. 8:11.

118. France, *Matthew*, 312.

119. Donald A. Hagner, *Matthew 14-28, Word Biblical Commentary*, vol. 33b (Dallas: Word, 1993), 632.

120. Ibid.

121. France, *Matthew*, 314.
122. MacArthur, *Matthew 16-23*, 313.
123. Important missiological thinkers have attempted to measure responsiveness through a "Resistance-Receptivity Axis." See Edward R. Dayton and David A. Fraser, *Planning Strategies for World Evangelization* (Grand Rapids: Eerdmans, 1980), 178-9.
124. Larkin, "Biblical-Theological Methods," 5.
125. Pentecost, *Parables of Jesus*, 155.
126. Peace, *Conversion in the New Testament*, 289-90.

III. MISSIOLOGICAL INSIGHTS

Chapter Nine

A Christocentric Understanding of Linguistic Diversity: Implications for Missions in a Pluralistic Era

Samuel H. Larsen

Background

Secular communication theorists commonly assume human biological evolution, and human language in its diversity is therefore presumed to have evolved from lower animal forms such as salamanders through higher animal forms such as primates.[1]

In Biblical studies, redaction critics have generally viewed the Babel narrative of Genesis as mythological. Their theories have not fared well in light of subsequent scholarship. For example, contemporary scholars rarely hold to Hermann Gunkel's hypothesis that the narrative resulted from the blending of two ancient stories, one of a city and the other of a tower, because of the strong literary coherence of the unit.[2]

By contrast, many evangelical Bible scholars attribute the diversity of human languages entirely to God's judgment at Babel (Genesis 11). Therefore these scholars view linguistic diversity negatively as a problem to be remedied rather than as a divinely-intended expression of creativity. With that view comes implications for both nation-states and the Christian community. Homogeneity of language and culture often becomes an ideal and goal.

Is there a Christocentric "third way" which is faithful to the biblical text, treating it as true history, and yet which views linguistic (and hence cultural) diversity positively?

Preliminary Observations

On superficial reading of the English translation, Genesis eleven might easily be construed to mean that diversity of language and culture did not exist after the Flood of Noah until the events of the Babel narrative. The text says, "Now the whole earth had one language, and the same words" (Gen. 11:1, ESV), and "the LORD said, 'Behold, they are one people, and they have all one language . . . Come, let us go down and there confuse their language, so that they may not understand one another's speech . . . Therefore its name was called Babel, because there the LORD confused the language of all the earth" (Gen. 11:7-9).

The events of the first day of Pentecost following Christ's resurrection seem to indicate that the Spirit of God reverses the condition imposed at Babel (diversity of language) as he works through the Gospel (Acts 2). F. F. Bruce writes, "The event was surely nothing less than a reversal of the curse of Babel."[3]

The vision of John while on the island of Patmos provides, through his eyes, a glimpse of heaven itself, where the multitude saved out of every ethnic and language group now sing in unison to the Father and the Son (Rev. 7:9-10). To be able to do so, one might surmise, requires them to share the language used in the song.

Many readers draw the implication that uniformity of language is finally restored in heaven. If uniformity is God's ultimate goal, should not God's people work toward it even now? Cultural and linguistic diversity is then viewed as a condition inferior to cultural and linguistic uniformity. Referring to the Babel account, Allen Ross concludes, "The text thereby demonstrates that the present number of languages that form national barriers is a monument to sin."[4]

Biblical and Theological Reflection

There is, however, another way to interpret the wording of Genesis eleven. The term "language" (Heb. *saphah*, "lip") may denote a fundamental language system ("common speech"), whereas "words" (Heb. *debarim*) may denote shared or core vocabulary.[5] The plural form of the Hebrew word for "one" used with the term for "words" in Gen. 11:1 occurs only four other times in the Old Testament (Gen. 27:44, Gen. 29:20, Dan. 11:20, and Ezek. 37:17), and in three of those passages translators typically render the term as "few."[6] For example, a child may speak his parents' language and use vocabulary common to them without understanding extensive grammar, vocabulary, or concepts, and having the ability to speak other languages known to the parents. Communication is still easily possible. Kiswahili is a trade language in East Africa and a second language to most Kenyans. Even very basic grammar skills and a minimal vocabulary enable one to communicate with others from different tribes (with their own distinct languages). Peter Berger argues that a society must necessarily possess a "sacred canopy" of shared essential language (common speech) and values if unity amid diversity is to be maintained.[7] The Babel narrative, therefore, may also be understood to mean that, amidst the diversity that was already emerging (culturally and linguistically), humankind retained a shared way of understanding (i.e., one language system, Heb. *saphah*) and a shared content or expression (i.e., a common core vocabulary, Heb. *debarim*). God then removed that shared umbrella, or "sacred canopy" of social cohesion in an act both of judgment and of grace. Ross writes, "The human race, although united by origin, is divided by language, territory, and politics as a part of God's design to bring blessing to the human race."[8] The call of Abraham, with the explicit promise of blessing for the nations through his line, immediately follows the Babel narrative and the connecting personal genealogy.

The developments recorded in Genesis four and ten support such an interpretation of the Babel narrative. Chapter four informs the reader regarding the emergence of individuals with skills in metallurgy, musicology, and animal husbandry, among others. Specialized technology implies specialized vocabulary and concepts. People name things and processes as they discover or develop them, and human finitude precludes the assumption that each human being can entirely know what every other human being has learned. Distinctive disciplinary jargons and terminological shorthand are natural developments, not sinful in themselves. Language diversity reflects diversity of interest and culture. Naming indicates dominion and insight into the real nature of things. A name denotes identity, relationship, or sovereignty. God calls the cosmos into being, and it responds by coming to be. Such "call-response" implies relationship. God then names nature and Adam. Adam in turn names the animals and Eve, reflecting God's own naming of day and night, of sky and seas, and of Adam himself. Cain names a city for his son (Gen. 4:17). All apparently name their children. The process of naming implies more than simply an assignment of symbols corresponding to modern English nouns, because verbal expressions may also be part of naming. For example, Hagar's name for Yahweh was "the Living One Who Sees Me" (Gen. 16:13-14).

John Ellis suggests, with Benjamin Whorf, that language is not primarily communication. Rather, he argues, categorizing is the fundamental activity of thought, reasoning, and language.[9] Language then fundamentally involves making sense of human experience. Yet even before Adam named the animals, God had spoken to him, which implies that the *imago*

Dei already included all the foundational structures of thought, reasoning, and language. The cultural mandate, as it has been called, of Genesis 1:26-28 was given to both Adam and Eve, and therefore presumably took place following God's commandments to Adam (Gen. 2:15-17) and the activity of Adam in naming the animals (Gen. 2:19-20). Adam's naming of the animals prior to the entry of sin into the world and prior to the creation of Eve suggests not so much that he created the characteristics of each animal but rather that he formulated a descriptive taxonomy. Edward Hall writes: "Science and taxonomy go hand in glove. In fact, implicit in every taxonomy is a theory of the nature of the events or organisms being classified."[10] In classifying the animals, Adam thereby created the first human culture, which he would have passed on to Eve and then their descendants. That culture, like Adam's DNA, may well have carried within it the potential for a wonderful variety of expressions within the boundaries set by the Creator.

Just as the genetic potential for all races and physical traits, along with all natural talents, was present in Adam's DNA, so also the potential for diversity in conceptualization and expression was also present. Hereditary aptitudes for pattern recognition, logic, mechanics, mathematics, psychomotor skill, music, and language were all part of the biodiversity built-in within the genetic DNA of Adam and Eve. The individual experiences encountered by their descendants, in God's providence, provided occasions for their individual aptitudes to express themselves. Not evolution, but God's creative design for differentiation within the boundaries of human kind best accounts for such diversity. Kreitzer, in a helpful recent treatment of the subject, argues cogently that, over time, geographical separation of human beings naturally results in cultural-linguistic diversity, a diversity which was intended by God from the beginning.[11] Yet even apart from geographical distance, other more intrinsic factors, as previously described, also may contribute to diversity of conceptualization and expression of human thought.

Genesis chapter ten, the "table of nations," tells the reader three times (vv. 5, 20, and 31) that the descendants of Noah spread over the earth "by their clans, their lands, their *languages* [Heb. *lashonotham*, their tongues], and their nations" (italics added). The process may have been well underway by Peleg's time. Peleg was at least five generations from Noah (perhaps more if one takes "begat," Heb. *yalad*, to mean "became the progenitor of" Gen. 10:22-25), and lifetimes were longer (not shorter, as claimed by many secular evolutionists) than at present. The global population by Peleg's day must already have been substantial, which may imply that clans and language distinctions were also well along in development, although they still shared a common speech and identity as well. Peleg's name means "division," and the text then explains, "for in his day the earth was divided" (v. 25). Many commentators take this reference to allude to the Babel narrative which immediately follows the list of nations. A plausible understanding of chapter eleven is that, as the descendants of Noah began to multiply and spread out, and as language distinctives proliferated, they consciously retained an essential intercultural core of vocabulary, syntax, and worldview which made continued communication readily accomplished. Resisting the command of God to "fill the earth" (Gen. 1:28), they sought to maintain for themselves a common capital and anthropocentric identity (Gen. 11:4). God frustrated their man-centered rebellion by removing the communicative common ground, plunging them into confusion and conflict, and driving them apart. Yet God's judgment was also gracious, because compartmentalizing sin restrains it, and because God's judgment resulted in the fulfillment of God's creative purpose and blessing as expressed in Gen. 1:28.[12]

Robert Candlish observes that the scattering recorded in Genesis eleven apparently was not anarchical, but rather followed a pattern: "The division of languages, therefore, was made subservient to an orderly distribution of the families of each of Noah's sons. They were scattered abroad; but it was in a regular manner, and upon a natural principle of arrangement—with a joint regard to kindred and to language—according to their families and their tongues."[13]

The Apostle Paul presented this truth to the Athenians, proclaiming the unity of human origins and the reality of God's sovereignty over the dispersion of the nations (Acts 17:26). Willem VanGemeren further notes that the resulting diversity was not itself sinful, nor did it represent the thwarting of God's creative and redemptive purposes. Commenting on Genesis eleven, he writes: "Multiplication, migration, population of the earth, and the rise of civilizations are natural expressions of the blessings of God. The Table of the Nations contains no comment or allusion to the natural superiority of any region, race, or political entity."[14]

Genesis 1:28 provides an essential background for understanding Gen. 11:4 (". . . lest we be scattered over the earth."). God's creative purpose for humankind was that they should "fill the earth and subdue it" (Gen. 1:28 KJV). In Genesis 2:8 God planted a garden and placed Adam in it. God pronounced the entire planet "very good" (Gen. 1:31), but the entire planet did not comprise the garden. The question naturally arises: How could Adam and his descendants "fill the earth and subdue it" without leaving Eden? Prior to the Fall recounted in Genesis three, a sinless Adam could have subdued the earth by extending the boundaries of Eden, following the pattern provided by God himself in the cultivated and divinely-ordered beauty and productivity of Eden. The Fall resulted in Adam's expulsion from Eden along with frustration as he attempted to interact with his environment (Gen. 3:17-19). Nevertheless, God's creative purposes expressed in his blessing (Gen. 1:28) were not overthrown. Following Gen. 1:28, the post-lapsarian promises of Gen. 3:15 and 12:2-3 bracket the Babel narrative and are redemptive and messianic, providing pivot points for God's global purpose for humanity as He unfolds that purpose in history. This purpose is a history which describes the struggle between two "seeds" (Gen. 3:15). The intervening Noahic narrative, chapters six through eight, powerfully illustrates the motif of judgment and renewal, grace, and the salvation of (and through) a believing remnant. Yet chapters ten and eleven demonstrate that the ultimate source of the problem, the corruption within human nature itself, is still present and capable of explosive malignant growth. Humans urgently need a new heart, a motif which is subsequently developed in the Old Testament (Deut. 30:6, Ps. 51:10, Jer. 31:31-34, and Ez. 36:25-27). Only the promised Seed makes this heart possible. Taken together, the passages generate a missiological framework. In Christ both redeemed humanity and creation itself are ultimately restored (cf. Rom. 8:19-23). Christ does not remove diversity, but confusion and conflict—both ecologically (within creation) and relationally (within the community of the redeemed).

The New Testament describes how believers are born spiritually into the family of God and are endowed with a diversity of spiritual gifts (Eph. 4:4-16). Together, believers form one Body in complementary unity. Indeed, gender also provides complementarity; Adam finds in Eve a help "meet" for him (Heb., "according to his aspects"). God created male and female and together called their name "Adam" (Gen. 5:1-2). Believers are equal in their standing before God (justification "in Christ Jesus," Gal. 3:28) but are not identical in their appointed service, or function, within the believing community (1 Cor. 12:29-30).

In his vision of heaven, John witnessed a numberless multitude "from every nation, from all tribes and peoples and languages" worshiping God (Rev. 7:9-10). The question arises: How did he know? The answer may be that the Holy Spirit simply imbued John with that insight. More likely, he could see and hear for himself. After all, John describes what they were wearing and carrying and what they were saying. Now, it might be easy to tell differences of facial appearance and stature, even though all wore white robes and held palm branches. The statement of languages proves more problematic however.

How could they speak in different languages and still praise God in a loud voice with a common doxology? The answer may be that John heard them expressing a concert of praise, wherein refrains of praise in the various languages reverberated in succession or else came in and out at well-synchronized points as a modern descant might do, or just as instruments would in an orchestrated symphony or as voices would in well-harmonized parts of a choral anthem. If John received, along with his vision, the restored ability to understand those languages, he would surely have been deeply moved by what he saw and heard. Indeed, he may have partially experienced the same phenomenon earlier at Pentecost (Acts 2), where linguistic diversity was not erased, but affirmed. The unifying truth of the Gospel comprised the content of the message on that occasion. Pentecost is, strictly speaking, more a healing of Babel than a reversal of Babel. The Spirit's outpouring at Pentecost resulted in true hearing, as well as speaking, because the message was not only linguistically comprehensible (v. 6), but actually registered on some three thousand of those present (v. 11). They responded to Peter's explanation and appeal: "So faith comes from hearing, and hearing by the word of Christ" (Rom. 10:17 NASB).

Others may raise the objection that there should be no distinctive or exclusive knowledge in heaven, that all citizens of heaven should share knowledge and vocabulary. The answer to this objection appears earlier in the book of Revelation, when the one who overcomes is told that Christ "will give him a white stone, with a new name written on the stone that no one knows except the one who receives it" (Rev. 2:17, ESV). Uniqueness, far from diluting unity, improves it. Quite apart from any effects of sin (which are no longer present in heaven), God's creatures are yet finite. Each one can comprehend only a tiny part of the fullness of the divine majesty. Several examples demonstrate the principle of improved unity through uniqueness. Together, in complementary fashion, the Body of Christ understands more fully (Eph. 3:18), much as the perspectival vantage points of the four Gospel writers serve to complement and reinforce one another. God creates the man and the woman and calls their name "man" (Heb. *adam*, Gen. 5:1-2). The perspective of both genders contributes to a more complete reflection of the image of God. Uniformity of perspective would not have served as well. Just as depth perception requires parallax, which in turn can only be provided by multiple angles of sight, so also the testimonies of the Gospel writers are not contradictory, but complementary. So, too, may be the languages of heaven.

Summary and Missiological Conclusions

The biblical data may not permit a conclusive verdict. However, a plausible explanation of the Babel narrative interprets God's judgment at Babel as bringing confusion and conflict, while at the same time accelerating the process of human linguistic diversity and providing an impetus for humanity to fill and subdue the earth.

Children gradually learn the vocabulary of their parents, but share from early childhood the core language skills needed to communicate. In the same way, human beings of differing languages still can and do communicate with one another, as long as they share at least a basic core of understandings and expressions, some *lingua franca*, by which they may express themselves. Without such a common medium of communication, the speakers may never ascertain any shared meanings.

If one understands the Babel narrative to be the event at which God removes the shared core of meanings (the "one language and same words" used in common) from humanity, the outcome is loss of the ability to cooperate and a resulting accelerated dispersion. That interpretation clearly falls within the possible ways of understanding the text and merits further exploration.

Missiological implications of such an understanding of Babel are significant. For one thing, cultural and linguistic diversity are then a blessing rather than a curse. God receives more glory from harmonious unity within diversity than he does in a bare singularity resulting from uniformity. Complementarity, rather than conformity, glorifies God more. Harmony is essential, however, for without it diversity leads to chaos. Moises Silva observes: "We need not infer that linguistic uniformity is a goal of redemption, but surely the ability to understand each other and thus to praise God in unanimity is very much part of his saving grace to us."[15] Creative ways of preserving diversity while promoting harmony in worship and service to God are then positive values and goals for the Church.

A second missiological implication which follows from the first is that the message of the Gospel must be, and is, translatable into every human language. The ascended Christ, having received the promised Holy Spirit in our humanity (Hebrew, "in Adam," Ps. 68:18; Eph. 4:8) as our covenant head, poured out the Holy Spirit at Pentecost (Acts 2), not in order to overturn the judgment pronounced at Babel but in order to bring healing from it.[16] The Holy Spirit, in turn, empowers the word of God as it is communicated to those who hear, even across cultural-linguistic barriers. Bible translations which respect the cultures and languages of the recipients are therefore both legitimate and necessary. Diverse styles of worship are also appropriate, subject to the boundaries God himself has given in the Bible.

Theologically, it is only in Christ, the Head, that the whole body (Church) finds its completeness and builds itself up together in love. Believers honor their Creator by recognizing their finitude and their complementarity within the community of faith. Yet even together, the Body of Christ is incomplete apart from the Head, Christ himself. In his human nature, he is one of us (incarnate and finite), but simultaneously, in his divine nature, he belongs to the Triune Godhead (divine and infinite). The Church is his body, the fullness of him who fills all in all (Eph. 1:23). Through their spiritual union with Christ, believers are, even now, enthroned in heavenly places (Eph. 2:6).

In Christ the Head, the whole Body fits together and finds integration and identity despite all its diversity (including language). Christ gives his people their common purpose and kinship, bringing relational healing. The Bible associates healing with hearing (Jn. 12:37-41). Missions must never substitute humanization for proclaiming Christ, for he is the heart of the Gospel. Christ—and Christ alone—must remain the center of creation, of redemption, of mission, and of eschatological glory.

Notes

1. Edward T. Hall, *Beyond Culture* (Garden City, NY: Doubleday, 1977), 192-3.
2. Gordon J. Wenham, *Genesis 1-15*, Word Biblical Commentary, ed. David A. Hubbard and Glenn W. Barker, vol. 1 (Dallas, TX: Word, 1987), 238.
3. F. F. Bruce, *Commentary on the Book of the Acts* (Grand Rapids, MI: William B. Eerdmans, 1974), 64.
4. Allen P. Ross, *Creation and Blessing: A Guide to the Study and Exposition of the Book of Genesis* (Grand Rapids, MI: Baker, 1988), 234.
5. R. Laird Harris, Gleason L. Archer, Jr., and Bruce K. Waltke, eds., *Theological Wordbook of the Old Testament* (Chicago, IL: Moody, 1980).
6. Wenham, 238.
7. Peter Berger, *The Sacred Canopy: Elements of a Sociological Theory of Religion* (Garden City, NY: Doubleday, 1967).
8. Ross, 230.
9. John M. Ellis, *Language, Thought, and Logic* (Evanston, IL: Northwestern University, 1993); Benjamin Lee Whorf, *Language, Thought, and Reality: Selected Writings of Benjamin Lee Whorf*, ed. John B. Carroll (Cambridge, MA: M.I.T., 1956).
10. Hall, 122.
11. Mark Kreitzer, "Toward a Covenantal Understanding of Ethnicity: An Interdisciplinary Approach" (Ph.D. diss., Reformed Theological Seminary, 2003).
12. Warren A. Gage, *The Gospel of Genesis: Studies in Protology and Eschatology* (Winona Lake, IN: Carpenter, 1984), 139.
13. Robert S. Candlish, *Studies in Genesis* (Grand Rapids, MI: Kregel, 1979), 176.
14. Willem VanGemeren, *The Progress of Redemption: The Story of Salvation from Creation to the New Jerusalem* (Grand Rapids, MI: Zondervan, 1988), 80.

15. Moises Silva, "Biblical Perspectives on Language," in *Foundations of Contemporary Interpretation: Six Volumes in One*, ed. V. Philips Long, et. al. (Grand Rapids, MI: Zondervan, 1996), 217.

16. Alan Richardson, *Genesis 1-11: The Creation Stories and the Modern World View* (London: SCM Press, 1953), 126.

Chapter Ten

Leadership and Teams in Missions—Jesus Style

Mike Barnett

Browse through your nearest mega-bookstore and you will be amazed at the number of titles on leadership. A flood of books and articles on leadership filled the literary shelves of our world throughout the 1990s and continues into the twenty first century[1]. Perhaps the most interesting aspect of this overflow of literature is that it is not limited to the business and management sections of our catalogs. Historical, biographical, psychological, political, athletic, international, organizational, and cultural perspectives on leadership abound. And yes, even the shelves of your local Christian bookstore will include a variety of options on leadership.

The impetus for this chapter flows from this professor's need to develop a viable seminary course on leadership and teams in the world of global missions and his prolonged frustration in not finding a text that moves beyond the singular perspective of the North American local church pastor or prophet. This chapter seeks to provide a framework for discussions on leadership and teams and how they apply to the world of missions today. Three models for leadership will be outlined and compared to three systems of organizational management followed by a discussion of three paradigms of missions leadership and management. Finally, a projected model of leadership and teams in missions will be proposed.

Three Models of Leadership

When we think of great leaders, we think of powerful, charismatic, strong-willed, and sometimes ruthless public figures. Great orators come to mind—those who can capture the imaginations of an audience and motivate them to action. Extraordinary leaders are usually inextricably linked to extraordinary circumstances or events. Some are infamous despots working for evil, while others are heroic leaders, singularly beloved as defenders of the good of humanity. When we consider outstanding leaders of modern history, we think of Abraham Lincoln, Vladamir Lenin, Mao Tse-tung, Winston Churchill, Adolf Hitler, Franklin Roosevelt, Mahatma Gandhi, Golda Meir, John F. Kennedy, and Anwar el-Sadat, all eminent communicators with charismatic personalities, doggedly determined to direct their publics through extraordinary times and circumstances.

What separates the despot from the heroic leader—the Hitler from the Gandhi? Surely both rely on demagoguery in its truest form, influencing and even manipulating the emotions of their followers. If we simply rely on leadership guru John C. Maxwell's definition that *"[l]eadership is influence . . . [n]othing more; nothing less,"* verifiable by whether or not the leader has someone following him,[2] then we cannot distinguish between a Mao Tse-tung and a Churchill. Both wielded massive influence and commandeered hordes of followers. But if we look at another criterion, perhaps we can delineate the despot from the heroic leader. In *The Leadership Wisdom of Jesus*, Charles C. Manz distinguishes the two according to their leadership style or *modus operandi*. He refers to the despot as the "strongman" and the heroic leader as the "visionary hero."³

Strongman

Strongmen (or women) use fear and intimidation to gain and maintain a position of autocratic influence and control over others. These are the infamous dictators of history who sometimes inherit their position of authority but frequently create it out of the context of their day, usually through much hard work and due diligence. Though they may have pure motives in the beginning, their style of leadership and system of leading inevitably result in despotism. Lenin tragically exemplifies one who initially sought the good of the masses but eventually succumbed to the temptations of tyranny. Occasionally a "benevolent" dictator or strongman emerges, but history is replete with examples of malevolent tyrannical leaders typical of the strongman model.

Of course, the realm of the strongman is not limited to politics. How many corporate bosses of the nineteenth and twentieth centuries ruled with a heavy hand, applying the proverbial stick rather than the carrot? Who has not worked for a corporate despot at one time or another? What about the typical frustrated sports coach who seeks self-worth at the expense of his or her students? How about sports legends like Bobby Knight, the former coach of the University of Indiana basketball team? Known more for his tirades and strongman antics than his superb winning record, Knight was forced to resign from the university because of his politically incorrect, autocratic tactics.⁴ If, as Manz proposes, strongman leaders depend on "fear-based compliance," and their followers jump at any opportunity to accelerate and celebrate their downfall,⁵ one wonders how many short-lived strongman leaders have left an unwritten legacy.

It should be no surprise that many strongman leaders reside in the world of Christian leadership. How many church denominations suffer at the hands of religious despots? The history of the church reads like a political soap opera as one theological or ecclesiastical faction after another postures for power—usually in the name of Christ. Church splits are often the result of a challenge of leadership wherein one or more strongmen or women ply their leadership "trade." Perhaps the level of intensity rises because it is the name of Christ which is being defended or undermined.

The strongman is still the stereotypical image of a leader. The concept of "leader" is still perceived as the "Boss" of the American business world or the "Governor" of English aristocracy, even in this age of empowerment and leadership paradigms as both art and science. The "leader" is the one who owns, runs, controls, and/or dictates the purpose, policies, and/or procedures of everything. In Africa, this is the "Bwana"—the one who pays for service, who employs the people. In the Arab world, the strongman is the "Zaeem," the proprietor, the one with the resources, the money, the time, the power, the name, the right, and the responsibility to lead the family, tribe, and/or community. The leader of Mediterranean culture is the "Godfather". And, yes, in many cases, the strongman remains the "Pastor" or "Preacher" of the Bible-belt church of America.

Visionary Hero

On the other hand, the Gandhis and Churchills of this world usually fit Manz's visionary hero model. Above all, the visionary hero has a just cause, an ethical motive, and is "able to create and articulate a captivating vision for others to follow."[6] These leaders do what is right in the face of evil and destruction. They may campaign for their position of power and influence, but they are often enlisted or promoted to their level of leadership in the midst of demanding circumstances. Though Churchill aspired to the highest government office of Great Britain, and prepared for it throughout his life, historians agree that but for the *blitzkrieg* of Nazi Germany, he likely would never have reached the office of Prime Minister. Churchill was the leader for the times. His vision saw beyond the despair of the people of Great Britain. His cause was just and right. He totally committed himself to doing whatever was required to assure victory. He knew the ravages and realities of war. He was a great visionary hero leader.

Visionary hero leaders are also found in the world of business. In *Built to Last: Successful Habits of Visionary Companies*, the authors identify what separates the very best companies in the world from the second best, the "gold medal winners" of corporate competition from the "silver medal winners." One of the key factors is that these companies, and their leaders, focus on "more than profits."[7] Theirs is a higher cause, a more noble purpose for the company. This often benefits humanity and/or society as a whole and is reflected in the company's core values. The industry giants George Merck II of Merck & Company (the pharmaceutical giant), Masaru Ibuka of Sony, David Packard of Hewlett-Packard Company, and Robert W. Johnson of Johnson & Johnson each led their companies to achieve something beyond profits or the bottom line. They cast a vision of conquering disease, pioneering electronic entertainment, providing technology services, or promoting the art of healing on a global basis and for the benefit of all humanity. Today, their companies are the gold medal winners who bested their competitors (Pfizer, Kenwood, Texas Instruments, and Bristol-Myers, respectively).[8]

The church has had its share of visionary hero leaders. These are the charismatic preachers and teachers of the twentieth century evangelical world of faith. Leaders such as Robert Schuller, Pat Robertson, Dr. James Dobson, Beth Moore, Bill Hybels, Rick Warren, Charles Stanley, Anne Graham Lotz, and Ed Young, to name a few, are not just "taking a walk" by themselves (see note 1) but are leading tens of thousands of Christian pilgrims on their faith journeys. They cast a God-sized vision, bigger than life itself, and in the process become celebrity-heroes of the faith. They author best-sellers, host radio and TV shows, appear on Oprah, counsel presidents and kings, and sometimes pastor the mega-churches of our age. They become a marketing "brand" with a reputation and message that is singularly identifiable. And many of them stay true to the higher cause and calling of the gospel. They are visionary hero leaders.

Servant Leader

The third model of leader is the servant leader. Interestingly, the modern concept of "servant leadership" grew out of the teaching and experience of a former business executive and university lecturer who focused on organizational management and leadership policy. Robert K. Greenleaf's *Servant Leadership: A Journey into the Nature of Legitimate Power and Greatness* is the classic text on principles of servant leadership. Though Greenleaf was a "non-theological" and self-proclaimed mystic when it came to religion, he understood the importance of the church and its role in shaping society, and he included in the church in his analysis of the concept of the servant leader.[9]

Greenleaf's servant leader is a "servant first," choosing to lead in order to serve, versus the "leader first" who later decides to serve others. The point of distinction is motive. The driving force of a servant-first leader is to insure that the needs of others are served above all else. In contrast, the leader-first leader may be driven by material gain, a hunger for power, or a need for influence.[10] The leader-first category fits the strongman model of leadership, whereas the servant-first category complements the ethical agenda of the visionary hero. In the shadow of the anti-establishment activism of the 1960s, Greenleaf's hope for the future rested on his "belief that among the legions of deprived and unsophisticated people are many true servants who will lead."[11]

Greenleaf posits eighteenth century American Quaker abolitionist John Woolman as his example of the servant leader who quietly persuaded people "one person at a time" and effected change "man by man, inch by inch" compared to the conventional public leader who measures leadership by the numbers of people he or she can muster. Greenleaf also cites Thomas Jefferson as a servant leader who knew who he was and set out to achieve his goal by "one action at a time" in order to achieve a great many accomplishments.[12] This pattern is not unlike Manz's best practice of "Mustard Seed Power," which violates the "more is better" mentality and promotes the concept that little things done well, step by step, can transform the world. Of course, Manz takes his mustard seed power idea from Jesus (Matthew 13). The servant leader does not set out to shine the light of fame and/or fortune on himself, but seeks to "concentrate on constructively spreading goodwill and serving as a positive model for others."[13] Indeed, this sounds like Jesus.

So, the servant leadership model is very much the Jesus model or Jesus-style of leadership. Motivated by an impulse to serve and save others, Jesus, the servant-first "suffering servant" (Isaiah 53), came to lead the spiritually and physically disenfranchised out of darkness and into light. He did it by modeling to the twelve, one by one, how to be servant-first leaders. He taught them, "If anyone wants to be first, he must be the very last, and the servant of all" (Mark 9:35 NIV). He warned them about strongman leaders who abuse their power and "lord it over" those they lead. But "not so" with servant-first leaders. They must become slaves to those whom they serve, "just as the Son of Man did not come to be served, but to serve, and to give his life as a ransom for many" (Matthew 20:25-28 NIV).

Jesus *is* the ultimate model of servant leadership. He kept to his agenda, one step at a time, planting tiny mustard seeds of hope and action which later spread throughout the known world. Though he was tempted to reach for fame, fortune, and power (Matthew 4), he chose instead to give his life for others. Imagine the Son of Man, Messiah, the Christ himself, kneeling and washing the feet of his students at the celebration of the Passover feast that night in Jerusalem two thousand years ago (John 13:5-17). What more vivid picture of radical servant leadership is there?

Summary

Three models of leadership were presented: the strongman, the visionary hero, and the servant leader. The strongman fits our general image of the leader—the Boss, Zaeem, or Bwana—in control, with the power, commanding and demanding others based on a self-serving agenda. These are the despots, the dictators, the tyrants playing out their parts on the world stage. Perhaps more importantly, these strongmen and women also act out their roles in the "off-Broadway" dramas of everyday life—in the office, school, marketplace, or church. Equally charismatic but without the sinister agendas, we have the visionary hero leader, a product of the times, seizing the moment to lead others through the trials of their circumstances for the well-being of all. Though they may relish in their victories, these heroes are about more than profits. They win the gold medals of life by standing for core values which benefit those under their influence. They are the heroes of our times. Finally, we have the servant leaders who are driven by the motive to serve others. They are, in essence, leaders by default, not by choice. Like the hero leaders, they work for good not evil, but their preoccupation is singularly to serve others for the sake of others that all might be transformed for the better. Jesus modeled this style of leader.

Three Eras of Organizational Management

As a complement to the three models of leadership discussed above, three eras of organizational management are presented along with analysis of how these models play out in church organizations and examples from the American presidency.[14]

Craft Shop and Family Farm

Students of organizational development often refer to the first management era as the "craft shop and family farm" system.[15] The small family-owned and family-managed shop or farm depended on the performance of family members for survival. The shop or farm focused on quality versus quantity of production and was limited in its ability to impact those outside the family circle. The head of the family was the leader, and every family member did his share to provide shelter, clothes, and food for the well-being of the family.

The craft shop or farm model had its advantages. It met the immediate physical needs of the family while nurturing the psychological needs of the group. It "'felt' like the family as people worked closely together in a highly interdependent manner with long-term relationships and stability that caused them to invest in and help each other."[16] It sounds a bit like "church," and in fact, the church in pioneer areas often developed along the same leadership lines as the small craft shop or farm.

Great leaders often manifest the leadership values, worldviews, and practices of their time and place in history. Perhaps Abraham Lincoln reflects the best of this craft shop and family farm paradigm. His rural upbringing along the frontiers of Kentucky, Indiana, and Illinois molded his character and conditioned his mind for the presidential challenge of saving the Union. To this day, we look upon Lincoln as a kind of father figure leader who led our young and vulnerable nation through its darkest hours.

Mass Production

The second era of leadership and management was the era of "mass production" exemplified by the innovations of Henry Ford and his automobile revolution. Ford based his assembly line method of production on the principles of the specialization of workers and the simplification and standardization of products. Quality was not abandoned, but efficient productivity and the ability to reach beyond the immediate circle of a family to the masses became the goal. The company was no longer an intimately related family group. Leaders evolved from caring father-figures to impersonal product champions while workers became interchangeable, like the parts they assembled on the line.[17]

Though this system met the physical needs of the immediate members of the company and reached beyond to the masses of society, it fell short of meeting the emotional needs of employees from the top down. Specialization resulted in fragmentation, which eventually undermined creativity, efficiency, and product quality. Such an impersonal system of management resulted in human costs of alienation, lack of fulfillment, and ultimately the loss of self-worth.

Is there a hint of the mass production paradigm in the growth of regional churches in the 20th century? Perhaps as the small farm church began to grow with its community, the need to serve the masses resulted in a kind of factory-line approach which threatened the sense of family and close-knit spiritual community. Standardization and specialization became the order of the day in churches as they divided into age-graded departments and ministries, each with its own kind of ministry manager, production budget, physical plant and so on. The pastor frequently became the CEO, charged with leading the entire organization from the top. Since he was no longer the specialized preacher and pastoral minister, the CEO-pastor often became the slave of many tasks and master of none. A further study of this apparent parallel development of social and church organizational leadership patterns is warranted.

Surely Franklin Delano Roosevelt reflects the leadership paradigm of his day. Roosevelt's aristocratic and often aloof character became the cherished symbol of the industrial and military power of a rebuilt nation defending freedom around the world. We became a nation of factory line specialists, first rebuilding our country under Roosevelt's New Deal, and later struggling to overcome Fascism. The leader fit the times and circumstances.

Team-Based Organization

The third era, which came into its own in the 1990s, was the "team-based organization" era of leadership and management. It was built upon the foundations of the previous two eras but utilized the concept of the team to advance quality and effectiveness. In fact, we are still in this third era of management paradigms today. It came to life with Eiji Toyoda (president of Toyota) as its catalyst in the 1950s. Toyoda discovered that the best results came when his employees "worked as a team, taking responsibility for improving their own work process!"[18] The team-based organization marked a shift from the capital intensive endeavors of Ford's simplified and specialized production model to a quick, responsive, adaptive, flexible system which flowed out of the creativity, skills, and strengths of the team members themselves. By the 1990s this team-based ideology had spread beyond the factory floors of car manufacturers to the board rooms of all types of organizations.

Once again, this paradigm shift in management is reflected in the life of the church. With the emergence of the "mega-churches" of the last quarter of the 20th century, a transformation of church leadership and "management" arose. Today the traditional role of the "small shop or farm" church pastor is endangered. The typical visionary hero leader may still fill the position of "pastor," but the role has become that of the entrepreneur who keeps the company of believers inspired, motivated, strategically focused, core-value-oriented and moving forward. No longer limited to the pulpit (literally and figuratively), nor to the management demands of the large church

CEO, these entrepreneurial pastors use books and other media to stamp their "brand" of church and core values on the hearts and minds of their company of followers. Such a church model requires a leadership team which often appears on the church bulletin as the traditional ministry staff but is increasingly home-grown, called, and trained from the ranks of the laity with all of their marketplace moxie and savvy. The "team at the top"[19] still looks to the pastor-entrepreneur for inspiration and vision, but the "Executive Pastor," in his new role, frequently leads the ministry team. Indeed, the teams at the bottom of these team-based churches sometimes reflect this pattern. In their attempt to turn "members into ministers," Saddleback Valley Community Church, in Orange County, California, offers a streamlined, team structure which resembles Mr. Toyoda's car company.[20] So the team-based paradigm of the 1990s has infected the church as well, and some argue that the new model is more biblical than the old! Alas, this is another discussion topic for the future.

Even the presidency of the United States reflected a paradigm shift in 2001 with the arrival of George W. Bush—a fairly unremarkable, somewhat unpolished, but surprisingly astute leader and experienced entrepreneur.[21] Bush's style of leadership contrasts with that of his predecessors. From the beginning, the story of the Bush administration was not about his leadership ability or charisma but the make up of his team. The public witnessed the assembling of a team of diverse, talented, experienced, and capable people who were leaders in their own right. The image was that of an empowered, potentially high-performance presidential team. A kind of corporate professionalism uncharacteristic of the White House emerged. History will ultimately judge the ability of this team at the top, especially in light of events since September 11, 2001, but the shift in style of management and leadership is clearly evident.

Summary

Three eras of organizational management have been presented: the small craft shop/family farm, mass production, and team-based organization. In each case, parallels to the world of the church were suggested and examples of American presidents offered as illustrations. Though this discussion of management models has been superficial at best, it provides a framework for discussing the next question: How do these leadership and teams models apply to missions today?

Leadership and Teams in Missions Today

A survey of leadership paradigms in modern western missions reveals a similar evolution to that of the leadership and organizational management models which have been previously discussed.

Missions Station

In the "Great Century" (nineteenth century) of colonial missions, the mission frequently functioned as a small craft shop or family owned and managed farm. In some cases the mission team was just that: Generally, the members of a single family, led by the father, were working together both for their own physical survival and the spiritual opportunity of their host community. Even in cases of cooperation between missionary families, a missionary outpost or station functioned as a small town community. One person tended the gardens, one the livestock, another the task of translation of Scripture, another education, preaching, teaching, and so on. Though the objective was to share the gospel to the masses, the craft shop model seldom reached more than a few host families outside the station. The strongman or visionary hero leader was at the helm, doing his best to guide the group in their mission of evangelization and/or church planting.

One of the best examples of this mission station paradigm was the "Serampore Trio" of William Carey, Joshua Marshman, and William Ward and their families near Calcutta, India in the early 1800s. These three missionaries comprised "one of the most illustrious examples of missionary teamwork in the history of the church."[22] One of the first mission stations in the modern missions movement, Serampore was modeled on the communities of the Moravian Brethren[23] and functioned as a kind of small town mission family. Everyone pitched in to ensure survival and to accomplish the mission. While Carey functioned as the senior leader, keeper of the gardens, social activist, and Bible translator, Ward focused on preaching and discipling, and Marshman and his wife Hannah focused on education and the development of schools. The Serampore station survived, and though it never saw the emergence of large numbers of converts or churches, it laid the groundwork for those who followed.

Institutionalized Missions

As more missionaries arrived on the fields, the need for a mass production of missions services and "products" led to the development of institutionalized missions organizations. This was the characteristic "Mission" body of the twentieth century. No longer the single or small cluster of families, a sophisticated administrative organism of product management emerged. Still led by a strongman or visionary hero, these missions often mirrored the systems of polity and decision-making of their sponsoring churches—complete with spiritual leaders, worship services, administrators, committees, retreats, annual budgets, business meetings, and even a well-used copy of Robert's Rules of Order.

In the best cases, this mass production model for missions opened the door to move beyond the coastal ports of safe havens into the unknown challenges of the inlands. The institutionalized mission provided necessary infrastructure and resources to support missionaries beyond their urgent concerns of survival and immediate community. Missionaries became mobile specialists, highly educated and trained in ministries of agriculture, medicine, education, translation, evangelism, church planting, project coordination, and so on. The institutionalization of missions followed. The mass production model resulted in more missionaries, resources, Bibles, schools, hospitals, relief and development projects, converts, and churches in more countries than ever before.

Like the mass production management model, the downside of the institutionalized mission was often the alienation and dehumanization of missionaries. Powerful institutionalized missions often "went to seed" as they became self-absorbed and fostered an ethos of inter-mission politics, posturing, cronyism, and turfism. This sounds a bit like some churches, does it not? In worst cases, doing the "main thing" of missions—evangelism and church planting—became secondary to doing the business of the mission. Perhaps the best caricature of this syndrome is the infamous "Annual Mission Meeting," usually conducted in the late summer months with all members of the mission attending. Horror stories abound of the great missionary battles fought not on the front lines of the fields of the harvest, but in the halls of the annual mission meeting, slugging it out for programs, budgets, houses, cars, and the right to remain in the mission.[24] Of course, the employee versus management confrontations of the mass production era of industry also manifested themselves in the institutionalized mission with a "them and us" mentality persisting between the missions agency and the missionaries as represented by their mission.

The institutionalized mission was the leadership and management paradigm of its day. In many cases it advanced the mission cause in a healthy and productive way. Like the mass production system of Henry Ford, it had its shortcomings. As the nature of missions changed, so did the needs for leadership and management. A new day was dawning—one of fast, flexible, and focused teams of missionaries.

Missions Team

Finally, the team-based organization paradigm of management appeared in the world of missions. As the evangelical missions community focused on the least-reached peoples on earth, the need for streamlined, tightly focused, strategic people group or population segment teams emerged. The trend for the personalization of missions and a "hands-on" experience called for missions teams that were able to communicate in real time with constituency and client alike. The information age and technology removed the institutional barriers of the past age. The missions agency bottleneck was shattered and creative "outside the box" strategic thinking became the order of the day. Right before their very eyes, the institutional mission and its bureaucratic agency became obsolete. The call for teams rang out!

Agencies began to scramble for team technology that would heal their organizational wounds and unleash their missionaries to complete the unfinished task of reaching all peoples on earth with the gospel. A new excitement about missions spread throughout the homelands of the Western sending agencies. A missionary was no longer seen as an eccentric, Lone-Ranger, Bible-in-hand and pith-helmet-on-head, preaching in the bush of Africa. Missionaries could be on the cutting edge of strategic thinking and acting. In short, anyone could be a missionary or at least on mission with God. It seemed that all you needed was a team!

Some best practices for missions teams were developed. As early as 1993, a team-based organization model came out of Frontiers, the Western-based agency which focuses on reaching the Muslim world. Frontiers' co-founder and former director, Greg Livingstone, proposed a "New Testament missionary team model" complete with an entrepreneurial team leader and various "people people" who carried on the front line tasks of "friend-makers," "hosts," "evangelists," "prophets," "teachers," and so on.[25] Livingstone would be the first to admit that the Frontiers team approach is not a magic solution to the challenge of teams, but his was one of the first bold, self-critical attempts at a new kind of team paradigm.

A significant move to team-based missions came in 1997 when the International Mission Board (IMB) of the Southern Baptist Convention moved from a mission-based to a team-based organization. The IMB assembled over sixty of its overseas regional leadership team members along with its executive US-based leaders for four weeks of leadership training. The session included a three-day ropes course session at Berry College in Rome, Georgia, and the rolling out of the team-based concept courtesy of the Miller/Howard consulting firm. It was the beginning of a painful but productive shift to a team-based model which strives for a structurally "flat" organization with de-centralized strategy development and implementation. Of course, such a radical change took its toll on personnel who were comfortable with the status quo but it was truly a bold move on the part of IMB President Jerry Rankin and his colleagues.

The results are still out, but the IMB is undoubtedly a more streamlined organization, focused on strategic purposes and goals more than the self-perpetuation of the system. Outdated policies were "put on the shelf" and projects that didn't fit the purposes or goals of individual teams were scrutinized. The transformation is still in process. The IMB shift provides an interesting case study in the dynamics of team development. According to Katzenbach and Smith's study on teams, at least five types of teams fall on the "team performance curve": single-leader work group, pseudo-team, potential team, performing or real team, and high performing team.[26] This author has witnessed and worked with all five types of IMB teams over the past seven years. The IMB and other missions agencies have truly entered the team-based era of missions leadership.

Leadership and Teams in Missions Tomorrow

Now the question presents itself: "Where does the servant leader fit in the paradigms of missions leadership and management?" Surely there have been examples of servant leaders throughout the history of missions, but has there been a real trend or movement toward this Jesus-style of leadership? Even in the "missions team" paradigm mentioned above, the leader still usually fits the role of visionary hero. Perhaps that is why many of these new missions teams are merely "pseudo-teams," that try to "become a team" simply for the sake of "being a team" without committing to the discipline of teamwork for the sake of achieving a common purpose or goal.[27] Real teams are "small group[s] of people with complementary skills committed to a common purpose and set of performance goals"[28] and who are devoted to fulfilling God's mission of establishing worldwide church planting movements (CPMs).[29] What if the missions community really learned to replicate "real teams"?

Empowered Teams

The secret to the success of team-based missions organizations for tomorrow may lie in their ability to develop servant or Jesus-style leaders to lead missions workers to become "empowered teams." In his book *The Empowered Leader: 10 Keys to Servant Leadership*, Calvin Miller comes close to the concept of an empowered team. He even poses the question of whether a book on "empowered leaders" can truly be about "servant leadership." In synthesizing the writings of earlier leadership gurus, he comes closer to capturing the essence of servant leadership, yet he still falls short.

Missions leadership is not primarily about being the empowered leader or finding what it takes to become an empowered leader. It is about accomplishing God's purposes through an *empowered team!* We need to move beyond the self-serving motive which encourages becoming an empowered leader because "you can best achieve what you want in life if you are servant enough to help others achieve what they want in life."[30] We need a "Greenleafian," "servant first," Jesus-style leadership model (see above), focused on God's mission. We need leaders who have a passion for "more than profits" or personal gain and recognition. Better yet, we need the Jesus-style suffering servants, mentoring others to deny the rewards of worldly leadership for the sake of the Father. If we are going to get to empowered teams, we need servant leaders.

Perhaps Henry and Richard Blackaby's *Spiritual Leadership: Moving People on to God's Agenda* more closely identifies the kind of motive that drives a servant-first leader. A true "spiritual leader" is one who leads in a way that others discover and engage in God's agenda for their life and work. By the way, "Blackaby^2" (as my students affectionately refer to them) are not talking about leading others on to "God's agenda" as determined by the leader! This is a discipline of leadership that depends on the Holy Spirit to move those leading and those led "from their self-centeredness . . . into a relationship with himself."[31] A servant leader is able to lead a truly high performance, "extra-ordinary" team. Katzenbach and Smith define such a team as one with a "high degree of commitment and intensity" which develops into a "genuine concern for each other's personal success and growth that often transcends the life of the team" itself.[32] Is it possible to develop such an extra-ordinary team?

A Case Study

In 1997, a team of five came together to lead a newly created region of the IMB which included about 350 missionaries working in the 10/40 Window.[33] Though they shared some common experiences, the five came from various missions backgrounds, regions, and philosophies. They were recruited by the regional leader and approved by the executive leadership of the IMB, as a part of the first phase of a global reorganization of the overseas division of the missions agency. They knew very little about the task before them when they met for the first time.

At that first meeting, the regional leader focused his team on the task at hand—to lead the IMB's efforts to reach the peoples of their region for Christ. A God-sized vision soon crystallized into a picture of church planting movements among every people group flowing through their region to all peoples on earth. Their region's role or mission in accomplishing this vision would be to serve as catalysts for these church planting movements. The die was cast. A clear vision and mission were established. Before they completed their three-day retreat, they came to the realization that they could not accomplish their mission and see the reality of church planting movements among all peoples through their region. It could not be done! At least they could not do it. When they arrived at this understanding of the immensity of the task before them, the regional leader knew they were ready to begin their journey, serving alongside each other and those of their region. In those first few days, the mustard seed of an empowered team was sown.

Make no mistake about it, they did not set out to be an empowered team, but it happened. As this team began to implement a plan to accomplish their mission, the realities of the task became apparent. They were to lead a group of missionaries who had been members of four separate and sometimes competing former areas to become a region of partnering colleagues focused on reaching all peoples through their region. At the same time, as a part of this global reorganization of the IMB, they had the task of leading the region's missionaries to embrace a "New Directions" paradigm of doing international missions. The challenge was awesome.

How did this team perform? Did they accomplish their mission? After three years they had become an effective leadership team, with a high sense of mutual respect, trust, and love for each other. They experienced the kind of leadership which serves others for the sake of the cause. They mentored other teams in and outside their region on the principles of an empowered team. They developed an ethos reflected in their core value of "empowerment which results in shared responsibility and accountability." They learned much together. They traveled in pairs in order to more effectively lead others. They laughed, cried, and prayed together along their leadership journey. They empowered the teams they served to establish a foundation for continuing the task of facilitating church planting movements among all peoples through their region. These teams became known for their cutting edge methods and were called upon by other regions for equipping and advisement. This regional leadership team of the IMB became a "high-performance" or "extra-ordinary" team model for their organization. In a recent annual report, the data made this undeniable: more people groups engaged, more personnel, new churches started, new partnerships and alliances, streamlined delivery of support resources, and so on. More importantly, by focusing their region on the challenge before them and leading out in the work, they turned the minds and morale of their newly created region to the task ahead. No, they did not finish their mission of establishing church planting movements among all the peoples of their region, but they prepared the way for the next leadership team to refine their strategy and advance toward the common vision.

Today, four of the five remain with the IMB. Two are now based in the global headquarters, charting new courses for the global strategy of the entire organization. Two remain in their region as the new regional leader and associate leader of the region. The fifth is equipping others from a North American base of missiological education and training. A few months ago, they had a spur of the moment "reunion" and spent an evening reflecting on their experience. All agree that they grew in their understanding of Jesus-style servant leadership and the principle of empowered teams.

Conclusion

This chapter has addressed the much discussed topic of leadership and teams. We looked at some general models for leadership juxtaposed with three historical eras of organizational management. We considered how these models and eras influenced the church, and we took a glimpse at some presidential examples. We reviewed three paradigms of leadership and management from the world of missions, and we contemplated the empowered team paradigm—a potential future paradigm for missions which capitalizes on the servant leader model and the missions team paradigm. I hope that now we at least have a better framework for continuing discussions regarding this vital aspect of missions. Better still, perhaps for some, we have a new hope in the potential for moving to the next edge of leadership and teams in missions, Jesus-style.

Notes

1. Some of the author's favorites include: Henry T. Blackaby and Richard Blackaby, *Spiritual Leadership: Moving People on to God's Agenda* (Nashville: Broadman & Holman Publishers, 2001). J. Robert Clinton, *The Making of a Leader* (Colorado Springs: Navpress, 1988); James C. Collins and Jerry I. Porras, *Built to Last: Successful Habits of Visionary Companies* (London: Random House Business Books, 1999); Max De Pree, *Leadership is an Art* (New York: Dell Publishing, 1989); Jon R. Katzenbach and Douglas K. Smith, *The Wisdom of Teams: Creating the High-Performance Organization*, 2d ed. (New York: Harper Business Book, 1999); Charles C. Manz, *The Leadership Wisdom of Jesus: Practical Lessons for Today* (San Francisco: Berrett-Koehler Publishers, 1998); John C. Maxwell, *The 21 Irrefutable Laws of Leadership: Follow Them and People Will Follow You* (Nashville: Thomas Nelson Publishers, 1998) and *Developing the Leader Within You* (Nashville: Thomas Nelson Publishers, 1993); Calvin Miller, *The Empowered Leader: 10 Keys to Servant Leadership* (Nashville: Broadman & Holman Publishers, 1995).

2. Maxwell, *Developing the Leader Within You*, 1. Note Maxwell's favorite leadership proverb: "He who thinketh he leadeth and hath no one following him is only taking a walk."

3. Manz, 155.

4. It is worth noting that Knight's strongman tactics have been well-received in Lubbock, Texas, where, in his first year as head basketball coach, he has put the Texas Tech Red Raiders on the national map of basketball powers. So, the strongman leader still finds followers—a topic for another discussion.

5. Manz, 155.

6. Ibid., 43-44.

7. Collins and Porras, 46. Chapter 3, "More than Profits," provides an excellent analysis of companies whose reason for being rose above the bottom line.

8. Ibid., 47-61.

9. Robert K. Greenleaf, *Servant Leadership: A Journey into the Nature of Legitimate Power and Greatness* (New York: Paulist Press, 1990), 218.

10. Ibid., 13.

11. Ibid., 14.

12. Ibid., 29-32.

13. Manz, 153-54.

14. For a classic analysis of social developments or "waves" see Alvin Toffler, *The Third Wave* (New York: William Morrow and Company, Inc., 1980), 29, 222, 415-20.

15. Jennifer M. Howard and Lawrence M. Miller, *Team Management: Creating Systems and Skills for a Team-Based Organization* (Atlanta: Miller Howard Consulting Group, A Towers Perrin Company, 1994), 4. This section of the chapter is largely based on the author's participation in a three-day Miller/Howard Consulting Group course for missions leaders at Berry College, Rome, Georgia, November, 1997.

16. Ibid.

17. Ibid., 5.

18. Ibid., 5-6.

19. The "team at the top" concept is developed in Chapter 11 of Jon R. Katzenbach and Douglas K. Smith, *The Wisdom of Teams: Creating the High-Performance Organization,* 212-238.

20. Rick Warren, *Purpose Driven Church: Growth Without Compromising Your Message & Mission* (Grand Rapids: Zondervan Publishing House, 1995), 365-392.

21. Webster's defines "entrepreneur" as one who takes "considerable initiative and risk" in managing an enterprise. Bush has experienced the risk factor and likely understands the value of teams and teamwork in a way unlike his predecessors. Like Rick Warren, many of the pastor-entrepreneur leaders take the initiative and risk of planting and growing a church from

scratch—thus fulfilling the true definition of entrepreneur. Of course, some might argue that the riskier venture might have been to try to transform an existing church!

22. Timothy George, *Faithful Witness: the Life and Mission of William Carey* (Birmingham, AL: New Hope, 1991), 124. See also William R. Estep, *Whole Gospel—Whole World: the Foreign Mission Board of the Southern Baptist Convention: 1845-1995* (Nashville: Broadman & Holman Publishers, 1994), 14-23.

23. Estep, 16.

24. The author served for 12 years as a strategy consultant and missions support leader, working with a variety of international mission agencies and missionaries from various regions and teams. The International Mission Board (IMB) of the Southern Baptist Convention included a special section about the dynamics of the mission body in their career missionary orientation well into the 1990s. A "mock annual missions meeting" was held in every orientation to prepare the new missionaries for the dreaded annual mission meeting.

25. Greg Livingstone, *Planting Churches in Muslim Cities: a Team Approach* (Grand Rapids: Baker Book House, 1993) 100-115.

26. Katzenbach and Smith, xxiv.

27. Ibid., xx-xi.

28. Ibid., xxxiii, 21.

29. For more on CPMs see David Garrison, *Church Planting Movements* (Richmond, VA: Office of Overseas Operations, International Mission Board of the Southern Baptist Convention). A CPM is defined as a "rapid and exponential increase of indigenous churches planting churches within a single given people group or population segment." (Garrison, 7.)

30. Miller, x.

31. Blackaby and Blackaby, 23.

32. Katzenbach and Smith, xxiii.

33. The author had the privilege of serving on this team from 1997-2000. For more on the 10/40 Window, see Patrick Johnstone, *The Church is Bigger Than You Think: Structures and Strategies for the Church in the 21st Century* (Ross-shire, Great Britain: Christian Focus Publications/WEC, 1998).

Chapter Eleven

The Inescapable Christ:
The Significance of E. Stanley Jones' Christology for Twenty-first-Century Missiology

John Moldovan

Time magazine called him "the world's greatest missionary."[1] A spokesman of the government of India called him "the greatest interpreter of Indian affairs in our time."[2] In his brief review of this missionary, Paul S. Rees wrote:

> Missionary to India for over 50 years...
> Missionary to the world...
> More than three and a half million copies of his books in circulation...
> Translated into 18 languages and set in Braille...
> Lifelong evangelist...
> Half of his ashes now buried in India, near the Christian ashram which he founded, and half in a church burial plot in Baltimore, near the spot where he was converted...
> A man drenched with Christ![3]

In his dissertation on Eli Stanley Jones, C. Chacko Thomas confirms that "Asbury College considers Dr. Jones one of the most outstanding, if not the greatest, among its alumni."

The President of the Alumni Association of the College, Warner P. Davis, while introducing Jones to one of his congregations, said: "If E. Stanley Jones were Asbury's single gift to the world, all of the prayers, sacrifices, tears, and money invested in this college would be well paid."[4] Even Jones acknowledges the impact of his ministry with satisfaction:

> I have received many honors in my life - seven honorary degrees; have been chosen "The Methodist of the Year," but incidentally was so busily engaged in evangelistic meetings I couldn't stop to go to the function to receive the honor, so my daughter graciously received it on my behalf; was twice nominated in the Norwegian Parliament for the Nobel Peace Prize, but felt gratified that Dr. Martin Luther King was given the honor instead, for I know really that he had earned it more than I; have been given "The Gandhi Peace Prize"; several of my books have sold over a million copies each - *The Christ of the Indian Road* and *Abundant Living;* I have met emperors, kings, presidents, and prime ministers. And yet, as I look back, all these combined do not weigh in appreciation as much as the one single fact of the honor bestowed upon me when I was set apart as the bearer of good news, an evangelist. Something was washed from my soul when I went through the twenty-four hours of being immersed in the honors of being a bishop.[5]

This writer has witnessed the impact of Jones' Christology on both believers and unbelievers in one of the least expected places, specifically in Romania, Eastern Europe. During the dark days of Marxist-Leninist domination, one of Jones' devotional books, *Abundant Living,* was secretly introduced to the Christian community. The content resonated extremely well with the intellectuals and the younger generation. It became a hit. Jones' meditations offered a new perspective on life, God, Jesus Christ, and spirituality. The translation of the book into Romanian multiplied readership rapidly. The translated manuscript was duplicated through manual typing. The first carbon copies were rushed secretly by special couriers to other key cities. Working nonstop, dedicated Christian typists ensured the production of at least nine carbon copies for each page. In a few weeks, copies of the book reached thousands, each reader being limited to twenty-four hours access. University students, doctors, engineers, housewives, factory workers, preachers, pastors, and many of their agnostic friends read the book in one setting, some of them during the night. Jones' realistic approach inspired and even mobilized the oppressed Romanian believers. His amazing passion for Christ enthused thousands of people.

It is not the purpose of this chapter to explore his entire legacy or defend E. Stanley Jones against his critics. Rather, the purpose is to present accurately his theology, particularly his Christology, and to reveal the relation of his Christology to his missiological practices. The chapter starts with a brief overview of his formative years, examines some aspects of his theology, focuses on his Christology, explicates positions taken, identifies inconsistencies, weaknesses, and distortions, and concludes with innovative approaches to missions and missiological applications of his Christology for the twenty first-century missiologist.

This study, however, exhibits some inherent limitations. First, it is not an analysis of a fully articulated Christology. Second, not every aspect will be treated. For example, Jesus' sinlessness, self-designations as the Son of Man and Son of God, the virgin birth, and his Parousia will not be examined.

The Formative Years

Eli Stanley Jones was born in Maryland in 1884 into a middle class family. He experienced an initial conversion at age fifteen after hearing a message delivered by an Englishman from John Bunyan's church in England:

> 'Young men,' Jesus said, 'He that is not with me is against me.'
> It went straight to my heart. I knew I wasn't with him but I didn't want to be against him. It shook me. I turned to my chum and said: 'I'm going to give myself to Christ. Will you?' He replied: 'No, I'm going to see life first.' Then I saw I would

have to go alone, and did. I climbed over the young men, went down the steps and up the aisle to the altar, and took my place among the seekers. I felt undone and wept - wept because I was guilty and estranged. I fumbled for the latchstring of the Kingdom of God, missed it, for they didn't tell me the steps to find. I stood up at the close when they asked if it was all right with us. I wanted the kingdom of God, wanted reconciliation with my heavenly Father, but took church membership as a substitute. My mother came into my room next morning and silently kissed me before I got out of bed. Her son was a Christian. But I soon found I wasn't. I felt religious for a few weeks, and then it all faded out and I was back again exactly where I was before, the springs of my character and my habit formation unchanged.[6]

The real conversion came two years later. Evangelist Robert J. Baterman, a converted alcoholic, on fire with God's love came to Memorial Church. Jones recalled:

I said to myself, 'I want what he has.' This time I was deadly serious. I was not to be put off by catch phrases and slogans. I wanted the real thing or nothing. No halfway houses for me; I wanted my home. For three days I sought. During those three days I went to the altar twice. On one of those times my beloved teacher, Miss Nellie Logan, knelt alongside me and repeated John 3:16 this way: 'God so loved Stanley Jones, that he gave his only begotten Son, that if Stanley Jones will believe on him he shall not perish, but have everlasting life.' I repeated it after her, but no spark of assurance kindled my darkened heart. The third night came . . . A ray of light pierced my darkness.[7]

Following his conversion and filling of the Holy Spirit, Jones was led to go to Asbury College in Wilmore, Kentucky.[8] He became student body president and was invited to remain as an instructor. At that time he received a letter from the Methodist Mission Board saying: "It is our will to send you to India."[9] He reflected:

I was given no orientation, no briefing on what to do as a missionary, no manual of instructions on how to travel. I was given a Hindustani grammar, forty pounds in British gold, a ticket to Bombay via Britain, a handshake, and sent off. I was to learn by experience, by trial and error...At Bombay there was no one to meet me...[10]

Jones arrived in India in 1907 as a Methodist missionary. In 1911, in Lucknow, he married a colleague, Mabel Lossing, and soon moved to Sitapur. Their only child is Eunice Jones Mathews. In 1928, Jones was elected a bishop by the Methodist General Conference in the U.S.A., but resigned before his consecration, determined to continue his missionary work.[11] From the 1930s, his work extended to six continents. He received seven honorary doctorates, wrote twenty-nine books, received the Gandhi Peace Prize in 1961, and was twice nominated for the Nobel Peace Prize.[12]

Basic Theological Views

David Bundy states that "Jones was no 'ivory tower' theologian and made no pretense of being an academic theologian."[13] Moreover, Stanley Jones "has freely admitted on several occasions that both his theological and ethical thought have been modified and adjusted many times during recent decades."[14]

The Bible

Jones was convinced that historically, "Christians have fastened on three infallibilities: The infallible Bible, the infallible Christian experience, and the infallible Church." He sees the place of authority in the Christian faith "at the junction of these three coming together and all three saying the same thing. The objective reality (the infallible Bible) becomes the subjective reality (the infallible Christian experience) and is corrected and corroborated by the collective witness (the infallible church)."[15]

When he states that "the Bible is infallible - vitally infallible," he believes that, "if you take the way it shows you, you will infallibly find God. For it shows you Jesus and Jesus is that Way. Jesus is the Way from God and therefore the Way to

God . . . But there is only one Mediator between God and man—Jesus, and the Bible leads you to Him."[16] However, Jones failed to see an infallible Bible as a proper source of authority. He observed that insistence on a verbal infallibility rests upon very precarious ground, for of the hundreds of manuscripts at man's disposal, no two are alike. This fact led him to the conclusion that "vital infallibility" of the spirit is better than "verbal infallibility" of the letter. With this fact in mind, he insisted that final revelation must come through a person and not through a book.[17]

To Jones "the Bible is not the revelation of God; that would be the Word become printer's ink. But the Bible is the inspired Record of Revelation - the Revelation is seen in the face of Jesus Christ; the Word become flesh. He is the final and perfect Revelation of God."[18] He wrote:

> I go to my Bible every morning with a pen in hand expecting some fresh insight to come - an insight which I can note on a margin. And it seldom or never fails to come. You are striking deeper and deeper layers of truth all the time. This is a Divine Book for it reveals the Divine Person. Out of the words arises the Word. This Book creates expectancy. I am satisfied and yet on the stretch. And I know there is no end to This. This is It and forever![19]

View of Sin

Stanley Jones described sin as "a paralyzing hand on all we think and do and are."[20] Thus, "sin is unnatural, it is an imposition, it has the same function in life as a foreign body does when it is introduced into the tissues – it causes inflammation, infection, and if not got rid of, then death."[21] Men, according to Jones, "have thrown overboard the chart, the compass, the steering wheel, and the consciousness of destination. They are free from everything – everything except the rocks, and the storms, and the insufferable inanity of being tossed from wave to wave of mere meaningless emotion."[22]

The ethical impact of sin is seen in the "tremendous cost to God, to society, and to the individual. Since a loving God must be a forgiving God, it is important for man to realize that there can be no cheap forgiveness."[23]

According to Kenneth R. Thompson, "the chief weakness in Jones's doctrine of sin is his confidence that man can have an easy victory over sin if he desires it. "When sin begins to bully me," wrote he, "I quietly ask it to bend its neck and let me see . . . I am on the winning side." Man is fighting against a dead foe. In an effort to support his idea, the seventh chapter of Romans was labeled as pre-Christian theology. Jones denied that Paul the Christian could have had such a struggle with sin as is described there. Only "the guilt-ridden piety of modern neo-orthodoxy" could be based upon such theology, stated Stanley Jones in his latest work."[24]

Salvation

Despite some moments of weakness in his understanding of salvation, Stanley Jones believed that salvation was by grace rather than by works. This fact appears many times in his books. In 1930 he wrote that "men are to be born 'from above,' the power is from 'on high,' and the Holy Spirit is to come 'upon us,' not from within us." A similar statement is found in *The Christ of the Mount*. "We cannot lift ourselves into the Kingdom of God however hard we may strive, for if we were able to gain it by our own efforts, then our righteousness would be self-righteousness and that would cut straight across the very spirit of the new kingdom."[25]

Following Gandhi's death in 1948, E. Stanley Jones stated his view of salvation more clearly: "But I looked on salvation, not as an attainment through one's efforts, but as an obtainment through grace. I came to Christ morally and spiritually bankrupt with nothing to offer except my bankruptcy. To my astonishment he took me, forgave me, and sent my happy soul singing its way down through the years."[26]

God and Christ

> Man cannot know what God is like unless He communicates Himself through a word. If one says, "I can know God in my heart intuitively and immediately, without the mediation of a word," then the answer is: "But your 'heart' then becomes the medium of communication and knowing the heart as one does with its sin and crosscurrents and cross-conceptions he knows it is a very unsafe medium for the revelation of God." God must reveal Himself . . . I cannot read Thee unless I get a Word from Thee.[27]

To Jones this Word is "not a spelled-out Word, it is a lived-out Word. He is indeed the speech of eternity translated into the language of time, but the language is a Life. God's method is a Man. Jesus is God speaking to the man in the street. He is God meeting me in my environment, a human environment. He is God showing his character in the place where our characters are formed."[28] Elsewhere, Jones says, "If God isn't like Jesus, I am not interested in Him. For the highest I know in the realm of character is to be Christlike . . . When the disciples said, 'Show us the Father - it suffices us,' 'Jesus quietly said: 'He that hath seen me hath seen the Father,' and it was one of the greatest moments in human history."[29]

Jesus is God's authentic self-revelation. "He is 'the image of the invisible God,' 'the express image of His Person.' In Jesus we have the Key, the Master-Key that unlocks everything in the universe - God, man, life, material, spiritual, individual, and the collective. So we work from Him down to life. In His Life we see life."[30]

Jesus is also "the Divine Transformer who takes the high voltage of the Divine and transforms it into usable form. In Jesus we do see God face to face and do not die, but live,"[31] for Jesus is "God approachable, God available, God simplified, God lovable, the Word has become flesh."[32] "Jesus did not only bring the good news; he was the good news. Philosophies point to truths; Jesus said, 'I am the Truth.' Moralists point to the Way; Jesus said, 'I am the Way.' Religions point to the Life; Jesus said, 'I am the Life.'[33]

Christology

Jones excels on this topic. He states, "My Song will not be primarily about special events, but about the special event, about Jesus Christ. I have something to sing about - and the something is a someone."[34] He adds, "I don't have to defend Jesus. I have to present him, and he is his own defense. You don't have to organize a society for the defense of the sun because someone throws mud at it. The sun shines - that is its defense. Jesus defends himself, for he appeals to the soul as light appeals to the eye, as love fits the heart."[35]

Jesus as Redeemer

One can detect Jones' deep sense of gratitude from reading statements like this:

> He is so like me that I feel I might put my hand on his shoulder and say, "Brother man." But the moment I am about to do it I am confronted with that something in him that is unlike me. He confronts me with an offer of salvation that only God can offer. So instead of putting my hand on his shoulder, I find myself at his feet. It is this unlikeness to me that saves me. We need both the likeness and the unlikeness. He is like me, therefore my Example; he is unlike me, therefore my Redeemer. If he were only like me, he could not be my Redeemer; if he were only unlike me, he could not be my Example. It is the combination of the likeness and unlikeness that gives me what I need.[36]

When Dr. Kagawa, the Japanese saint, read the story of the crucifixion for the first time he was overwhelmed with emotion: "Is it true that cruel men persecuted and whipped and spat upon this Man Jesus?" he asked. "Yes, it is true," he was told. "And is it true that Jesus when dying on the cross forgave them?" "Yes, it is true." Then Kagawa burst into prayer: "O God, make me like Christ." And that became his life prayer.[37]

Resurrection

Jones believed in the physical resurrection of Christ. He wrote, "Do not tell me that He arose spiritually and that this is the meaning of the resurrection....For if the only victory here is victorious spiritual survival after death, it leaves behind the whole question of the worth-whileness of the whole fabric of the earth-side of existence."[38] Moreover, "God's last word is not the cross - it is the Resurrection. The Resurrection is God's seal of approval on the Cross. It is God saying: 'Well done, come up higher.' And He went to the right hand of final power."[39]

Jones' Criticism of Liberal Theologians

Tillich, the theologian, on returning from the Far East, said, "We should emphasize Christ, in the interest of universality, not Jesus." Jones disagrees:

> That is a serious misconception. It is Christ who limits Jesus. The idea of Jesus being the Jewish Messiah has cramped Jesus - the Incarnation of the Universal God, He was the Jewish Messiah, but He was very much more - and very different from the Jewish conception. You cannot say "Christ" until you have first said "Jesus," for Jesus puts His own character content into Christ.[40]

Jones has similar reservations about Bultmann:

> Bultmann has a large modern following. He told a friend of mine, head of a theological college, that "it would make no difference to my theology if Jesus never lived." He has accepted the Word become word, but not the Word become flesh, so it is something other than the Christian Gospel. But if Jesus never lived, then His teaching had no historical backing, no illustra-

tive content . . . The ideas of the Gospel are guaranteed by the fact of Jesus. Cut out that guarantee and your ideas have no guarantee.[41]

Regarding liberals, Jones explains: "They proclaim truths but not the Truth. They are syncretic but not evangelistic. They announce news, but not the Good News. They teach as the scribes, who echo the past, and not as the Christ who assumes control over the present and the future."[42]

Jones also acknowledges the danger of inclusivism:

> In an institution training men and women to go out for Christian service in foreign lands the question of Jesus saying, "I am the Way, the Truth and the Life" was explained by one of the teachers as being "an oriental metaphor, for there are many ways." And the head of the institution said: "Jesus has many names - Mohammed, Krishna, Buddha, Confucius." This is the moral and spiritual fog into which we get when we lose the Norm.[43]

Jones' scathing criticism continues:

> I know Jesus is under fire, under the intensest fire that has ever come upon him in any age. This fire is more cruel than any other, for it is from behind: he is being wounded by his own followers, so-called. I pick up a church bulletin in a university town and see the announcement: "Professor _____ will conduct a class on 'The Problem of Jesus.'" I inwardly reply: "Is Jesus a problem? He solves my problems; he has solved, does solve, and will forever solve my problems." So I smile - and sing. Another professor of a theological seminary said in an address: "We know little or nothing about Jesus; therefore I can dismiss him cavalierly." I am not angry; I smile a pitying smile and reply, "The conclusion comes out of the premise. You dismiss him cavalierly, for you know little or nothing about him. Did you know him by surrender and faith and obedience, you would not then dismiss him cavalierly, but you would fall at his feet with the doubting Thomas and say, 'My Lord and my God.'" So I dismiss this witness cavalierly. He knows little or nothing about Jesus; hence dismissing Jesus means he dismisses himself from serious consideration.[44]

Historical Jesus

Jones once replied to a professor regarding the historical Jesus, saying, "Was he the creation of the imagination of the early Christians? Does the demythologizing process now going on succeed in making Jesus himself a myth? That raises more problems than it settles."[45] Jones continues:

> Did the early church produce him? Who were the early church? For the most part they were the ignorant scum of humanity transformed. Paul said: "Make no mistake: no fornicator or idolater, none who are guilty either of adultery or homosexual perversion, no thieves or grabbers or drunkards or slanders or swindlers, will possess the kingdom of God. Such were some of you," (I Cor. 6:9-11). What produced the early church out of that material? The impact of the living Christ. Could they in turn produce Christ out of their imaginations? "Out of their imaginations" - out of imaginations soaked in the impurities of a decaying age? Then again, the inventors would be more astonishing characters than the hero. Bad men could not have created him, and good men, however good, would not and could not create him. For the "attempt to impose divine qualities upon the framework of human nature has always resulted in a monstrosity" - "always" except in the case of Jesus of Nazareth. For in him divine qualities were not imposed upon human nature, but exposed through human nature. . . If the apostles or the early Christian church created Jesus, who created them? The moment they would try to create Jesus out of their imaginations those imaginations would be corrupted and made incapable of producing such a character. Everything said about Jesus was merely an extension of the vitality in Jesus himself.[46]

Jones extends his line of argument with passion:

> What Jesus said in history became true in experience. He said he was a Savior. They tried it and found themselves saved, not from hell, but from what they had been, to what they wanted to be and ought to be. When Jesus said, "Come unto me and I will give you rest," they came and found it exactly as he said. They were at rest from guilt and frustration and emptiness. Everything . . . he said in history was verified in experience. The two kinds of reality, objective and subjective, were coming together

and verifying each other. It was so then; it is so now; I challenge anyone, anywhere, to expose his inner life to Jesus Christ in repentance and faith and obedience, and I will tell what will happen - tell with an almost mathematical precision. Such a person will be changed, profoundly changed, in character and life; and he will know it in every fiber of his being.[47]

Stanley Jones the "Modernist"

Dr. Bob Pierce, addressing a large gathering of conservative Christians, said: "They say Stanley Jones is a modernist. I've seen him on his knees, poring over the Bible, for four hours in a rat-infested shed in India. What kind of modernist is this?"[48]

C. Thomas Chacko defends Jones' stance on various issues:

> He still holds with the Fundamentalists the outstanding things about Christ: the virgin birth, the atonement of sin, the miracles of Jesus, the inspiration of the Scriptures and the new birth, while he is with the Modernists in the following the scientific method of asking for the facts in religion and of applying the Gospel to the social as well as to the personal.[49]

Jones also defends his views as orthodox:

> I belong neither to the Fundamentalists nor to the Modernists. I trust I belong to Christ and am a Christian holding the Fundamentals of the Christian faith and holding them with an open mind, so that they may be under the constant correction of the mind of Christ. The ultimate standard is Christ's living mind . . .[50]

Jones' Innovations in India

The Christ that Stanley Jones presented would be "the disentangled Christ - disentangled from being bound up with Western culture and Western forms of Christianity. He would stand in his own right, speaking directly to the needs of persons as persons without any . . . entanglements."⁵¹ The following story illustrates this approach:

> A friend of mine was talking to a Brahman gentleman when the Brahman turned to him and said, "I don't like the Christ of your creeds and the Christ of your churches." My friend quietly replied, "Then how would you like the Christ of the Indian Road?" He saw him dressed in Sadhu's garments, seated by the wayside with the crowds about him, putting his hands upon the heads of the poor, unclean lepers who fell at his feet, announcing the good tidings of the Kingdom to stricken folks, staggering up a lone hill with a broken heart and dying upon a wayside cross for men, but rising triumphantly and walking on that road again. He suddenly turned to the friend and earnestly said, "I could love and follow the Christ of the Indian Road."⁵²

Roundtables

This strategy is explained as follows:

> The meetings for the Christians are usually in the churches, and the night meetings for the non-Christian public are usually held in public halls, theaters, school halls, or out-of-doors in compounds of various kinds. The non-Christian on the whole will not come in large numbers to churches, so we go to a neutral place and call them "lectures." Prominent non- Christians usually preside the first few nights. This is an asset and a liability: an asset in that it tends to naturalize the meetings, as one of their own is presiding, and a liability in that there is a custom in India to make "chairman's remark" at the close of the address. These "remarks" give the chairman the opportunity to blunt the point of the address by saying, "Very good, but all roads up a mountain lead to the same summit. So all religions lead to God." That is the stock reply to the presentation of Christ as the Way. I leave it without reply, for the last few nights are under Christian chairmen. I usually take a broad subject such as the world situation on the first night and the last night end on the cross . . . I have to answer those prejudices, bringing them out at the end to the foot of the cross. Sometimes my non-Christian chairmen, instead of trying to cancel what I say, say things that

add a plus to the address. For instance, a Hindu chairman said: "If what the speaker has said tonight isn't true, it doesn't matter; but if it is true, then nothing else matters."[53]

Ashrams

The ashram program was developed in an attempt to allow the people of the twentieth century "to see the Kingdom of God in operations on at least a small scale. It was the hope of Stanley Jones that even a small scale demonstration of the kingdom would encourage the over-all growth of the kingdom that now "is."[54] "Jesus Christ is the Guru of this Ashram" appears on the walls of the Sat Tal Ashram, the original Christian Ashram.[55]

Jones elaborates on these meetings:

> We step out of the Bible into the world around us to see how we can function as a church. Then after those two hours we have a Work Period, where we work with our hands . . . I usually end up the morning after the Work Period with a message on one of the main emphases of the Ashram-Jesus Christ and his uniqueness, the Kingdom of God, self-surrender, the Holy Spirit, evangelism.

> After lunch we have the Family Meeting in which we meet as an Ashram Family and ask the group to bring up any constructive suggestions for change - what can we do better? We remind them that if they do not bring up criticisms at the Family Meeting, they should not bring them up anywhere else, so that there will be no secret criticism.[56]

> After the Family Meeting there is recreation until 4:30, when we have Prayer Groups. The Prayer Group is not for the discussion of prayer; that would be the Word of Prayer become word; but groups that really pray - the Word of Prayer become flesh. The leader doesn't discourse on prayer; he simply directs the praying of the group. After supper there is a vesper service, and I finish up the day with an evangelistic service at night in which we give the group a chance to fix publicly the decisions made during the day.[57]

Significance for the Twenty First Century Missiology

The association of Christ and Christianity with Western civilization and the British rule proved to be a serious obstacle in presenting Christ to the East. Jones tried to detach Christ from the Western trappings. He called Christians in India to a deeper dedication to Christ. His task, as he understood it, was to present Christ and let the people of India make their own judgment.

Jones has also been regarded as a forerunner in interpreting Christ to the educated non-Christians. His devotional books have had a special appeal to seekers and new converts. Jones expressed his ideas clearly. Readers cannot easily forget his short but brilliant statements or his apt illustrations from science and psychology. He comes across as a sincere communicator.

The impact of E. Stanley Jones' Christology is projected in the areas which follow.

Effective Contextualization

Jones' immersion into the Indian culture offers an excellent platform for effective, receptor-oriented communication. Even a casual observer may quickly realize the relevance of his message, as Jones compares the Hindu and Christian ways of salvation.

> The Hindus give the three ways of salvation as: The Gyana Marga, the way of knowledge, or mind; the Bhakti Marga, the way of devotion, or emotion; the Karma Marga, the way of works, or will. They give you the choice of any one of the three ways. Jesus is all three ways in one: "I am the Way," a way of acting, of doing, of going, the Karma Marga; "I am the Truth," the way of knowing; the Gyana Marga; "I am the life," the way of emotion - the Bhakti Marga.[58]

Jones' acculturation is also seen in his conversation with a Chinese engineer: "'What do you believe about Jesus?' He replied: 'I believe he was the best of men.' 'All right,' I replied, 'let us begin there. If he was the best of men, he is your ideal, your standard. Then you will want to cut out of your life everything he cannot approve.'"[59]

"The Disentangled Christ"

Missiologists are making serious efforts to avoid the introduction of a Western Christ to culturally distant, unreached people groups. New, creative approaches must be considered. Part of Jones' success is due to methodology. His skillful innovations include the Christ of the Indian Road, the Roundtables, and the Christian Ashrams. Yet Jones points out that the obsession with modernity and cultural relevance could lead to severe problems. He warns: "If the church marries itself to the spirit of the times, it will be a widow in the next generation."[60] Jones affirms the uniqueness of Christ and rejects inclusivism:

> Arnold Toynbe is an able historian, but he missed his step when he said he no longer believed in one Incarnation, that he preferred the attitude of the Hindus who say that Vishnu incarnates himself many times. So he says he has given up an exclusive faith for a more inclusive faith in this regard.[61]

Jones believed that "one of the greatest dangers to the Christian movement in the East is the danger of syncretism. At the top there is a fading out of any clear-cut issue between Christ and other ways of life. There is a tendency to put flowers gathered from many places into a religious bouquet. The bouquet may be beautiful, but since it has no roots of its own, it withers and dies."[62] In his view,

> The gospel reaches down into the soil of each nation and picks out elements akin to its own nature. But here again the end is not a syncretism, for the law of life in Jesus Christ is the determining factor in the disposition of these assimilated elements. "Syncretism combines, eclecticisms pick and choose, but only life assimilates." The gospel repudiates syncretism, it refuses an eclecticism, but it does assimilate, for it is life.[63]

Christocentrism

Unlike John Hick who insists on a "Copernican Revolution," Stanley Jones stresses the Christocentric position. The center of Jones' messages is always Christ. "I try to make Him (Christ) my last word on everything," he says. One of the outstanding Hindu leaders once remarked, "We always know where Stanley Jones is coming out, for no matter if he begins at the binomial theory, he will come out at the place of conversion - conversion to Christ."[64] In 1928 E. Stanley Jones asserted that he "could not be satisfied with a standard any less certain than that found in Jesus. While Hinduism mingled the sublime and the ridiculous and offered no norm by which ethics might be judged, he found that the norm had been fixed for Christianity and that norm was Christlikeness."[65]

Emphasis on Recovering the Social Action

Long before the 1974 Conference in Lausanne, Switzerland, where John Stott made his ardent appeal for balance, Stanley Jones combined in his message the two aspects of the Christian Gospel: the personal and the social. The editor of *The Christian Century* writes, "[Dr. Jones] is one of the most precious assets of American Christianity. We have no other evangelistic voice who senses, as he does, the social implication of our Christian faith, and we have no social gospeller who is such an evangelistic voice . . ."[66]

Evaluations and Conclusions

Belief in the innate goodness of man led Stanley Jones into many pitfalls. Thompson elaborates:

> After an extended preaching tour of America he stated that he went across America for more than a year and a half and had not seen a single person speaking in an abusive tone to anyone. Such statements must be classified as sentimental optimism.

The same type of idealism is revealed in his conclusion that the young people of the high schools of America "never strike a false moral note."[67]

Thompson later remarks, "Excessive optimism concerning the goodness of man led Stanley Jones into many pitfalls as he predicted the early realization of the kingdom of God on earth."[68] The chief difficulty faced by the interpreter of the theology of Jones is his inconsistent use of certain terms.

In the early 1930's Jones came under the influence of Sherwood Eddy, who was promoting a society based upon the principles of socialism. As a result, Jones was too generous in his comparison of communism and Christianity. He asserted that Christianity has much more in common with communism than with fascism or Nazism. Both communism and Christianity were said to "aim for the well-being of the individual and the community. Both of them would try to embody the second commandment, 'Love thy neighbor as thyself,' and both would define the neighbor as a man apart from race and birth and color and class."[69]

The naïve optimism of Jones "was even more apparent as he stated his opinion in 1937 that 'thoughtful Communists cannot hold to their dogmatic atheism much longer.' He falsely assumed that the 'scientific' basis of communism would soon drive the intelligent adherents of communism to God."[70]

Later, Jones realized his naiveté. He came to see that "since communism has no God, it has no stable moral universe and is ready to use any means to achieve its goals. This moral opportunism is just one of the fatal defects of the Communist system."[71]

Jones' tendency to interpret scripture in a manner which fits into preconceived social ideas, the use of illustrations which are extreme in their sentimentality and sometimes misleading in their implications and excessive repetition of "pet" expressions and illustrations, represent some of his weak points.[72] One may also wonder whether the Ashram as a Kingdom of God movement is much better than the Church as the Kingdom of God movement.

Nevertheless, Stanley Jones was one of the most popular American preacher-evangelists of his generation. The focus of his message was Christ. The contagion of his faith originates in his personal experience of Christ. His determination to be an effective missionary led him to witness "before high and low, kings and peasants, what Christ has done for a bankrupt life."[73] "It is no exaggeration to say that Stanley Jones is more than an individual - he has become, in a fine sense, an institution."[74]

Notes

1. *Time,* 12 December 1938, 47.
2. *The Christian Century* 81 (12 February 1964): 216.
3. S. Paul Rees, "Drenched with Christ," *World Vision* 17, no. 4 (1973): 23.
4. C. Thomas Chacko, "The Work and Thought of Eli Stanley Jones with Special Reference to India" (Ph.D. diss., State University of Iowa, 1955), 12.
5. E. Stanley Jones, *A Song of Ascents: A Spiritual Autobiography* (Nashville, TN: Abingdon Press, 1968), 372.
6. Ibid., 26.
7. Ibid., 27.
8. Ibid., 64-5.
9. Ibid., 73.
10. Ibid., 75.
11. W. Richard Taylor, "E. Stanley Jones 1884-1973: Following the Christ of the Indian Road" in *Mission Legacies. Biographical Studies of Leaders of the Modern Missionary Movement,* ed. Gerald H. Anderson, et. al. (Maryknoll, NY: Orbis Books, 1994), 339.
12. James K. Mathews, "Jones, E. Stanley (1884-1973)" in *Biographical Dictionary of Christian Missions,* ed. Gerald H. Anderson (New York, NY: MacMillan Reference USA, 1998), 339-40; and M. Fackler, "Jones, Eli Stanley (1884-1973)" in *Who's Who in Christian History,* ed. J. D. Douglas and Philip W. Comfort (Wheaton, IL: Tyndale House, 1992), 282-3.
13. David Bundy, "The Theology of the Kingdom of God in E. Stanley Jones," *Wesleyan Theological Journal* 23 (1988): 59.
14. Kenneth Ralph Thompson, "The Ethics of Eli Stanley Jones" (Ph.D. diss., Southwestern Baptist Theological Seminary, 1960), iii.
15. Jones, *Song of Ascents,* 104.
16. E. Stanley Jones, *Word Became Flesh* (Nashville, TN: Abingdon Press, 1963), 243.
17. Thompson, "Ethics of Eli Stanley Jones," 79.

18. Jones, *Word Became Flesh*, 243.
19. Ibid., 283.
20. Thompson, "Ethics of Eli Stanley Jones," 65.
21. Ibid., 67.
22. E. Stanley Jones, *The Christ of the Mount: A Living Exposition of Jesus' Words as the Only Practical Way of Life* (Nashville, TN: Abingdon Press, 1931; reprint, Festival Edition, 1981), 9 (page citations are to the reprint edition).
23. Thompson, "Ethics of Eli Stanley Jones," 65.
24. Ibid., 68.
25. Ibid., 71.
26. Ibid., 72.
27. Jones, *Word Became Flesh*, 19.
28. Jones, *Christ of the Mount*, 30.
29. Jones, *Word Became Flesh*, 24.
30. Ibid., 67.
31. Ibid., 48.
32. Ibid., 25.
33. Jones, *Song of Ascents*, 98.
34. Ibid., 21.
35. Ibid., 107.
36. Jones, *Christ of the Mount*, 122-3.
37. Jones, *Word Became Flesh*, 288.
38. Chacko, "Work and Thought of Eli Stanley Jones," 124.
39. Jones, *Word Became Flesh*, 200.
40. Ibid., 139.
41. Ibid., 237.
42. Jones, *Christ of the Mount*, 121.
43. Jones, *Word Became Flesh*, 42.
44. Jones, *Song of Ascents*, 19.
45. Ibid., 100.
46. Ibid.
47. Ibid., 103.
48. Ibid., 44.
49. Chacko, "Work and Thought of Eli Stanley Jones," 111.
50. Ibid., 112.
51. Jones, *Song of Ascents*, 110.
52. E. Stanley Jones, *The Christ of the Indian Road* (New York: Abingdon Press, 1964), 23.
53. Jones, *Song of Ascents*, 112.
54. Thompson, "Ethics of Eli Stanley Jones," 113.
55. Jones, *Word Became Flesh*, 265.
56. Jones, *Song of Ascents*, 227.
57. Ibid.
58. Jones, *Christ of the Mount*, 104.

59. Jones, *Song of Ascents*, 103.
60. Ibid., 133.
61. Jones, *Word Became Flesh*, 40.
62. Jones, *Christ of the Mount*, 120.
63. Ibid., 110.
64. Chacko, "Work and Thought of Eli Stanley Jones," 83.
65. Thompson, "Ethics of Eli Stanley Jones," 82.
66. Chacko, "Work and Thought of Eli Stanley Jones," vii.
67. Thompson, "Ethics of Eli Stanley Jones," 61.
68. Ibid., 124.
69. Ibid., 150.
70. Ibid., 155.
71. Ibid., 159.
72. Ibid., 254.
73. Jones, *Word Became Flesh*, 315.
74. Chacko, "Work and Thought of Eli Stanley Jones," vi.

Chapter Twelve

How Do They Think? Understanding and Teaching Religious Belief Systems in Twenty-first-Century Missions

Norman E. Allison

Background

This chapter demonstrates the use of a systems model to enable students who are training for cross-cultural ministry to use specific models when examining the structural properties of religious belief systems. This subject represents a valuable area of preparation that should be taught more widely in undergraduate and graduate studies for prospective or current cross-cultural workers.

Through the application of logical models to case studies, the course trains students to understand not only how religious beliefs are structured in the minds of people, but also how these beliefs express themselves in the daily lives and rituals of people in every part of the world. The ultimate purpose of the course is to train cross-cultural workers to understand more thoroughly and empathize more deeply with the people among whom they will serve.

At Toccoa Falls College (undergraduate), Cultural Anthropology is the minimum prerequisite for this course. Students have been trained in this and prior courses (Applied Anthropology, Peoples of the World, Ethnography, World Religions, etc.) to recognize the worldviews of other people. In Religious Belief Systems (RBS), the professor and students work to deepen this skill so that students begin to see how to view the people of a second culture in such a way that they see the world through the eyes of those with whom they share the Good News, and they begin to understand the world as the people of their second culture see it, that is, to think as they think.

Many theologians express concern regarding the use of anthropological theory, citing the danger of adopting a purely relativistic approach to the study of the beliefs of a people. They are correct in being concerned, as they should be for their own discipline as well. From an evangelical Christian perspective, however, the overriding application of biblical absolutes to theoretical models should prevent relativism. In recent years, some observers have expressed concern that missiologists have gone too far in the application of anthropology to missiological issues. This author does not join in that concern. In fact, the greater concern should be that many Christian workers, even cross-cultural workers, have little or no interest or training in anthropology.

Whatever one's training may include, no one may take his assumptions for granted without ongoing evaluation. Christian anthropologists must always apply biblical absolutes in such a way that they will form the essential guidelines for any application of theory. From the first few days of class in the Religious Belief Systems course, students know the explicit biblical assumptions which will guide their course of study, and they are cautioned to question any movement away from those guidelines.

From another direction, contemporary discussions in anthropological literature express continuing concern regarding the imposition of Western structures of understanding on non-Western cultural data. In the aforementioned course the instructor works to see that *emic*[1] structures are given a high priority, and he encourages his primarily monocultural students to examine non-Western beliefs and values without the inherent ethnocentrism so often seen in the history of their predecessors. Discussions often involve questions designed to reveal whether or not the students are modifying their perception to consider non-Western solutions to case study problems. As the semester progresses, one notes movement away from monocultural assumptions and reactions.

The history of anthropology is replete with numerous theories designed to help individuals understand the mosaic of peoples and their cultures around the world. These theories tend to come and go with time. As for this author's approach in dealing with the complexities of communicating the Gospel in other cultures, exposure to various alternatives has led me to adopt a mixture of theoretical approaches. Although my perspective and my methodology may be seen as eclectic, I follow what is known as the "general systems theory"[2] approach to cultural analysis, modified by a "functionalist"[3] mentality, a bit of symbolic and cognitive theory, and a few other strange ideas—all further molded by my evangelical Christian worldview. So if my approach may be a little difficult to classify at times, this is the reason!

In recent years, many anthropologists seem to be moving away from understanding the intricacies of culture through structural systems. In fact, in this postmodern world, all theories, definitions, and methodologies seem to be open to new interpretations. In a recently published article for the American Anthropological Association, under the subtitle, "Postmodern Suspicion of Structure," one professor writes,

> In anthropology, we see a move away from the panoramic sweep of cultural systems, whether of a positivist stripe or hermeneutic grandeur . . .

> The trend in anthropology is away from cross-cultural comparison and a search for statistical or other universals. How ironic that, as the forces (and structures) of globalization increase, anthropology turns more toward local knowledge and practice.[4]

Nevertheless, as some behavioral scientists in this postmodern era move to change how they and others should understand the societies of the world, there is still a strong affinity among some scientists—this author included—for the use of the "systems" approach in the study of religion and related beliefs and practices. The data in this chapter follow that approach.

In addition to the influences previously noted, this author's thinking has also been challenged and shaped by the writings of Christian anthropologists Alan Tippett, Paul Hiebert, and Charles Kraft, along with missiologist David Hesselgrave and others. In fact, some of their ideas are so mixed with mine, I have difficulty in sorting them all out as I teach this course and write this chapter! But I will attempt to give credit where I am aware of using source materials.

This author's personal study of religious belief systems began during the ten years I spent working among the Arabs of Jordan and Lebanon. One of the many things I learned as I lived among these gracious people was how little I knew about the way they thought and how little I understood the worldview that guided their lives.

Later, knowing I would stay in the USA to teach, the Lord arranged for me to study cultural anthropology at the University of Georgia. There, I took a concentration in Belief Systems. Among many scholars introduced to me by Dr. Charles Hudson, my major professor in this concentration, was a writer by the name of Robin Horton, professor of Philosophy and Religious Studies at the University of Port Harcourt, Rivers State, Nigeria. A book entitled *Rationality*, edited by Bryan Wilson, first exposed me to his writings.[5] In that volume, Horton examined the similarities underlying African thought and Western science, and then compared differences. More recently, Horton has expanded his work in his own book, *Patterns of Thought in Africa and the West: Essays on Magic, Religion, and Science*.[6]

The Course

The design for this course, Religious Belief Systems ("RBS" to students), gives a background in theory and then employs a simple beginning model developed for the study of religious beliefs in any culture. This model remains simple so as to be useful to undergraduate students, most of whom have limited experience in dealing with other cultures. It is also easy to remember and apply in whatever cultural system they work.

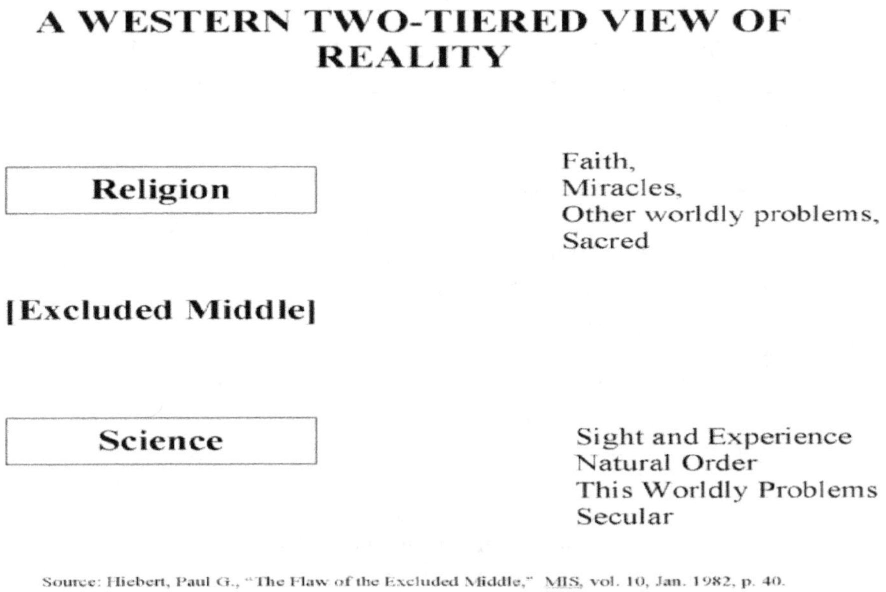

A WESTERN TWO-TIERED VIEW OF REALITY

Religion	Faith, Miracles, Other worldly problems, Sacred
[Excluded Middle]	
Science	Sight and Experience Natural Order This Worldly Problems Secular

Source: Hiebert, Paul G., "The Flaw of the Excluded Middle," MIS, vol. 10, Jan. 1982, p. 40.

Figure 1: A Western Two-Tiered View of Reality[7]

In class, the professor emphasizes that dealing with the subject of Religious Belief Systems really involves dealing with the way people think. The students are not just examining beliefs and values, even though that is an important part of their study. They must focus on how these are structured in the human mind. The course simplifies many of the intricacies related to the subject in order to focus on a way of communicating with undergraduate students which will interest and enlighten them, and in order to give them tools which may be developed further as they work with the complex beliefs of societies around the world. Some of the students may question whether or not the course and the professor have been successful in this goal, but most of them express a high level of interest.

Early in the course they read Paul Hiebert's classic article, "The Flaw of the Excluded Middle"[8] and discuss it in class. Students begin to see, many for the first time, that the Western, two-tiered view of the universe typically leaves out an entire dimension present in the worldview of people in non-Western cultures. The model given by Hiebert in the original article is titled "A Western Two-Tiered View of Reality."

For those who may not be familiar with this concept, the *Evangelical Dictionary of World Missions* describes it this way:

> Hiebert built his analysis on a two-dimensional matrix. The first dimension is that of three worlds or domains: 1) a seen world (that which is of this world and seen), 2) the unseen of this world (that which is of this world but not seen), and 3) an unseen transempirical world (that which pertains to heavens, hells, and other worlds). The second dimension is that of two types of analogies people use to explain the powers around them: 1) an organic analogy (powers are personal, e.g., gods and spirits) and 2) a mechanical analogy (powers are impersonal, e.g., gravity and electricity). Combining the seen/unseen/transempirical worlds and organic/mechanical analogies into a matrix, Hiebert's model highlighted the difference between Westerners, who tend to see only two worlds (the seen world and the transempirical world) and many non-Westerners who recognize the middle world, comprised of unseen powers (magical forces, evil eye, mana) and spirits which are very much a part of everyday human life (e.g., a person is ill because of a curse or a spirit attack). The blind spot in the Western worldview Hiebert labeled the flaw of the excluded middle.[9]

How Do They Think? 299

With conceptual models like this, the students begin to realize the importance of understanding that people in different societies actually do see the world around them very differently. The students also begin to comment that the work God has called them to do is a bit more demanding than they had thought previously.

From this point, the professor introduces a very simple model which is based on a three-level triangle that looks at the process of human thought as it moves from sensory perception at the base through increasing levels of abstraction. The model is simple because it must reiterate to students that a religious belief system will nearly always reflect two consistent themes, regardless of the system's complexity. The model looks like this:

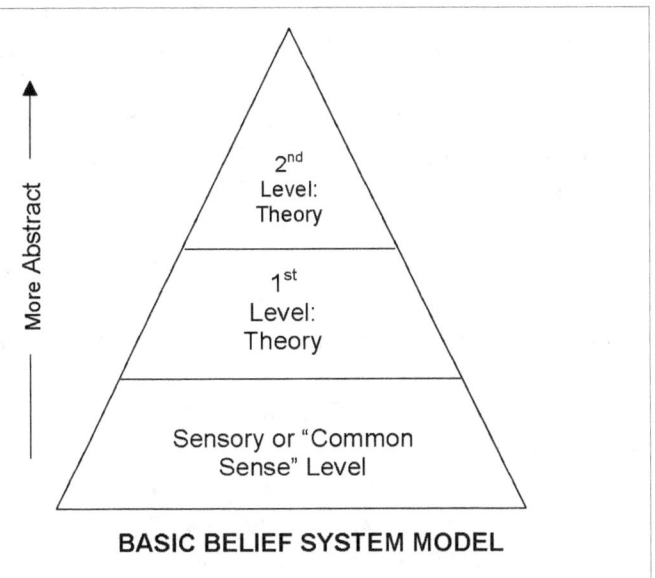

Figure 2: Basic Belief System Model

This model shows the students that:

1. Human thought processes tend to move from the level of "sensory perception" at the base to a more

"abstract" category and then on to higher levels of abstraction (more than two, but this keeps the model simple).
2. More and more is explained by less and less as one moves toward the more abstract upper point of the triangle.

The professor will re-introduce these very fundamental concepts periodically, enabling the students to use this model as a basic building block throughout the course.

Quite often in cultural anthropology, scholars stress *differences* between people in different cultures because monocultural people are prone to assume that other people are just like they are, with a few variations. This is one of the major reasons for using "The Flaw of the Excluded Middle" early in the course. This article often profoundly modifies student thinking about worldviews. In addition, as the students study different belief systems, they view a number of case studies illustrating an unlimited number of different ways people devise to organize their religious beliefs. However, at a certain point in the course, similarities between traditional (or folk, or primal) beliefs and those of people who have been taught in a Western scientific context need to be stressed as well. So the professor must move to a variation of this model to make comparisons (See figure 3).

The following premises help students think through the implications of this model:[10]

First, *the theoretical character of thought in traditional belief systems is essentially the same as that in Western scientific thinking.* In other words, "common sense" in both systems of thought (traditional and Western) is the simplest tool for dealing with circumstances in everyday life. However, when problems are not solved with common sense solutions, both systems allow for thinking to move into a higher, more abstract level.

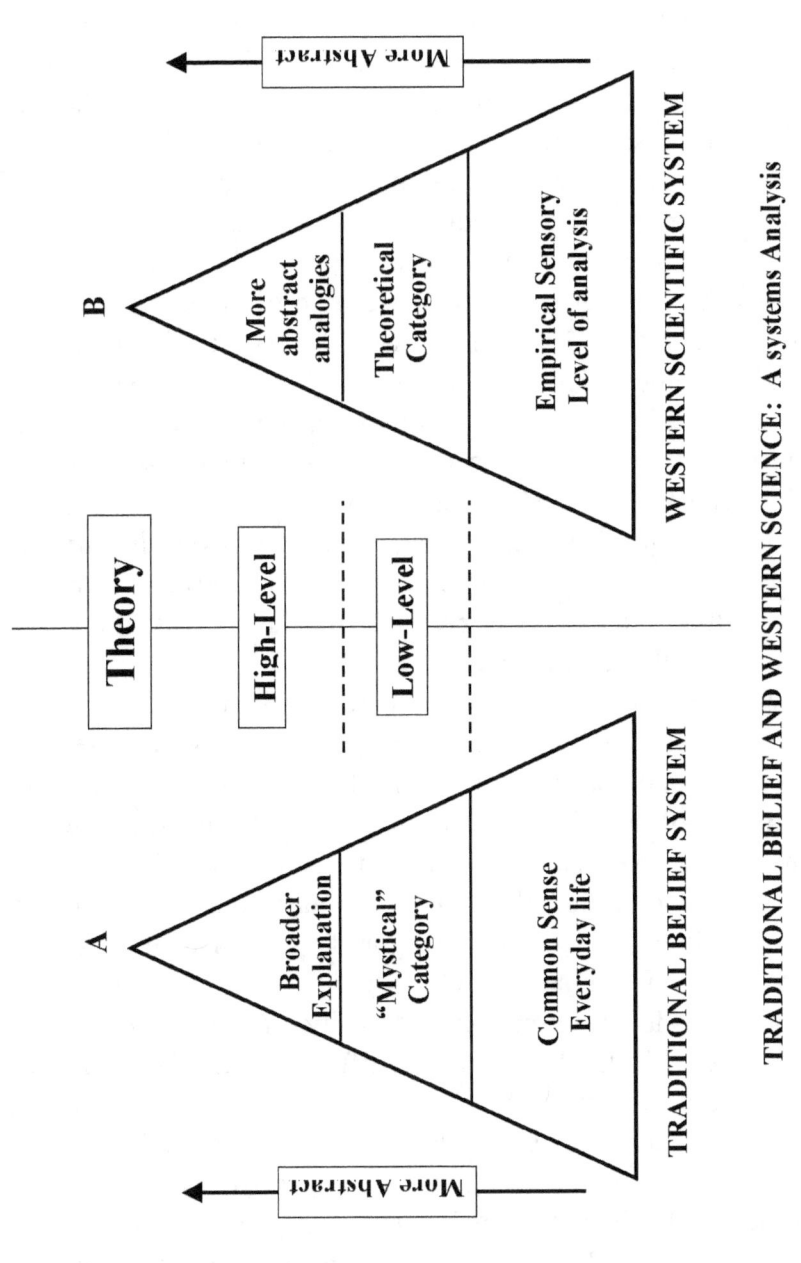

Figure 3: Traditional Belief and Western Science: A Systems Analysis.

Model A, the Traditional Belief System: An example from Robin Horton's work among the Kalabari people of Africa serves to illustrate this process. Horton describes how the Kalabari have a variety of herbal treatments for diseases. Several of these may be tried in order to bring about recovery. If the herbal remedies produce no result, they begin to say, "There is something else in this sickness." In other words, when the level of common sense is too limited, they call the diviner and the search moves into the "mystical" category to find the cause. This category is familiar to the Kalabari (they do have a "middle" level) so they think and interact with the spirit world on a daily basis. The diviner often looks for a possible causal relationship between the social lives of the individuals (anger, envy, etc.). His worldview is very holistic, and it is his responsibility to determine the cause of an illness or misfortune and usually to prescribe the cure, so his solution is a move into the middle level.

What has been described here is a jump in the minds of the diviner and the people involved, from common sense to mystical thinking in the traditional or folk belief system. For this type of belief system, most answers are found in the common sense everyday thought modes, but if solutions to problems are not found there, it is not uncommon to make this jump. Since the mystical category is so holistically entwined with the common sense level in traditional systems, the transition to this level is normally not a difficult one to make.

Model B, the Western Scientific System: Using Horton's illustration to show similarity between the two modes of thought, picture a physicist looking intently through his microscope. He observes small, fast-moving particles going through a sheet of metal foil in his laboratory experiment. These particles are too small to analyze, so he needs to compare them with some known quantity. As he observes, he sees that these particles' movements have a similarity to the movements of planets in a solar system. In his thinking, he has shifted from the observable but unknown to an analogy made with a known quantity. He has, in fact, moved into the first level of abstract theory to find an answer to his problem. There are differences between the two systems, but the similarities in arriving at solutions are basically the same.

Second, *the level of abstract theory (high/low) used varies with the context.* Interestingly, a person's choices as he moves into the abstract levels of theory will depend on the width of the context he wants to consider. If he believes it necessary to use only a limited area of experience (beyond that of common sense), he may use what is generally called a "low-level theory." Of course, this is not the only factor (limitations based on intelligence, range of experience, etc. are important), but this is how one normally arrives at solutions. If this person has deeper concerns, he may use a higher-level of theory.

Since this class is concerned primarily with understanding non-Western belief systems, readings from *Nuer Religion*, by E. E. Evans-Pritchard further enrich the students' understanding.[11] The class discusses Evans-Pritchard's premise that "a theistic religion need be neither monotheistic nor polytheistic. It may be both. It is the question of the level . . . of thought, rather than of exclusive types of thought."[12] If one understands monotheism to be exclusive in a system of belief, this statement may sound like a contradiction in terms. However, in a number of belief systems, like that of the Nuer, one high god and many spirits can and do play complementary roles. The "level of thought" referred to by Evans-Pritchard would equate in our model to a "monotheistic god" at the high level, and a polytheistic realm of spirits at the low level of theory (which compares to the middle range of Hiebert's model—the range excluded by Westerners).

In traditional belief systems, spirits provide explanations in broad but clearly defined contexts. This vital worldview belief relates primarily to one's immediate community and environment, and to daily concerns. A supreme being, however, while related to a higher level of theory, tends to provide a means of explanation which relates to theories of the origin of life, the reason for existence, etc.

An interesting validation of the triangle-shaped model is that more and more is explained by less and less as one moves up toward the peak of the triangle. The "mystical" or "1st level of theory" explains a broad range of issues which confront people on the daily sensory level. The "2nd level of theory" provides an even broader explanation as thought is generalized into fewer abstract categories.

Treating sickness further illustrates how high/low levels of theory vary with context. In non-Western systems, when a sickness does not respond to herbal treatments of various kinds, the practitioner may re-diagnose and try another alternative, but if there is still no result, he concludes that there is something else in this sickness. In other words, the context provided by common sense is too limited, so there is a shift to mystical thinking to resolve the problem. The Western analogy might be the use of prescription medications to cure an illness, but if this has no benefit, one may shift to prayer to resolve the problem.

Later in the course, another topic, closely related to the understanding that has just been developed, deals with the comparison of High and Low Religion to Great and Little Tradition. The professor generally uses the model depicted in figure 4 to explain the relationships.

High Religion has been defined as "a cognitive domain that is expressed in a highly institutionalized social organization."[13] Christianity, Buddhism, Hinduism, and Islam all represent High Religions.

How Do They Think? 305

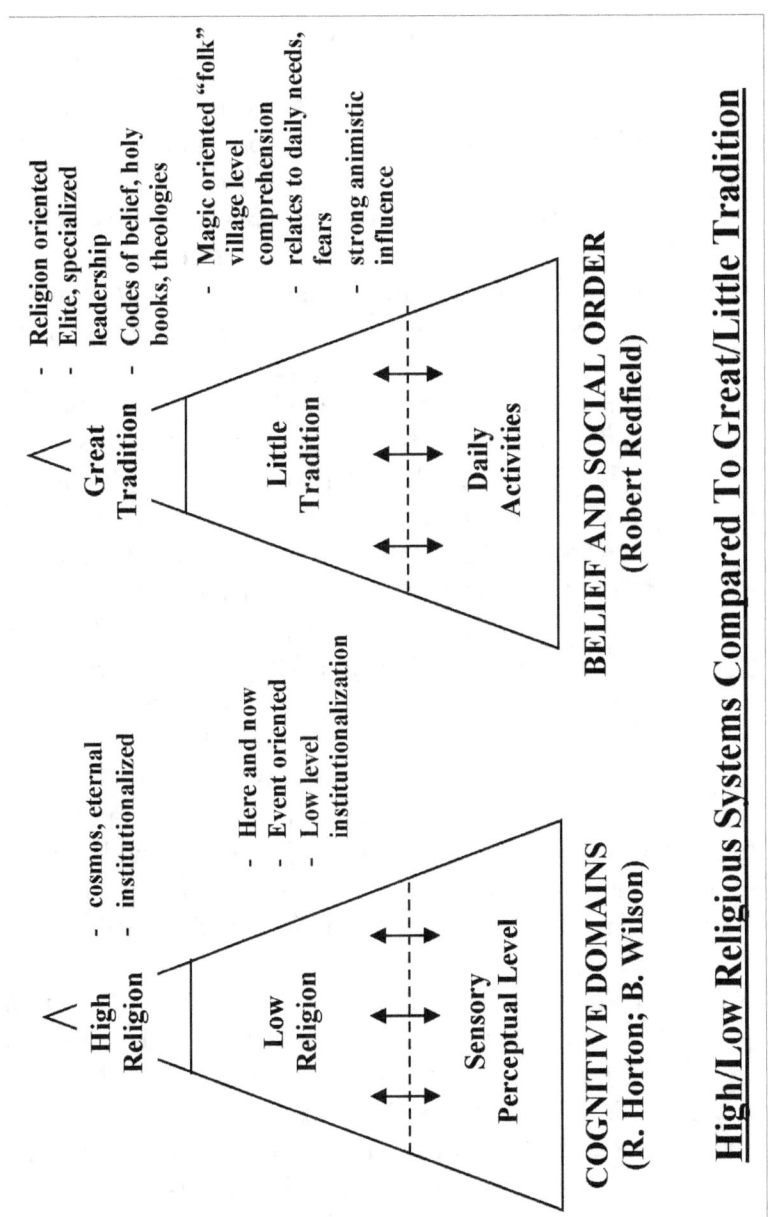

Figure 4: High/Low Religious Systems Compared to Great/Little Tradition

The characteristics of a High Religion are:

1. It deals primarily with *cosmic questions* such as the origin and destiny of things and the ultimate meaning of life.
2. It has *written texts* that solidify or "fix" an authoritative body of beliefs. Since these texts are then unchangeable, as time passes, commentaries must be written to make these meaningful and applicable to new times and changing cultures.
3. It is *institutionalized.* A High Religion is characterized by specialization with different leadership and religious roles; it has formally defined orthodox positions; it has central institutions such as temples or churches and schools for training leaders, and it has bureaucratic organizations of many forms.
4. For the most part, High Religion provides for *moral systems* in which the gods (usually male dominant) are good and in conflict with demons or "devils" who are evil.

By contrast, the category of Low Religion is a cognitive domain in religion that is less institutionalized, and centered more in immediate people-oriented needs and practices. A Low Religion tends to have the following characteristics:

1. It deals with the *immediate problems of everyday life* rather than ultimate matters. It is concerned with crisis, disease, death, drought, etc.
2. It is often *informally organized.* The leaders may not even be specialists but only perform their religious services alongside their everyday work.
3. It has *no written texts.* Beliefs are found in myths, dramas, and religious performances, and since these are not "frozen" by being put into an unchanging

form, they can change over time without the people being aware of it. Therefore, they can be reinterpreted for each new problem or occasion.
4. A Low Religion is often *amoral*. Emically, the spirits and beings in this world are understood as being good or bad (more analogous to people). They help those who serve them and harm those who forget them.

Robert Redfield's model somewhat parallels the model from R. Horton and B. Wilson. Redfield was a professor at the University of Chicago and did his field work in Mexico. He studied concepts of folk society and folk culture, attempting a closer integration of the social sciences and the humanities. He classified a framework for categories or domains of religion as Great and Little Tradition.[14] Redfield took a slightly different direction in relating belief to social order, but his approach resolves essentially the same way. If one focuses with Redfield on the cognitive domain of High Religion, especially in the context of the society's social institutionalization, several levels of organization may be discerned.

The Great Tradition refers to great centers of organized religion; its central cathedrals, mosques, etc., training centers, formal bureaucracies, holy writings, and organizational structures. One finds the highest arenas for religious activity here. Also the clergy, the theologians, the leaders, and the scriptures of the religion are located here.

Most of the books written about the world's major religions deal with Great Traditions, giving extensive information about how they are rationalized, delineating their systematic codes of beliefs, their commentaries, their organization, etc. Most students who plan to work in second cultures are directed to these kinds of sources. Such sources are, of course, important to give the *ideal* perspective of the religion in question, but they give only a partial picture of the true nature of actual belief.

The Little Tradition refers to the actual expressions of the Great Tradition worked out in the daily lives of people at the folk level. This is the religion of the average believer, often in the lives of people at the rural, peasant, or small village level. A significantly high percentage of the population of most societies around the world functions at this level. At this level one finds a great deal of variance in the content, and even in the structure of the peoples' belief systems, although the primary contrast is between the Great and Little Tradition. Little Tradition beliefs correlate poorly with what is defined as orthodox by the Great Tradition. The Great Tradition tries to control the lower levels and determine for them what is orthodox and correct, but in most areas of the non-Western world this is difficult. The "fit" is better if channels of communication between the top and the bottom are good, but this is most often not the case.

Redfield also notes that ideas most often spread horizontally in the Little Tradition, through the folk channels of communication. They may also move up from the Little Tradition and find acceptance in the Great Tradition, or they may be passed down from the Great to the Little Tradition. Change is introduced in a number of ways, but it is usually very slow compared to changes in the Western world. In addition, Redfield adds that the leaders at the level of Great Tradition may be unaware of variations at the Little Tradition level.

The course professor must draw these and other concepts together as well as consistently refer back to "The Excluded Middle" in Western cognitive orientation. This middle realm of belief, as this chapter has demonstrated, is important and even vital to the belief systems of non-Western peoples, structurally and practically. If the missionary neglects it or disregards it, he will face potentially serious problems in communicating the Gospel to people in other cultures. Having been trained in Western educational modes of thought, our automatic reaction is to exclude this middle level and look for answers in other categories of thought.

Historically, and even today, when many cross-cultural workers enter a new society, they are not aware of the kinds of differences that people make in categorizing religious beliefs. The workers focus on learning the language and proclaiming the Gospel and generally assume God will take care of the rest. An understanding of religious belief systems provides a crucial tool in the process of contextualizing the Gospel in a new society. For example, two typical mistakes—to be seen as inferences—may be drawn from these various models.

First, most Western-trained missionaries and preachers, having a Western cognitive orientation centered in the High Religion realm, tend to concentrate almost entirely on issues of High Religion which they believe are essential to bring about changes in the lives of people to whom they take the Gospel. This is especially true if they have no training in cultural anthropology. Because high religion is the central area of concern in *their* lives, and because they are *specialists* in areas dealing with a high content of theory, they unconsciously expect this high level to be the focal point in the lives of others. Often, they frame their communication in "high religion" sorts of concepts, primarily in theological language, a major component of their own education. Even though the presentation may be simplified by those working in a second culture (at least by *their* standards), it often seems irrelevant to the daily lives and needs of average people.

Second, Western-oriented people often do not notice the Low Religion of a particular area, or if they do, they usually discount its importance. In the scientifically-trained worldview of the Western missionary, hearing that sickness is caused by witchcraft or evil spirits seems like superstitious nonsense. The missionary knows that germs cause sickness. Even though he knows the Bible teaches the interrelationship of the seen and unseen world of spirits, and though intellectually he believes the Bible, he is conditioned in his automatic responses to such phenomena by his own scientific training. He mentally takes the supernatural of Low Religion and puts it into the natural category of his own Western belief system, or excludes it entirely as "superstition." Of course this is mainly due to the "excluded middle" in the Western worldview and the failure to understand the importance of that entire area in the lives of non-Westerners.

Obviously the form of Christianity that comes to non-Western peoples often fails to answer the questions raised in their daily lives. These questions *were* answered by their old Low Religion. For this reason, new converts usually turn back to the old religion to meet these needs. Or they may take some religious symbol from the new religion, like the cross, and substitute it for the former Low Religious symbols and their corresponding use (e.g., as magical).

There are some uncomplicated solutions to these problems; however, they have profound implications. One must emphasize that:

1. Cross-cultural workers must communicate in the forms of Christianity that speak to these immediate, daily, real needs. It is usually much more appealing to people in traditional or folk cultures to relate the Gospel to points of need they feel now, than to begin with the cosmological issues of belief found in the High Religion domain of Christianity. The Bible speaks to those felt (and deeper *true*) needs, and those biblical solutions must be studied, learned in an *emic* context, and applied in new cultures.
2. Cross-cultural workers must discover the cognitive domains of explanation in particular societies and speak to all of those domains. If they only work with one area, such as the High Religion, people will be only partially converted. Many, if not most, "Christians" in the non-Western world seem to be High Religion converts, but functioning folk religionists. The Western cross-cultural communicator's lack of understanding may be partially responsible

for this very large and continuing problem among people who claim to be Christians in every society around the world.

The issues dealt with thus far comprise the core of this course, but there is much more. The topics covered in class and through assigned readings are:

1. History of the Anthropological Study of Religious Belief Systems
2. Animism-The Starting Point
3. The Flaw of the Excluded Middle
4. Western Beliefs vs. Traditional
5. Witchcraft, Sorcery, and Magic
6. Religious/Magical Practitioners
7. Nuer Religion
8. Worldviews & Kinship-Based Cultures
9. Sins: Cultural or Theological
10. Symbolism and Ritual
11. Power Concepts
12. Spirit Possession
13. Power Encounter
14. Kalabari Worldview
15. High and Low Religion
16. Cognitive Categories & Conversion

The professor also uses several videos to give a visual representation of what is primarily theoretical to these students who have limited cross-cultural experience.

The course papers done by students in this class have produced some surprising results reflecting what they have learned and applied in the course, many of them in ways that take the application of this knowledge beyond what they are expected to grasp in this undergraduate class. As the course progresses, students receive more complex case studies and demonstrate models of those belief systems, adding more content to the simple model with which the class began. The students are encouraged to think through the intricacies of the specific system they are studying and to diagram and analyze the belief system as carefully as they can. Their final course paper must include the model they construct and explain the rationale for the way elements are placed in the model.

The objective of this chapter is to give the reader a taste of what Toccoa Falls College teaches in the School of World Missions, specifically in the analysis of religious belief systems. One of the major reasons this author teaches this course is to emphasize how and why students should do more in-depth study as to how people of other cultures *think*.

Listening to a former student, now a missionary, speaking of his work among the Fulani in Guinea, this author was interested to hear how he had applied some of the principles learned in class. He and his wife have worked there for fifteen years. He emphasized that two factors remained important in reaching the Fulani. First, relationships had to be established. "People," he said, "must know you before they will believe what you have to say. And you have to *demonstrate* that you believe what you say." Then he added, "Western people tend to start with the roof, but with the Fulani, we have to build a foundation first."[15] I took this as a confirmation that he had applied lessons he had learned in the School of World Missions at Toccoa Falls College.

As students of Religious Belief Systems communicate the Gospel in other cultural frames of reference, they will be better able to understand systems of thought and belief as they work within the worldviews of the people they have gone to serve. I trust that the reader will also consider the benefits of such training for all students in ministry, especially those planning to be cross-cultural workers.

Notes

1. Any analysis should be conducted on the basis of and understanding of culture from the inside. This insider's viewpoint is known as an *emic* perspective. The perspective of the informed outsider is called an *etic* perspective. The terms were developed by linguist Kenneth Pike, for many years associated with the Wycliffe Bible Translators, and are now widely used by anthropologists.

2. General systems theory grew out of the work of Austrian biologist Ludwig von Bertalanffy (1901-1972). It encourages anthropologists to examine cultures as systems composed of both human and non-human elements. It presumes that the normal state of a system is equilibrium and describes the various methods by which systems deviate from and return to states of balance. Roy A. Rappaport (1926-1997) was a major proponent (cf. "Ritual Regulation of Environmental Relations Among a New Guinea People." For additional background, see Paul Hiebert, R. Daniel Shaw, and Tite Tienou, *Understanding Folk Religion* (Grand Rapids: Baker, 1999), ch. 2.

3. Here I am referring to what is known as the "psychological functionalism" of Bronislaw Malinowski. Briefly stated, the theory is that cultural institutions function to meet the basic physical and psychological needs of people in a society. See Bronislaw C. Malinowski, *Magic, Science, and Religion* (Garden City, NY: Doubleday, 1954 [1925]).

4. Ashley E. Maynard, "Problems of Translation," *Anthropology News* 44, no. 2 (2003): 8, 11.

5. Robin Horton, "African Traditional Thought," in *Rationality*, ed. Bryan R. Wilson (New York: Harper and Rowe, 1970).

6. Robin Horton, *Patterns of Thought in Africa and the West: Essays on Magic, Religion, and Science* (Cambridge: Cambridge, 1993).

7. Ibid., 40.

8. Paul G. Hiebert, "The Flaw of the Excluded Middle," *Missiology* 10 (1982): 35-47.

9. A. Scott Moreau, ed., *Evangelical Dictionary of World Missions* (Grand Rapids: Baker, 2000), 363.

10. The following statements are drawn largely from Horton, "African Traditional Thought," and Horton, *Patterns of Thought*.

11. E. E. Evans-Pritchard, *Nuer Religion* (New York: Oxford University, 1956).

12. Ibid., 316.

13. Bryan R. Wilson, ed., *Rationality* (New York: Harper and Rowe, 1970).

14. Robert Redfield, *The Little Community and Peasant Society and Culture* (Chicago: University of Chicago, 1973).

15. Kenneth Blackwell, speaking at the First Alliance Church, Toccoa, Georgia, February 2003.

www.ingramcontent.com/pod-product-compliance
Lightning Source LLC
Chambersburg PA
CBHW071230070526
44583CB00017B/2120